HOW TO SAVE
THOUSANDS OF DOLLARS
ON YOUR HOME MORTGAGE

Randy Johnson

John Wiley & Sons, Inc.

New York • *Chichester* • *Weinheim* • *Brisbane* • *Singapore* • *Toronto*

Published by John Wiley & Sons, Inc.
Published simultaneously in Canada.

This publication is designed to provide accurate and authoritative information in regard to the subject matter covered. It is sold with the understanding that the publisher is not engaged in rendering professional services. If professional advice or other expert assis-tance is required, the services of a competent professional person should be sought.

Library of Congress Cataloging-in-Publication Data:
Johnson, Randy, 1937–
    How to save thousands of dollars on your home mortgage / Randy Johnson.
        p.   cm.
    Includes index.
    ISBN 0-471-19253-8 (pbk. : alk. paper)
    1. Mortgage loans—United States.   I. Title.
HG2040.5.U5J64   1998
332.7'22—dc21   98-13348
                                                                CIP

Printed in the United States of America.

10 9 8 7 6 5 4

CONTENTS

adjustable rate mortgage

read

FOREWORD

The truth seems hard to find in much of society today. This is painfully apparent in the mortgage lending business. The combination of borrowers' infrequent use of the product, lenders' abundance of information, and the complexity of the mortgage process often leads to obfuscation, half-truths, and sometimes outright lies.

This is why Randy's book, *How to Save Thousands of Dollars on Your Home Mortgage,* is a must for anyone thinking about applying for a mortgage loan. Randy's years of experience assisting borrowers through the home financing process have resulted in this useful tool that will enable you to find the truth, fragment by fragment, in the mortgage business. Some of this information will surprise or shock you. It *will* leave you better prepared when you need to shop for a mortgage loan. Randy's unique perspective will provide you with the information needed to make a wise decision on a mortgage loan that's best suited for your needs.

The truth can be found; it just takes a little help to find it.

Steven Renock
President, CU Mortgage Corp.

INTRODUCTION

Where ignorance is bliss, 'tis folly to be wise.
                                        —THOMAS GRAY

Most people think that the most expensive purchase they will ever make is their home; in fact, their mortgage is, if they have to borrow money like most people do. Consider this: If you buy a $100,000 home and finance $80,000 with a 30-year loan at an interest rate of 8 percent, you'll make a $20,000 down payment, whittle down your $80,000 mortgage, and end up paying a whopping $131,324 in interest. That's a total of $231,324 for your $100,000 home!

Now that I've got your attention, I'll assume that your goal in picking up this book is to save as much money as you can on your mortgage. Unfortunately, most people do not get the best mortgage. Why? The mortgage business has become so complex that most laypeople are bewildered by the terminology, baffled by an incredible array of choices, and confused by marketing material. Add the government's mandated disclosures forms—the Good Faith Estimate of Closing Costs and Truth in Lending forms—and many people are more confused than when they started.

THIS BOOK CAN HELP

In the mortgage business, ignorance isn't bliss—it's just expensive. Although two-thirds of Americans have mortgages, most remain out of their depth when it comes to mortgages, lenders, and programs. The field is so specialized and changes so rapidly that the typical homeowner, who needs this information only every 5 or 10 years, simply cannot keep up with it. The good news is that you can learn most of the information you need to make wise decisions and negotiate a better deal for your family. The mortgage business is rooted in common sense: When you get down to basics, you'll find that you can understand it, too.

In this book, you'll learn specific strategies to help you process information more effectively, to find out who the best lenders are, and to drive a harder bargain with those lenders. The information presented here has been gained in the trenches. I've been originating mortgages since 1980, and I've helped thousands of borrowers answer the same questions, solve the same problems, and overcome the same obstacles you face. I live in an affluent area, Orange County, California, where the median income is one of the highest in the nation. I've secured loans for Fortune 500 CEOs, CPAs, university professors, attorneys—almost 2,000 families in all. In general, these people have bought several homes and are smart, well educated, and knowledgeable about many topics. But very few of them know much more than the basics about mortgages. My point here is that even people who are experienced homeowners are at a disadvantage when it comes to getting the best mortgage. How much of a disadvantage? Let me share this with you. Whenever I meet with mortgage professionals I ask them, "How many buyers get the wrong loan or pay too much for it?" Invariably they tell me between 70 and 80 percent; no one has ever said that it is less than 50 percent! Bluntly, this means that the way the mortgage industry conveys information to its customers leads them to make mistakes more than half of the time.

HOW TO WIN AT THE MORTGAGE GAME

Mortgage lenders extract more money from the wallets of American families every month than any other industry in the country. The typical family spends 25 percent and up of its income on mortgage payments. So for consumers to be underinformed or misinformed about basic issues related to the largest single item in their budget is a sad commentary on the mortgage industry and alarming news for anyone planning to own his or her own home. That said, let me assure you that I can help you become one of the 20 percent who make the right decisions about their loans.

Specifically, this book will explain the following:

- The structure of the industry
- Why lenders do what they do
- How lenders market loans
- How to determine the best type of loan for your family
- How to find the best lenders
- How to negotiate the best deal for you
- How to lock in the rate on your loan at the best time
- How to avoid being victimized
- How to use the most modern technological development—the Internet—to help you secure a loan

As a mortgage lender, I've spent 17 years originating loans. I know tricks and tips available only to an insider, and I'll pass them on to you. Using these ideas to optimize the type of loan you get and where you get it, you should be able to save at least ½ percent every year. On a $300,000 loan, that's $1,500 every year—serious money in most households and a terrific incentive to read this book.

The material in this book is for all home buyers. I have a special place in my heart for first-time home buyers and have tried to include as much as I can to help that group. But as large and important a group as that is, there are many more folks who are buying their second or third home, so I include a great deal of information for them as well. In all cases, I have tried to give you the facts, but with a special slant—how professionals in the industry view them. I call it *insider information,* material you can find nowhere else. I have also included material on special up-to-date topics, including reverse amortized mortgages, equity-line loans, even how to get a loan on the Internet.

My goal is to transfer my knowledge to you in a very accessible and easy-to-understand format. I consider each of my readers as one of my clients and intend to give you the same help and benefits as if you were sitting right here in front of me in my office.

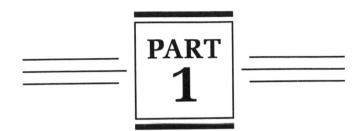

BACKGROUND

THE STRUCTURE OF THE MORTGAGE INDUSTRY

Did you ever figure that banking, loans, mortgages, interests of any kind, are about the most nonessential industries in the world?

—WILL ROGERS

KEY POINTS

- Various segments of the industry offer different types of loans for reasons that are important to them. This is meaningful to you because you want to get the loan that is best for you from the lender who specializes in that type of loan.
- No one lender offers every type of loan.
- No one lender has the best price on every type of loan.
- Lenders that have the lowest rates also usually have the strictest rules. Lenders that offer niche products (for example, loans to borrowers who don't meet high credit standards) have higher rates.

In spite of what Will Rogers said, I am proud of my industry. When I was born, approximately one-third of Americans owned their own homes. Today, that number has doubled, largely because people can finance the purchase of their homes by securing a reasonably priced mortgage.

WHY THE MORTGAGE MARKET IS DIFFERENT

Most people think that getting a mortgage is a lot like buying any other product; they also believe that the mortgage companies they talk with are lending their own money. In most cases those assumptions are wrong. Usually, lenders make loans that they can sell to some other company, either immediately or at some time in the future. When they sell the loan, they get their money back. Then they can lend out the money again, sell that loan, lend it out again, and so forth. What lenders are really doing is lending out *someone else's money,* and it's that *someone else* who determines the price. The bank adds on a profit margin, just as your supermarket tacks on a profit margin to Cheerios. Just as the base price of Cheerios is really determined by General Mills and not by your local supermarket, the price of money is not really determined by your local lender.

Historical Perspective

Prior to 1980, banks and savings and loan associations (S&Ls) *did* lend their own money, usually fixed-rate loans at 6 or 7 percent. Then, in the late 1970s, rate restrictions on the banking industry were lifted. Shortly thereafter, inflation rose to 14 percent, and short-term interest rates went even higher. The prime rate went to 23 percent. If you owned a bank and received $100 in interest income on a loan and had to pay out $200 to the depositor whose funds supported the loan, it wasn't very much fun. If you had 10,000 loans just like that, you can see that you wouldn't be in business very long. Indeed, a lot of lenders who had been around for a long time went under, merged, or were taken over and liquidated in what was probably the biggest disaster to hit the thrift industry since the Great Depression.

As a result, lenders and their regulators realized that if they were to stay in business more than a few years, they had to acknowledge that borrowing highly volatile short-term funds and lending out those funds at long-term fixed rates was like playing Russian roulette. So they invented the *variable rate mortgage* (VRM) and, later, the *adjustable rate mortgage* (ARM), which is the loan you see offered today. The ARM loan effectively locks in a lender's profit margin at a specific rate, say 2.5

percent. If the lender pays depositors 5 percent, the borrower pays 7.5 percent. If the lender pays depositors 10 percent, the borrower pays 12.5 percent. The lender always maintains the 2.5 percent profit margin.

A lot of people think that somehow this isn't fair, but I disagree. Financial institutions from banks to brokerage houses to insurance companies are really conduits. They take money, warehouse it in some form, and give it out at the other end. Banks and S&Ls lend their depositors' money to businesses and people in various forms—credit cards, car loans, business loans, mortgage loans, equity lines, and so forth. Essentially, they run a pipeline and charge a fee for the service. To make this clearer, let us assume that you want to borrow $100,000 to buy a home, but instead of going to a lender, you approach all your neighbors and try to borrow $100,000 in $1,000 and $2,000 chunks. How much do you think you'd collect, especially after you told them you would pay them back over 30 years? I think you see my point about the value of the service the lenders provide.

In running the pipeline, the lenders are simply not set up to take a lot of risk. That's why most of the bank loans I just mentioned are either short-term loans and/or tied to the prime rate or to something that ties the loan yield to the institution's cost of money. That's why banks or S&Ls that offer mortgages do not want to do fixed-rate mortgages. It exposes them to the risk of fluctuating rates. Consequently, if a bank or an S&L is originating loans for its own portfolio (that is, it is lending its depositors' funds), it will do so on adjustable rate mortgages (ARMs). In fact, banking regulators usually will not allow banks or S&Ls to hold fixed-rate loans in their portfolios because doing so may someday endanger the very existence of those institutions, as we saw in the 1980s when almost half of them went under.

RISE OF THE SECONDARY MARKET

No doubt the problem is becoming clear to you. Borrowers wanted fixed-rate loans, but the lenders, who were then mostly portfolio lenders, wouldn't offer them. This demand for fixed-rate loans gave rise to the *secondary market*. Most people have heard of the Federal National Mortgage Association (FNMA), more commonly called Fannie Mae, and the Federal Home Loan

Mortgage Corporation (FHLMC), called Freddie Mac. These quasi-governmental companies buy fixed-rate mortgages from banks, S&Ls, and mortgage bankers. They then assemble them, putting 100 or 200 similar mortgages into groups known as *pools,* which might total $10 or $20 million. Then they sell interest in the pools to institutional investors such as pension plans and mutual funds. Indeed, your company's pension plan probably owns interest in a number of such pools.

In the mid-1980s, when some of the big Wall Street brokerage firms saw FNMA and FHLMC siphoning off segments of their market by selling mortgage-backed securities to the pension plans that had been buying bonds from them, they decided to get into the act. I recommend to you Michael Lewis's entertaining and revealing book *Liar's Poker: Rising Through the Wreckage of Wall Street* (W. W. Norton, 1989), which describes the early years of that business. An entire book could be written on the secondary market, but for our purposes, suffice to say that it is the means by which your local bank, S&L, or mortgage banker can sell the fixed-rate loans it originated, thus getting its money back. The purpose of the *secondary market* is to provide liquidity to the primary lending market, or the originator of your loan.

Because of the *secondary market,* be assured that if you get a fixed-rate loan from a bank or an S&L that says it is lending its own funds, it's probably not true. It is funding your loan *this week* only because it can sell the loan *next week,* thus shifting the risk to someone else. This means the pricing is set by the *buyer* of your loan, *not* by the company that gave you the loan. Remember, the company you are dealing with is just adding a profit margin to whatever rates they are given by the company purchasing the loan.

The industry is essentially split down the middle as to where the money comes from: ARM money generally comes from deposits down at the corner branch, and fixed-rate money comes from pools of mortgage-backed securities assembled by FNMA, FHLMC, and Wall Street firms.

   TIP Even though lenders specialize in various kinds of loans, they probably won't turn you away if you ask for something other than their specialty. The cost of acquiring a customer is significant, and once you step through the door, an institution will do its best to sell you something—it wants to make money from you one way or another. That's why it is important to find a lender that specializes in your type of loan.

LOAN SERVICING

The second reason for the separation between *originators of loans* and *the real source of money* is what is known as *loan servicing.* You mail your monthly payments to a company that may in fact be the original lender, but then again may just "sound like" a lender. It sends the money on to the real owner(s) of the loan, perhaps a bunch of pension plans. They do all the accounting, nag you if you're late on a payment, and handle the foreclosure if you default on the loan. This is an enormously profitable business. Why? Look at it this way. Your electric company provides you with service, and every month it sends you a bill (just as your lender does). You mail your check and the electric company does the accounting. For illustrative purposes, let's say its billing department's budget for doing that is 20 or 30 cents per customer per month. Does that sound about right?

Typically, the servicer of a mortgage receives an annual fee of ⅜ percent of the loan balance, or $375 on a $100,000 loan. That's $31.25 per month, over 100 times as much as the electric company's billing department gets for doing substantially the same thing: sending out 12 statements, receiving 12 checks, and doing some reports. No doubt it has already occurred to you that $31.25 is a lot money for very little work and no risk at all. And if your payment is late, you pay a 5 percent late fee, say $35. The servicer gets to keep that! Furthermore, if you don't make payments on your loan, the servicer is also in charge of foreclosing, or at least handling the paperwork; it has nothing at risk because the loan is owned by someone else. The servicer is reimbursed for whatever expenses it incurs.

Is it clear to you why so many nonbank companies (GMAC, GE Credit, Countrywide, and others) are in the mortgage business? They don't care about the mortgages in quite the same way a portfolio lender does; they just originate and sell loans. *What they want is the right to service those loans.* Many lenders originate loans only because they want to replace the loans that were paid off last year. Thus the different types of originators of loans—banks, S&Ls, mortgage bankers, and mortgage brokers— are each originating mortgages for slightly different reasons.

WHERE THE MONEY COMES FROM

If the various classes of lenders are motivated by different factors, the same thing applies to the real sources of money, too. The mortgage business is very competitive, with very slim profit margins. Let's compare a bank or an S&L with a pension plan. If the bank is a portfolio lender, it lives and dies on its *yield spread,* the difference between the yield on its loans and what it pays its depositors. A pension plan, which might be a buyer of mortgage pools in the *secondary market,* is different. It accumulates a pool of assets, and its job is to grow the pool to be able to meet the requirements of the plan's retirees in the future. That doesn't mean that the plan administrator isn't interested in the yield; it's just that he or she does not have to worry about things like cost of funds or profit margins.

On a given day, the administrator or manager has investments in various securities such as stock, bonds, and mortgage-backed securities that have a certain diversification and maturity. Let's say that the manager is concerned today about funding the needs of the pool of retirees and how they will be paid in the year 2005. In 1997, the manager might buy some Treasury notes or corporate bonds that mature in the year 2005. For periods further out, the manager will have investments in longer-term securities. For shorter-term needs, the manager might buy, for example, Treasury bills that mature in only one year.

Now some smart bond salesperson might say to the fund manager, "Look, you've got $100 million in T-bills that yield 5 percent. Why not trade $20 million of those for $20 million of mortgage-backed securities that are tied to T-bills but that have a yield that is 2 percent higher, or 7 percent?" The manager knows how T-bills perform and might think that a 2 percent greater yield is adequate compensation for the additional risk of owning a security backed by mortgages rather than the U.S. government. Such managers would also be interested in securities of varying maturity—3-year, 5-year, 7-year, 10-year, 15-year, and 30-year. Put enough of them together and you have more products for the secondary market. This market, the market for securities backed by residential mortgage loans, is huge, even larger than the market for corporate bonds.

From this you can deduce that the yields required by this market are going to be based to a large degree on what other securities of similar risk are selling for, which is why the rates on mortgages during any particular period will vary similarly to other investments. The closest investment is the 30-year Treasury bond, called the *long bond*. If the yields on T-bonds move up 10 basis points (a basis point is ¹⁄₁₀₀ percent, so 10 basis points equals ¹⁄₁₀ percent), the bond seller is going to have a tough time selling mortgage-backed securities unless the yield is also raised 10 basis points.

Finally, realize that these securities are rated as to quality just as corporate and municipal bonds are. Buyers are willing to accept lower yields on higher-quality securities. So how is quality determined? It's more arcane than you would imagine, but at a fundamental level, each issuer says, "I have this big rule book and our loans are high quality because we only fund loans that meet these strict criteria." That's not unreasonable. Certain money sources are interested only in A-quality loans, and they have the strictest criteria. Others are less strict, and they will do loans that we'll call B/C loans—loans of lesser quality because the borrowers have poor credit or some other problem.

In the industry, purchasers of loans are commonly referred to as *investors*. Many such investors have relationships with the loan originators, under which they make bulk purchases of loans, say $10 million at a time. Others want to approve every single loan *before* it is even funded. If you have ever applied for your loan at some local company and a representative called you back a day later and said, "We've approved your loan but we need to get investor approval," that's what they're talking about.

CREDIT ENHANCEMENTS

An investor can lower the risk of its pools of mortgages by buying special insurance that protects the buyer of the loan in the event of loss. Typically, lenders will not do loans where the loan balance is more than 80 percent of the "appraised value of the house," the ratio known as *loan-to-value,* or LTV, unless they have such insurance. For conventional loans, they get *private mortgage insurance,* or PMI. Government loans, such as FHA and VA loans, are insured or guaranteed with *mutual mortgage insurance,* or MMI. When a lender approves a 90 percent LTV loan, it sends it to one of the insurers. That company, or agency, also underwrites the loan to determine whether it's of good enough quality to guarantee or insure against loss in the event the borrower defaults and the lender has to foreclose.

Some lenders also buy pool insurance on their mortgages, even though the loans are not over 80 percent LTV. This insurance is just a form of PMI, although the borrower does not pay for it directly as with normal PMI. Pool insurance insures the ultimate owner of the mortgage, such as a pension plan, against the risks of default in the portfolio. The issuer of the security thinks that with the added protection, its buyers will be satisfied with a lower yield than on comparable securities without this *credit enhancement,* as it is called.

CONCLUSION

Before we move on to the nitty-gritty, I want you to be aware of the battle that is going on in the mortgage market, a battle for market share. Fifteen years ago, the S&Ls had the overwhelming majority of the market. Many of the big banks didn't even offer mortgages. As a result of consolidation and the growth of the secondary market, the S&Ls' market share is far less than it was in the old days. While they will continue to be factors in the market, the biggest mortgage lenders today are companies such as Countrywide Funding, Norwest, GMAC, GE Credit, InterFirst, and the big banks like Chase, Citicorp, and NationsBank. Mergers will continue, and the big lenders are going to get even bigger. Even though big New York banks fund billions of dollars of mortgage loans, they know that they cannot provide service to retail customers in every location. So they work through smaller banks, mortgage brokers, and mortgage bankers, buying loans from companies like mine that have established a reputation in the local communities. We find customers for them, so you can think of us as mortgage retailers—similar to dealerships for automobile manufacturers.

Lenders compete with each other in the larger sense in that they are all trying to maintain or increase their business. However, I have never sensed that they compete for individual loans; rather, they think in terms of market share, not individual customers. On the plus side, the big companies have brought incredible liquidity to the national mortgage market. No one is denied the ability to buy a home because there isn't any money available. Home buyers anywhere in the country have access to the national mortgage market, where they can get loans at reasonable rates. The big lenders have also been largely responsible for the incredible array of products offered today. But let me ask you this: How can a lender that funds $100 million of loans every day care about each customer? It can't. In exchange for liquidity, reasonable rates, and product choices, customers have had to give up the concept that someone at a large institution cares about whether they actually get the house or not.

How do lenders approach the market? A lender decides which kinds of loans it prefers to specialize in and goes after that market. One lender might want to do loans for first-time home buyers who are buying directly from home builders. That segment comprises a huge share of the market, and certain lenders specialize in it. Others just want to do loans for wealthy customers. Still others want to secure loans for the midmarket, such as certain large banks that seem focused on selling something to the more or less captive audience represented by their depositors. Others specialize in loans that, for some reason or another, don't meet a stricter lender's requirement; because they are not as fussy and often deal with people who have been turned down elsewhere, they get a higher yield.

It is important that you understand this, because you will get a better deal from a lender that is targeting your group. This is no different from buying clothes. Nieman Marcus offers one level of quality and Wal-Mart offers another. Because each specializes in a particular style of merchandise, you'll be frustrated if you go to the store that doesn't carry the kind of merchandise you want. Let me give you an example as it relates to mortgages: If you want to borrow $500,000 and you go to a lender that specializes in first-time home buyers who want $100,000 loans, the loan rep won't chase you away. (The loan rep isn't that stupid. He or she will even tell you how great the company is.) But this company would be out of its area of specialization, and other lenders who specialize in large loans will offer you a better deal. By the same token, some lenders specialize in adjustable rate mortgages; others excel at funding fixed-rate loans. You can see what I mean.

I'm going to assume that most of my readers meet the standards of creditworthiness established by the secondary market and are interested in FNMA/FHLMC or in *jumbo loans,* those larger than the FNMA/FHLMC limit, which is currently $227,150.

You'll get a better deal if you deal with a lender whose main business is selling loans to that market. Such lenders have become efficient in funding these types of loans and will have lower costs.

If you have a property with a physical defect or other problem, if your credit is somewhat impaired, if your income is difficult to document, or if your housing-to-income expense ratios are higher than those lenders prefer, a portfolio lender will be better for you. Such a lender will approve your loan in-house, because that's where it will stay. You might have to settle for an adjustable rate mortgage, but that's not necessarily bad, as we will cover in upcoming chapters.

But before we develop strategies to get you to the right lender and help you assess your needs, Chapter 2 will give you some important background on how the industry has shaped consumer opinions about mortgages.

HOW LENDERS INFLUENCE BORROWERS' CHOICES

The truth has a horrible sweat to survive in this world, but a piece of nonsense, however absurd on its face, always seems to prosper.
—H. L. MENCKEN

KEY POINTS

- Information is power. Lenders have more information than borrowers, and this gives them a tactical advantage.
- Lenders have a vested interest in limiting or filtering information to the borrowers in such a way as to make their loans look better than loans offered by other lenders, whether they are or not.
- Many forces shape our opinions about lenders and loans, forces that are not totally rational. These forces usually act to the lender's advantage and the consumer's disadvantage.

HOW WE GET INFORMATION

Let's face it, no matter what we are shopping for these days, we are confronted by a lot of choices, whether it's laundry detergent, VCRs, cameras, automobiles, or carbonated beverages. If you are like me, when you start shopping for a big-ticket item, you consult *Consumer Reports.* That doesn't always make the choice any easier, because so many products have similar performance characteristics. If the top product rates a score of 90, often there are 10 other models rated between 80 and 90, any of which would probably meet your needs. Furthermore, the product rated as the "Best Buy" is seldom the market leader. Why? Because most of our buying decisions are based largely upon the reputations of companies and their image of their products rather than on facts, reason, and research. Every time you go into the supermarket, you choose products based on all the information you have gathered over the years. To illustrate my point, ask yourself the following questions:

- Can you write down the reasons you chose your long-distance carrier?
- Can you summarize the benefits provided by your health insurance program?
- Can you explain why you chose the particular brand of computer you have?

Don't feel bad; neither can I. The fact is that even these commonplace items have become so complex that we are compelled to make decisions about them based, not on careful research, but on the images created largely by the marketing and advertising departments of huge companies. That is how we get most of our information today. Simply put, when we make most of our buying decisions, we are winging it. But is this how you want to make choices about the largest item in your budget? Not likely.

The mortgage industry conveys information to the public in a manner that borders on the reprehensible. Chapter 1 revealed that 70 to 80 percent of all borrowers choose the wrong loan or pay too much. Lenders would like you to believe that they are providing you with all the knowledge you need to make a wise choice and that you are on an equal footing with them. Trust me, this is not the case. Lenders have an enormous amount of information that simply isn't available to you. Consider your own industry. I'm sure that there is much information widely known inside your company that is not known to your customers. The same is true in the mortgage industry.

For example, there is a database I subscribe to, and every day I download new data on the programs, the rates, and the fees of about 120 lenders. There are more than 80,000 entries, and they change every day. And that's not all. Lenders who do not want to publish their rates on this service because they want them known only to their select list of approved brokers send their rates to me by fax every morning. That's another 10,000 choices.

Of those 90,000 possible combinations, the average borrower will find only 10 or 20 or 30 while shopping for a loan. If the borrower is really thorough, the number might be as high as 50. That's less than ⅒th of 1 percent of the total amount of rate information available. It does not take a rocket scientist to tell you that there is a better program and rate in the remaining 99.9 percent of the market missed by the average borrower.

CONTROLLING YOUR ACCESS TO INFORMATION

Many lenders, perhaps most of them, have a vested interest in always having more information than you, the customer. Simply put, it is easier for lenders to deal with people who are *not* very knowledgeable; they can make more money from such people. These lenders shape your opinions about mortgages by filtering information regarding their companies and their products to make them look better. If you are asking, "You mean mortgages are sold like beer and laundry detergent?," the short answer is yes.

Let me offer the following evidence. Adjustable rate mortgages (ARMs) were introduced in 1983. Since then, borrowers have had a choice of loans tied to about five different indices. The loan that had the largest share of market was the one tied to the 11th District cost-of-funds index (COFI). In the ensuing 12 years, economic data were gathered to determine what each of these loans cost the borrowers. Guess which loan was the most expensive to consumers? Right—the 11th District COFI loan. The second most common ARM was tied to T-bills, and it was almost 1 percent cheaper than the COFI loan during that period. The cheapest loan was tied to six-month CDs and, sadly, it never enjoyed more than a 5 percent market share. Shocking? Perhaps, but it's true.

The lender-borrower relationship is what the mathematicians call a *zero-sum game:* What one party loses, the other wins. If the borrowers choose more of the high-cost loans, the lenders end up with the highest-profit loans—in spite of the fact every-one shops for the cheapest loan. Most borrowers end up with the most expensive loan, and the cheapest loan is the one in "last place." Obviously, something is fishy in the mortgage industry, and it can be summed up in this simple statement: *Most loan programs are sold, not bought.*

A loan officer for a bank or an S&L is really a salesperson whose job is to sell that profit-motivated company's program to the buyers. That company's marketing materials are designed to make that program look good, even if it isn't, which means if a company offers only loans tied to COFI (in the previous example, the most expensive ones), guess what the promotional material will tout? You guessed it: the COFI loan. A good salesperson can and will sell his or her product regardless of the facts.

It gets worse. All lenders offer a variety of loans, some of which we'll loosely call lower-profit-margin products and others that are higher-profit-margin products; obviously the company would rather have more higher-profit-margin products, so they pay their salespeople (loan officers) a higher commission rate on the higher-margin products. Many retail businesses call these *spiffs*. When the loan rep sits down with you, which product do you think you will hear about first? The one on which he or she gets the spiff. If the rep is a good salesperson, many customers will buy that program. Only if they show resistance will the rep finally unveil other products that are priced more attractively.

CONCLUSION

As a home buyer, you want the best deal you can find for your family; you want to spend the least amount on mortgage interest consistent with your ability to take risk. You want to make a rational choice. Unfortunately, much of the time the loan prod-ucts made available to you in the marketplace are not the best ones. Chances are, the big company where you bank does not offer the best products or the best pricing. But it probably *does* spend a great deal of money on advertising to put it foremost in the minds of its depositors and other consumers. The out-of-state lender that may have better mortgages cannot afford to compete with the local banks that offer checking accounts, savings accounts, car loans, mortgages, and a lot of other services. The persuasive power of the major advertisers to shape opinions is truly awesome, as you can see every day for products ranging from sportswear to autos to soft drinks.

What you must learn, and what I am here to impress upon you, is that the mortgage market offers many, many choices, but the good ones are often difficult to find. The purpose of this book is to help you cut through all the marketing hype and find a better deal for your family.

HOW LENDERS
MARKET LOANS

*A long habit of not thinking a thing wrong gives a
superficial appearance of being right. Time makes
more converts than reason.*

—THOMAS PAINE

KEY POINTS

- Lenders are just like other profit-making companies, and
  you should be just as cautious when dealing with them
  as you are in your other business dealings.
- Loan officers, or loan reps, are salespeople, some of
  whom will say anything, tell you they can solve any
  problem, even promise you rates that do not exist, just to
  convince you to fill out the application.
- When you are dealing with huge bureaucracies, remember, it is not the nature of such organizations to care
  about the individual customer.

A ROSE BY ANY OTHER NAME . . .

I find it fascinating and somewhat amusing that commercial
banks and savings and loan associations refer to themselves as
institutions. Where I grew up, institutions were organizations
such as colleges and universities, churches, hospitals, and museums. Banks may want you to think of them as "institutions," but
they are businesses whose objective is to make a profit. They

want you to believe that somehow they have a higher standard of ethical behavior, that they can be trusted more than other profit-making organizations.

The truth is that lenders' employees are people just like those in your company. They work for a living and they all take orders. Some are better than others, but their job is to make money without putting the enterprise at any undue risk, just like the company you work for. It's not that they aren't trustworthy; they very well may be, but you shouldn't assume they are or that they exist primarily to help you. They are out there to help themselves. If they can do that by funding your loan, they will.

MIND GAMES

I don't mean to depress or discourage you. I just want you to have your antenna out when you're listening to a lender tell you how wonderful his or her company is. The competitive pressures to succeed are enormous, just as they are in your business. Consequently, at some point someone in the marketing department may start taking a little liberty with the truth, or maybe he or she uses buzzwords to confuse people. Let me give you an example.

At times, ARMs account for perhaps 50 percent of new mortgage loans. Many borrowers shy away from ARMs because they are afraid that rates will "skyrocket" (almost everyone fears that word), and if they do, the borrower may no longer be able to afford his or her home. These people imagine that someone will come and evict them and they will have lost both their home and their equity.

Truly, no lender wants to be put in a position of repossessing people's houses. Lenders want you to be able to continue to make payments on your loan. After all, that's their business. To regulators, a foreclosure is visible evidence of a failure of the system. Bankers and regulators do not like failures, so all ARMs have some mechanism for preventing the payment from going up too quickly. In addition, all ARMs have a *ceiling rate,* a rate at which it stops going up regardless of what is happening in the economic world.

Those factors are common, however, to all ARMs. A lender can't brag about something that is available from every one of its competitors. Therefore, lenders talk about what they offer that is different, such as which index the company uses. Although at any given point in time, all the indices move more or less in the same direction, there are differences, the most significant being that some move more quickly than others. Let's call one type a *leading index* and the other type a *lagging index.* The lagging index moves in the same direction as the leading index, but more slowly, and it never gets as high on the upside because it's catching up. It also never gets as low on the downside.

From 1983 to 1995, interest rates were generally in a period of decline. If you were a portfolio lender and you wanted to maximize the yield on your loans, you would choose to offer loans tied to the lagging index because your yield would be higher in a market when rates were declining. If a leading index fell 1 percent, the rate on the lagging index might fall only ½ percent. That extra ½ percent is good for you as a lender, but would have a correspondingly higher cost to the borrowers. So the big question the portfolio lenders had to answer was how to get people who were looking for a low-cost loan to buy a high-cost loan. Well, they certainly couldn't come out and say, "Compared with other loans, this is a pretty expensive loan. To make it up to you, we'll give you a free checking account and this stuffed bear."

The marketing pros realized that customers had a strong negative reaction to the word *volatile.* Therefore, they instructed their sales reps (loan officers) to ask consumers, "Do you want a volatile loan or a stable one?" Well, sure enough, most people said they wanted a stable loan. So convincing was this message that even fairly smart people never came to the following logical conclusion: *"Wait a minute! You make it sound as if volatility is bad and stability is good. Volatility is only bad half of the time, when things are getting worse. When things are getting better (as when rates are falling), volatility is good. For the next few years, I want to be on the most volatile index I can find."* It wasn't ignorance that prevented customers from recognizing the fallacy in the marketing ploy. It was a combination of misplaced trust and not enough information.

An interesting footnote to all of this is that interest rates bottomed out in 1993–1994, with the T-bill yield dropping to about 3 percent. Some of these same institutions saw that the next interest rate move was going to be up. During a period of rising rates they would want loans tied to a leading index, not a lagging index. Loans tied to a leading index would be the first to move up and thus be the first to make more profit. So they deemphasized the lagging index loans and began to offer ARMs tied to T-bills, a leading index. For the consumers, agreeing to this type of loan was a huge mistake at the time. When rates are at lower levels than they have been for 20 years, that's the time to secure a fixed-rate loan, and there were plenty of fixed-rate loans offered at rates of 7 percent and below during this period. The only way consumers could be induced to take those T-bill ARMs was by offering them a very low start rate (called a *teaser rate*), some of them at less than 4 percent. Fixed-rate loans were being offered at 7 percent (by different lenders), so 4 percent looked good. Sure enough, in early 1994, rates took off, and those T-bill loans are today yielding 8.75 percent. How do those 7 percent fixed-rate loans look today?

Let's take this full cycle. During periods of declining rates, it's to the lending institution's advantage to offer only lagging index loans that are then the most profitable loans. When rates are down and likely to increase, it's to the lender's advantage to offer leading index loans that are going to be the most profitable in the coming period. My point is that lenders do this all the time. They are just like fishermen trying to catch the salmon swimming upstream. The job of the marketing department is to come up with bright, shiny lures to catch the quarry when they go by. They are constantly offering extraneous stuff to fool the consumers. You've heard about "zero-point loans," haven't you? Doesn't it sound as if you're getting something for free? Don't believe it. Every analysis I've ever done shows that the zero-point loan (covered in Chapter 19) is actually more expensive after a short period. Further, if customers had it explained to them thoroughly, very few would choose it. It's just another lure, and, sadly, it still works today because people hear the word *free* and conclude that it must be a good deal. Don't get hooked.

Of course, your bank or S&L may actually have a good loan for you, but you must make that decision based on facts, not on the company's say-so. In fact, except when some big bank is trying to buy market share, I don't consider banks to be very good real estate lenders. Many banking executives I know will say, "*We do not want to be the lowest-cost lender. We provide a lot of services to our clients and they are willing to pay a little more for that service.*" Perhaps those services may be worth the extra fees, but frankly, I doubt it. You should go where you can get the best deal.

TELEMARKETING AND DIRECT RESPONSE MARKETING

The most recent developments in the mortgage business are methods of marketing that are very successful to some lenders: telemarketing and direct response marketing. *Telemarketing* is when your phone rings at 7 P.M. and someone says, "Would you be interested if I could lower your monthly mortgage payment by $200?"

Direct response marketing is a euphemism for junk mail. Some lenders send out 200,000 pieces of mail every week. I cannot say this strongly enough: Beware of any lender using these methods. These are usually sweatshop-type operations specializing in B/C loans to credit-impaired borrowers. Whatever they offer, I'm sure you can find a better deal with a lender you find by using my recommendations.

THE FUTURE OF MARKETING IN THE MORTGAGE INDUSTRY

I enjoy my job. I like helping people buy their own homes. I like helping them understand their options. And I especially like helping some of those who need help the most. All the best people in the business feel as I do. Unfortunately, there are not many of us left. Most of us decry the loss of many of the industry's best counselors, replaced by mass marketing and less-than-reputable marketing methods.

Many of the major companies in the industry do not do a very good job of attracting and retaining a cadre of bright, well-educated, eager, and hardworking young people who make this business their career. Many now treat mortgage loan consultants as *entry-level positions* and use the mortgage department as a training arena. They hire recent college graduates, pay them $7.50 per hour, then run them through a three-week training program. Are you going to take advice from these people? I hope not.

Other companies, particularly the larger mortgage bankers and mortgage brokers, will hire almost anyone, fully expecting that 80 percent of them won't last more than a year or two. And they don't. In my view, the high turnover rate proves that their training is poor and that they never learn enough to become successful! They may do some business, but they aren't around long enough to truly learn the business, and they sure don't do a competent job of helping their clients.

I've told you all of this because I want you to have a realistic view of the situation. These organizations are run by people who make rules. Then they hire hundreds or thousands of people and tell them to follow those rules. If the rules say that they should approve your loan, they will do so. If the rules don't allow them to approve it, they won't. Your goal is to understand how to manipulate the situation to your benefit and to get what you want. The information in this book will help you accomplish that goal.

HOW TO CHOOSE
THE RIGHT LOAN

You'll never have all the information you need to make a decision. If you did, it would be a foregone conclusion, not a decision.

— DAVID MAHONEY

KEY POINTS

- The more risk protection you want, the more you'll have to pay.
- Every family has a different propensity for risk.
- The ideal loan is the one that balances these factors in your household.

FITTING THE LOAN INTO AN OVERALL FINANCIAL PLAN

I wish I knew who said, "Everyone is going to end up somewhere. If you have a plan, you'll end up where you want to be," because I agree. Once in a while, I have clients referred to me by a financial planner who has laid the groundwork. Such clients have a well-thought-out idea about what they want. Unfortunately, these people are all too few. If you haven't already done so, I strongly recommend that you hire a professional who can help you plan for your financial future. Such counseling should include mortgage planning because it is such a large part of everyone's financial picture.

In my experience, people go through the following phases in their economic lives:

20–30	Young people, first-time home buyers
30–40	Maturing people, often with growing families
40–50	Approaching middle age, perhaps with children in college
50–60	Approaching retirement, building equity and investments
60+	Retired or close to it, in their last home

Each of these groups has different considerations when seeking a loan. Furthermore, people at every stage of life suffer the ups and downs of the economic cycle; things are either getting better or worse; rates are either up or down and are heading one way or another. Those factors, too, influence what constitutes the proper type of loan for people at any given point in time. Perhaps that sounds obvious to you, but let me remind you: *Most people get the wrong loan or pay too much for their loan.*

People tend to go to one kind of institution or another based upon marketing hype, past experience, or because they don't understand the alternatives. A friend of mine runs the conduit through which a lot of credit unions sell their loans. Credit unions are pretty much fixed-rate shops, and most do not have employees who are adept at explaining complex loans to their members. Typically, regardless of where we are in the business cycle, between 90 and 95 percent of their loans are 30-year fixed-rate loans. When you go into a big S&L that is probably a portfolio lender, you'll find that it has a one-size-fits-all philosophy. "Our loan is perfect for you!" the rep will say. It may be easier to train the sales staff to sell a single product, but, in my view, that's a patently absurd approach to the market.

While reading this chapter, therefore, you should be particularly sensitive to your personal needs and goals so you can select the exact type of loan that will suit you precisely.

TYPES OF LOANS

The following are broad categories of generic loans currently available:

Conforming FNMA/FHLMC, currently less than $227,150
- 30-year fixed, 20-year fixed, 15-year fixed loans, fully amortized
- 5/25 loans, fixed for 5 years, then fixed for another 25 years
- 7/23 loans, fixed for 7 years, then fixed for another 23 years
- A large variety of ARMs

Jumbo loans, greater than $227,150
- 30-year fixed, 20-year fixed, 15-year fixed, 10-year fixed, fully amortized
- Interim fixed 3/1, 5/1, 7/1, 10/1 ARMs (also called FIRMs) fixed for the first named number of years, then turning into an ARM tied to the one-year T-bill index
- ARMs tied to T-bills, CDs, LIBORs, 11th District cost-of-funds, and prime rate

Again, these are just the broad categories. With specific differences, there are probably 300 or 500 different loans. Let's look at it from the lender's perspective to understand why the industry offers so many choices.

THE PRICE OF MONEY PLUS THE PRICE OF INSURANCE

Lenders are really concerned about three things: money, insurance, and risk. On any given day there is a basic price for money, which is related to what lenders have to pay their depositors or the price at which they can sell a loan. That determines the lowest absolute cost to the consumer.

The insurance part of the price is what you pay for long-term rate protection. If you ask the lender to guarantee your rate for one year, you'll get one price. If you ask for 15 years of protection, you'll pay more, a premium based on how risky the market perceives the additional 15 years of rate protection. You can conclude that the 30-year fixed-rate mortgage would have to be the most expensive product the industry offers, and you're right.

Finally, lenders assess the more obvious risk factors. The more risk the lender perceives, the more you pay. If a prospective borrower has a poor credit history, the lender perceives that it has a greater risk of not getting its money back, so the risk part of the price goes up. At higher loan-to-value (LTV) ratios, there is less equity to protect the lender's interest, so the rate goes up.

✳ *Here's the first lesson in choosing a loan:* Buy rate protection only for the length of time you'll be in the property. If you select a 30-year fixed-rate loan and you are in your home for only seven years, you paid a lot of extra money for 23 years of rate protection that you didn't need. How much is that? Well, the industry offers loans that are fixed for just seven years, and they are priced approximately ½ percent below the 30-year fixed-rate loan. On a $200,000 loan, that ½ percent amounts to $1,000 per year. Choosing a 30-year loan initially instead of a 7-year loan would cost you $7,000. To easily dodge one of those expensive "risk adjustments," buy rate insurance only for the amount of time you are going to be in the house. Not every home buyer knows this in advance, but many people do, and I just gave you 7,000 reasons to consider this carefully. Millions of people make this mistake simply because they don't have someone like me to explain it to them.

THE YIELD CURVE

People in financial circles talk about the *yield curve* because it is a very important concept in the management of large sums of money. Basically, it shows how the market values the yields on government obligations with varying maturities. (Other financial instruments, such as mortgage loans, will vary along with Treasury bills, notes, and bonds.) Figure 4.1 shows what the curve looked like in early 1994. This curve can be of value to borrowers in determining the general tenor of the times; it reflects how the market values the premium you might pay for longer-term rate protection. For example, the yield curve in Figure 4.1 is relatively steep, reflecting a large difference between short- and long-term rates. By comparison, the curve in Figure 4.2 shows that the market differentials are low, making the cost of long-term borrowing not much more expensive than that of short-term borrowing. The yield curves are superimposed so you can see the difference.

Finally, Figure 4.3 shows a comparison between the yields on Treasury instruments with the cost to a borrower of a one-year

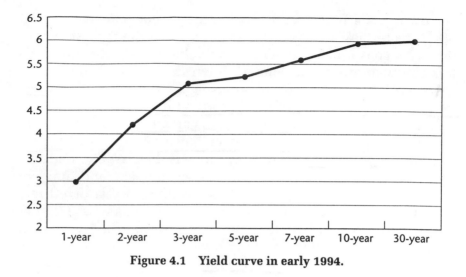

Figure 4.1   Yield curve in early 1994.

ARM (index plus margin, not start rate), various FIRMs, (loans such as 3/1, 5/1, 7/1, and 10/1 ARMs), and finally, a 30-year fixed-rate mortgage.

We look at these data to see how expensive, or cheap, various loans are at a given point in time. If you make the assumption that lenders could invest in Treasury bonds if they wanted to, it follows that they will invest in (fund) mortgages only if they feel that the yields they can obtain on mortgages are enough higher than the yields on Treasury obligations of comparable maturity to

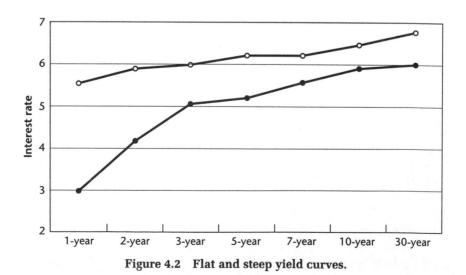

Figure 4.2   Flat and steep yield curves.

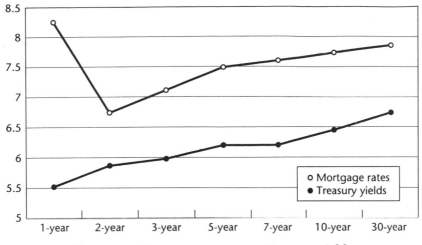

Figure 4.3   Mortgage rates versus Treasury yields.

warrant the risk. If the lender offered to do loans at the prices reflected in the higher curve, the difference between that curve and the Treasury yield curve could be interpreted as the markup, or profit margin, of that particular mortgage loan. You want a loan with the lowest profit margin (I hope!), and Figure 4.3 helps you understand the opportunities more easily.

As you can see, Figure 4.3 shows that the largest markup on the one-year T-bill ARM that, by definition, has a markup equal to its margin of 2.75, making it a very expensive alternative. The markup for the FIRMs is lower, which is another reason I am so fond of them. This kind of analysis is a little obtuse for many people, I know, but the data are not hard to get. The Treasury yield curve is printed in most newspapers on a weekly basis. It is also available at various sites on the Internet, notably http://www.dbc.com.

FIXED RATE VERSUS ADJUSTABLE RATE

The first question many people ask is, "Am I better off with a fixed-rate loan or an adjustable rate mortgage?" The answer is twofold:

1. If you are in a period of rising interest rates, get a fixed-rate mortgage. Even though you'll pay a higher rate ini-

tially, you'll save in the long run when the rates move higher.

2. If rates are falling, get an adjustable rate mortgage.

That may sound too simple, but it's true. Anyway, it's the first issue to deal with. I can hear someone asking, "How do I know whether rates are rising or falling?" Well, I can't predict the future any more than you can, and if you find someone who claims to, run, do not walk, in the other direction! However, I will point out that this is a cyclical world—the tide comes in and the tide goes out. If rates are or have been high, the next move will probably be down. Conversely, when rates have been down for a while, the next move will probably be up. Whether you are reading this book in 1998 or 2008, you probably have a pretty good feel for where rates have been and where they are going. Trust your intuition, but try to avoid making an emotional decision that leads to an unwise choice. Let's leave it at that.

REAL RISK VERSUS PERCEIVED RISK

Next, we need to evaluate risk factors—*your* risk, not the lender's risk. There are two types of risks: real and perceived. Real risk factors include being on a fixed income, having limited liquid assets, and so forth. People who work as ministers, teachers, or government employees have very little ability to change their income. It's unlikely that a minister whose mortgage payment goes up $500 per month is going to start moonlighting by tending bar on Friday nights. With some rare exceptions, my view is that ARMs are totally inappropriate for anyone on a fixed income.

I define *perceived risk* as the propensity to accept risk. Over the years, I can't think of any one thing I have done that is more important than helping people identify their propensity to accept risk. According to the people I interview, about 90 percent describe themselves as being "more conservative than average." That's a little silly when you think about it because by definition, exactly 50 percent of people are more conservative than average and the other 50 percent are less so. Let's call the first group "less willing to take risk" than average and the second group "more willing to take risk" than average.

Most people in the first group are going to be predisposed to get a fixed-rate loan. They are more cautious, probably have more cash and investments, and probably have fewer credit cards than average. In terms of their employment, you'd see more of these people gravitate toward jobs that are more secure. The people in the second group, to varying degrees, have the opposite characteristics.

Unfortunately, most people don't know which group they belong to. They become indecisive and uncomfortable even talking about risk. Let me tell you a funny story. A firefighter came into my office one day. Rates were moving favorably downward, and most people were interested in ARMs. So we talked about ARMs. His initial reaction to the ARM loan was, "That sounds scary!" I retorted, "Wait a minute. You're a guy who runs into burning buildings, and you think *this* is scary?" He quickly added, "Well, I won't run into just *any* burning building." The point is that he knew enough about burning buildings to be able to tell which ones he could safely run into and which ones to stay out of. He had found a comfort zone about burning buildings. My job was to explain ARMs to him so that he could find a similar comfort zone about them. Once he felt comfortable, we proceeded to obtain an ARM for him.

Risk Wrap-Up

It may be stating the obvious, I know, but the ultimate protection against financial woe is wealth. But very few people—even those who are—think of themselves as wealthy. Of course, everything is relative. Someone making $50,000 may think that a person making $500,000 doesn't have any worries. Well, people who make $500,000 worry too; they just worry about different things. At every level in our economy, there are people who are "comfortable" and those who are "stretched" all the time, another facet of my propensity-to-accept-risk factor. A person's income or the amount of money a person has accumulated has very little to do with this factor.

I'll end this section with an illustration showing how you can use common sense to work through the decision-making process. With certain exceptions, people on fixed incomes should not have adjustable rate mortgages. Here's a true example of one such exception. A teacher has inherited about $200,000, which she has invested in CDs and T-bills. She wants a loan, but fixed rates are unfavorable and ARMs are priced attractively. I analyze her situation with her. I point out that if rates go up, say, 1 percent, her $100,000 mortgage will get more expensive, by $1,000 annually. She is worried about this until I point out that the interest income on her investments goes up, too, by $2,000 for every 1 percent increase. That's twice as much. Because the increase in her interest income exceeds the increase in the cost of her mortgage, an ARM actually can't possibly hurt her. This sounds like a commonsense deduction, but it is not intuitively obvious when you first start thinking about it.

Risk Assessment Calculator

To assist you in determining where you stand with regard to risk, get out a pencil and paper and start making notes based on the following categories. Give yourself 1 point, 3 points, or 5 points depending on how closely you fit the description.

	1 point	3 points	5 points
Age	Over 50	30–50	Less than 30
Employment	Still looking	Okay or uncertain	Very stable
Income	Scraping by	Okay	Very comfortable
Income potential	Stable	Growing	The sky's the limit
Resources	Little or no savings	Doing okay	Lots of investments
Credit balances	I was afraid you'd ask	Some, but under control	Pay in full each month
Future burdens	Children entering college	Under control	None
Insurance	What the employer provides	Some	Plenty or no need
Investment profile	CDs at my bank	Mutual funds	Stocks, bonds, others
Return expected	2%–5%	5%–10%	More than 10%

Now add up your score.

	10 to 20 points	20 to 35 points	More than 35 points
Profile	Risk-intolerant	Can take some risk	Can take more risk
Alternative name	Cautious	Moderate	Aggressive

You can see that if you are young and moderately advanced in your career, even though you may not have a lot of financial strength, your potential for rising income puts you in a position to take some risks. On the other hand, if you are approaching retirement, you are past the point of wanting to bet the farm on whether interest rates will go up or down. I hope you'll agree that it is worthwhile to think about these factors and to put them down on paper. Refer to this exercise as you continue to read.

INDIVIDUAL CASE HISTORIES

I find that people can relate to individual experiences better than to generalities. Some of the following examples are composites, but the basic facts have been taken from my case files. I hope you find one that mirrors your situation and helps clarify your thinking.

A Young Couple

Joe and Alice Freeman graduated from school a few years ago and are into their careers. They both have secure jobs. Joe and Alice want to start implementing their financial plan by purchasing a home and feeling secure before they consider expanding their family in a few more years.

Here are some of the variables they should consider when selecting a loan. HUD / (veterans)

- FHA and VA loans are considered by many people to be the best loans for people with low down payments. While they are the loan of choice for some, the interest rates on these loans has been higher than comparable conventional mortgages, which, in my mind, makes them a loan of last resort—to be sought only after other choices have been explored.

NO

high interest

- A common, and nonnegotiable, requirement of most low-down-payment loans is that the borrowers must have saved 5 percent themselves! After they have saved their 5 percent, they should try to get gifts from parents to increase the down payment to 10 percent or even 20 percent. Although there are a large number of first-time-buyer programs designed to accommodate people with 3 or 5 percent down payments, the cost of private mortgage insurance is high. They could pay their parents 14 percent tax deductible and it would be about the same as paying non-tax-deductible premium payments to a PMI company.

- Many of the first-time-buyer programs are set up only for 30-year fixed-rate loans. In contrast, studies show that most first-time buyers own their homes for only about seven years. For many people, a two-step loan will meet their needs. As of this writing, FNMA and FHLMC will do 7/23 loans at 90 percent LTV, but not 5/25 loans. However, there are many lenders who will do interim fixed-rate loans, such as a 5/1 or 7/1 ARM, at LTVs of 95 percent for loan amounts up to $300,000. Joe and Alice should ask themselves serious questions about how long they are likely to be in this property. If it's for five years or so, they should opt for an interim fixed-rate or two-step loan.

The following steps will prepare anyone in Joe and Alice's situation for home ownership.

- Stay in a modest apartment or small home. Don't squander down payment money on temporary housing.

- Start putting money aside every payday. If possible, live on one paycheck and save the other.

- Defer buying a new car.

- Don't allow credit card debt to build up.

- Eat at home and enjoy inexpensive entertainment and vacations.

- Discuss the possibility of financial help with parents and other family members who are in a position to help.

- When you get close to the time to buy, check your credit report and repair errors.
- Find a good lender and get preapproved.

A Single Mother

Jane Roberts is a recently divorced mother with a young child. She has a good job, and in her divorce settlement she was awarded both spousal support and child support payments. The previous family home was sold, and Jane's share of the proceeds will be used as the down payment on a new home for herself and her child.

Jane should evaluate how long she is likely to be in the home, but I would probably recommend that she stick with a 30-year fixed-rate mortgage. In my view, single mothers are sort of like ministers, teachers, and others who are not in a position to take much risk. She should choose a risk-free loan.

Many lenders have loan programs available under the Community Reinvestment Act that are available only to people who make less than a designated percentage of the average income in a particular county. Jane's income as a single mother may very well qualify her for such a program, which has more flexible underwriting guidelines.

There are several other considerations unique to Jane's situation.

- She will have to give the lender a copy of her interlocutory decree she received from the court showing the mandated support payments. Many lenders also require evidence (via copies of checks from the ex-spouse) that she actually *receives* the support payments. You may wonder who bothers to keep them. My point! Keep them or provide bank statements that show those regular deposits.
- Jane should get her own credit card account. She should close all joint accounts she has with her ex-spouse and establish credit in her own name. That way, if her ex-husband is (or becomes) a problem maker, it won't damage her credit. Creditors for which there is an outstanding balance may not release her liability on the existing

account, but she can require that the card be closed to further purchases; when the existing balance is finally paid off, the account can be closed.

- Because child support payments are not taxable income, many lenders will increase them through a process known as *grossing up*. That will increase the loan amount for which Jane qualifies.

- If she is paying child-care costs such as a day-care center, she should not put this information on the application unless the lender requires it. If she puts it down, lenders will count it as a negative and it will reduce her ability to qualify for a loan. If she doesn't mention it, most lenders don't care or ask.

Middle-Aged Couple Buying a New Home

John and Brenda Francis have just celebrated their youngest child's college graduation. They no longer need their large family home and have decided to move to a smaller home. The significant financial characteristics are as follows:

- Because they will no longer be paying college expenses, John and Brenda have more disposable income.

- They probably have significant equity in their current residence.

- They are close to retirement.

Fifteen-year loans are ideal for people in this situation. John and Brenda probably do not want to make mortgage payments for the next 30 years because they will not be working for 30 more years. For a home that is smaller and less expensive, they can get a 15-year loan for which the monthly payment is actually less than the one on their previous home. Even if the payment were to be larger, they can accommodate a larger payment in their budget. As a retirement plan, owning a home free and clear is a great first step for many people. Just think about what your budget would be like without a mortgage payment!

Although biweekly payment plans have gotten a lot of publicity lately, if you read Chapter 17, you will learn that there is very little difference between a 15-year loan paid monthly and biweekly payments on a 30-year loan—except that the 15-year loan is typically ⅜ percent cheaper! That ⅜ percent makes the 15-year loan a much better choice.

Moving from Nebraska to Marin County

Peter and Nancy Grant have just sold their home in Omaha for $150,000 and are moving to Marin County, California, near Peter's new office in San Francisco. The Grants have discovered that comparable housing in California costs $300,000. They are experiencing the housing industry's equivalent of *sticker shock!* Even if Peter gets an immediate raise, it might not be enough for them to comfortably make a mortgage payment over twice the amount of their payment in Omaha.

The first step is to inquire about Peter's employer's relocation policy. Many companies have a mortgage-differential payment program that pays some of the increased mortgage payment, based on regional cost-of-housing variations, phased out over a five-year period of time.

We should operate under the presumption that Peter's income will be rising because, in general, only employees who are advancing would be candidates for a move. That means they have the ability to take greater financial risk than other people. They are also more likely to be transferred again. Consequently, this is one of those cases where a pure ARM with a low introductory rate or an interim fixed-rate loan such as a 3/1 ARM or 5/1 ARM would be the best choice.

If 30-year loans are at 8 percent, ARMs might have a start rate of only 6 percent, and a 3/1 ARM might be at 7 percent. An ARM with the potential for negative amortization might have a start rate even lower, perhaps 4 or 5 percent. Peter and Nancy can reduce their payment shock significantly with these loans and, for them, the future risk is almost certainly within acceptable boundaries.

Elderly Couple Selling Home

Bill and Fran Jensen are retired and selling their home to move to a retirement community. Let's assume the following:

- They have developed significant equity in their current home.
- Their income will be modest compared with that of their preretirement years.

The first decision is whether to have *any* loan on the new property. With the tax law changes in 1997, most people will no longer incur a capital gains tax on the sale of the old residence when buying a property of lesser value. Therefore, there is no need to get a loan to save cash for paying taxes.

In my mind, this decision depends on the tax situation of the borrowers and the availability of investments that earn a return higher than the cost of the mortgage. Let's review these issues.

If Bill and Fran's income is mostly from Social Security and pension benefit payments, it is likely that their marginal income tax rate is low. This means that the value of tax deductions such as mortgage interest are minimal and they should consider paying cash for the home. A couple with investment income or income from rental properties in addition to Social Security would be in a higher tax bracket, and the deductions would be correspondingly larger. Other things being equal, they should get a mortgage.

As for investment alternatives, if the cost of borrowing is, say, 7 percent, and if Bill and Fran have a portfolio of stocks and mutual funds that yield 12 percent, they would be better off having a mortgage and adding to their investments. There are even situations where the after-tax cost of borrowing, 4.5 or 5 percent, may be such that they can invest in tax-free investments such as municipal bonds and still come out ahead.

For people who do not have significant savings or who are used to the 3 or 4 percent the banks pay on savings deposits, it makes no sense to borrow at 7 percent and put the money into investments that yield only 4 percent.

As for the type of mortgage, 30-year fixed or 15-year fixed mortgages are the only appropriate loans for people who are not in a position to take any risks.

Single Woman Who Doesn't Plan to Get Married

Sheila Fisher is a single woman who does not plan to get married. She is secure in her career, has made maximum contributions to her company's 401(k) plan, and has developed a portfolio of investments. She is thinking about cashing in some of her portfolio for a down payment on a home.

First, she should carefully plan which assets to liquidate. If she sells stock to get the down payment, she should remember to set aside enough to pay any capital gains tax that might be due as a result of the sale. As discussed earlier, she should attempt to make as large a down payment as she can to avoid or minimize PMI premiums. She should tap parents and relatives if possible. She should also consider borrowing against her 401(k) plan or IRA. While this is usually perilous, many retirement plans allow special consideration for loans when the purpose is to purchase a principal residence. Specifically, the loan may be paid back over a longer period of time than the usual five-year period without incurring tax penalties. If Sheila has a sizable balance in her plan and wishes to use a portion of that for a down payment, she should check with her plan administrator and tax adviser.

Traditionally, the industry's approach has been that women can take less risk than men and should stick to fixed-rate mortgages. I have done lots of loans for career women, and I've concluded that many women are better able to accept risk than men. If Sheila's career is such that she has opportunities for upward mobility, she can be bolder in her approach to mortgage selection than if, for example, she is a teacher whose income is likely to remain relatively fixed. I would recommend that she consider taking advantage of the lower rates of two-step loans (5/25 and 7/23) and 5/1 and 7/1 ARMs.

Bachelor Who's Loaded

Tom French is a bachelor who made a lot of money early in his career and invested it wisely. His busy career put buying a home on the back burner. In addition, falling real estate values deterred him, but now the market in his area is turning around, and he is thinking that investing in real estate would be a good idea.

He's right. Every study I have ever seen shows that the long-term cost of owning a home is less than the cost of renting. If housing values are increasing, this is good timing. A person with abundant assets can afford to be very opportunistic about carrying a mortgage. Specifically, Tom is definitely not a candidate for a 30-year fixed-rate mortgage. If rates are at low levels, which I will define as being able to get a 5/1 ARM for 7.5 percent or less, Tom should take a loan and buy down the rate, as long as he can get a ⅛ percent reduction in the rate for every additional ⅜ percent point.

If rates suddenly jump higher than they have been in the past year, say above 8 percent when they have been below 7.5 percent, there is a likelihood that rates will eventually drop. In that case, Tom should choose a 3/1 ARM or a 5/1 ARM with zero points and refinance when rates drop.

If rates are 7 percent or less, then he should give serious consideration to getting a 15-year loan and buying down the rate, as above. If his income is commensurate with his accumulation of assets, the larger payment is incidental.

Minority Couple

Bill and Martha Williams live in the inner city of a large metropolitan area where they grew up. Bill has a good job in the construction industry. They are doing well financially, and they have saved enough money for a down payment on a home. As their children approach school age, they are considering moving to the suburbs, where they believe the educational opportunities are better. They are worried about the higher cost of housing in the suburbs and whether they will qualify for a loan. They are also concerned about whether they will be treated fairly by a lender.

Although I hear that redlining—withholding loans in certain areas considered to be poor risks—is still around, I believe that the federal Equal Credit Opportunity Act and similar state legislation have reduced the bias in lending in recent years. Nonetheless, it is not unreasonable for Bill and Martha to be wary about this issue. Most national lenders are under constant regulatory scrutiny to ensure they don't engage in discriminatory lending practices. Under the provisions of the Community Reinvestment Act (CRA), lenders are urged to increase their lending in certain areas deemed to have been adversely impacted in the past. Lenders also target people whose income is less than the average income for their community.

In my view, these lenders will bend over backward to lend to people meeting the minority criteria because it will help them meet their mandated targets for such loans. In particular, such borrowers may actually receive preferential treatment. When they choose to, lenders can be somewhat flexible about income, credit, and qualifying ratios. (In Bill's case, his income as a construction worker will fluctuate more than someone on salary, and fluctuating income is always a cause for concern among lenders.) Having said that, there are no doubt other lenders who will not work as hard as they should for certain borrowers, so you should choose a lender carefully.

The area of community lending is very complicated. One lender has a 10-page matrix that explains all the rules of the various alternatives. Picking the right one is not an easy task. Bill and Martha need to find an expert in this field. They should seek advice from their Realtor® and then call the larger lenders in their area. They should be very specific about their needs so they can be connected with the right people. (The average loan rep will not be knowledgeable in this field.) Finally, most CRA programs are available for only 15- and 30-year fixed-rate loans.

LOAN-TERM WORKSHEET

Finally, for those who feel more comfortable doing a personal, hands-on risk assessment, I want to give you a tool to help you make one of the most troublesome mortgage decisions: whether to take a 30-year fixed-rate loan or one of the cheaper, short-term alternatives. I've designed a little worksheet, shown in Figure 4.4, to help you weigh the value of one loan alternative against another. It is independent of the actual prices because it is concerned with *differences*, not the rates themselves. Let's work through an example. Then you can make copies of the blank worksheet or, better yet, generate your own matrix on a spreadsheet program like Excel or Lotus 1-2-3.

Remember, the more risk protection you want, the higher the price. In this worksheet, you'll quantify the risk protection you are getting and the amount you are paying for it. That way, you can determine the value of your protection. Let's assume that you need a $200,000 loan and are thinking that you may be in your house for six or seven years. You want to calculate the difference between a 30-year fixed-rate loan and a 5/25 loan that will be rewritten to the market rate (higher or lower) at the end of the fifth year.

		Insert your numbers here	Sample
	LOAN-TERM WORKSHEET		
A	Loan amount		$200,000
B	Loan #1		7.50%
C	Loan #2		7.00%
B − C = D	Difference in %		0.50%
D * A = E	Difference in $ per yr		$1,000
F	Years in home		5
E * F = G	Savings in initial period		$5,000
H	Potential additional years		2
F/H = J	$ per additional year		$2,500
J/A = K	Additional % factor expressed as %		1.25%
K + C = L	New breakeven % rate		8.25%

Figure 4.4   Loan-term worksheet.

Step 1: Analyzing the difference. Make sure that you adjust the pricing so that each alternative has the same origination fee (that is, the same points). You have the following two pricing alternatives.

Row	Item	Entry
A		$200,000
B	30-year	7.5%
C	5/25	7%
D	Calculate the difference in rate	0.5% = 0.005
E	Calculate difference in $ per year	$200,000 × 0.005 = $1,000
F	Total years in home	5 years
G	Total savings	5 × $1,000 = $5,000

Let me explain. If you take the 30-year loan at 7.5 percent, you paid $5,000 more, which represents the "insurance premium" you have paid over that five-year period. The value is that if you are still there after five years, you will pay only 7.5 percent for another 25 years, regardless of what the interest rate market does. Now we want to figure out if that's a good deal for you.

Step 2: Is this a good deal?

Row	Item	Entry
H	Potential additional years	2
J	Calculate $ per year	$5,000 / 2 years = $2,500
K	Item J divided by loan amount	$2,500 / 200,000 = 1.25%
L	Calculate new breakeven rate	7% + 1.25% = 8.25%

To summarize, if you take the 5/25 loan, you save $5,000 in interest. If it turns out that you are still there in years 6 and 7, as long as the rate on the 5/25 loan doesn't adjust to more than 8.25 percent at the end of the fifth year, you made the right choice. If the rate adjusts to higher than 8.25 percent, the added interest cost will be more than the $5,000 you saved, and the 30-year loan would have been the better choice.

I think you can see where I am going here. This model can quantify the problem for you and make the decision process easier. It is difficult to deal with this question on a qualitative basis. It is a lot easier for most people to use the worksheet and then make one of the following two determinations:

"I'd rather save the $5,000 and take my chances."

"I think that rates may be at 10 percent five years from now, and $5,000 looks like a cheap premium to me."

Ultimately, the goal is to be comfortable with your decision. The worksheet shown in Figure 4.4 has helped hundreds of my clients. I hope it helps you as well.

5

FOR FIRST-TIME
HOME BUYERS

Chance favors the prepared mind.
—Louis Pasteur

KEY POINTS

- First-time home buyers are very important to the mortgage industry.
- Lenders and agencies create new ways of expanding opportunities for home ownership, frequently by making it easier to get a loan.
- There are a wide variety of loan programs requiring very low down payments.
- First-time home buyers have traditionally relied on financial assistance from parents. Lenders are in favor of this, but they have some specific rules that are important to know.
- Significant advantages accrue when borrowers get preapproved for a loan.

First-time home buyers have always been a mainstay of the housing industry, accounting for anywhere from 20 to 40 percent of the industry's volume. As a group, however, they present some unique problems to lenders. First, they are the least knowledgeable of all borrowers, and they frequently do not have extensive credit histories beyond, perhaps, a car loan. Second, many do not have, as the industry phrases it, "demonstrated habits of thrift." This means that they usually have not yet saved enough for a down payment on a home. Even with gifts of money from parents and other sources, they are almost invariably cash-strapped at closing. Third, rarely do they settle for a home priced within their means. Finally, in spite of the almost constant injunctions from the mortgage industry, from home builders, and from Realtors, first-time home buyers seldom prepare themselves properly for the process of buying a home and getting a mortgage. (If this describes you, I hope you will take this as my recommendation to get a credit report and commit to being preapproved by a lender when the time is appropriate and *before* you start house-hunting.)

Still, in the face of those difficulties, because they are such an important part of the business, the real estate community will always bend over backward to try to get first-time buyers into a home. And from a very basic standpoint, I am all for this. I believe that the dedication of people to save money for the down payment and to make payments for a home in the face of economic hardships is a driving force behind the American economic system.

PROGRAMS, PROGRAMS, PROGRAMS

Much of the information the average consumer gets about the mortgage industry comes from the media, gathered by people who get paid for writing articles or news or radio reports to engage the public's attention. When HUD or FNMA or some lender comes out with a new program, these media pros will get the press releases and distill and filter the facts about the new program. Too often, an unsuspecting public becomes victim to what I will call "programmitis." They become mesmerized by the features of a particular program to the extent that they don't consider the alternatives. They are sold on a program because it sounds good. Of course it sounds good. The company promoting it probably spent $50,000 trying to make it sound good.

One such concept was the *graduated payment mortgage* (GPM). The idea behind this program was to have a payment that started out low and then increased gradually as the homeowner's income (ideally) increased over the years. Doesn't that sound like a good program for a first-time home buyer? I thought so, too. The problem was that lenders charged a little more for this program because it was "different" and harder to bundle and sell on the secondary market.

Furthermore, because of the industry's aforementioned poor sales force, more complicated programs are not adequately explained to people. In many cases, lenders will not even attempt to explain a program if they think that they are going to fail at it.

This chapter is devoted to programs and ideas that I know to be important to you. (Programs of little merit will be ignored.)

Community Home Buyer Programs and Other Affordable Loan Programs

As a result of the Community Reinvestment Act (CRA), the lending industry is under some pressure from Congress to expand home ownership opportunities, particularly for those geographic areas and demographic groups considered to have been underserved by the industry in the past. As a result, lenders today offer a wide variety of loan programs, the characteristics of which would have been thought of as ridiculous, even dangerous, 10 years ago.

The following program parameters will give you an idea what to look for. Most of these programs are restricted to 30-year fixed-rate mortgages (or, infrequently, 15-year mortgages if qualifying isn't an issue) for primary residences, and usually the borrowers may not own other real estate. Certain programs require that the borrowers attend special classes to inform them of the issues of home ownership. Finally, there are down payment requirements; in most cases, borrowers must contribute at least 5 percent (in some cases, 3 percent) from their own savings.

- *Income-driven programs.* The borrower's income cannot exceed the HUD-determined median income average for the area. In other words, income-driven programs are geared to help people with lower-than-average incomes. In some high-cost areas, the minimum income requirement is increased. For example, in California, the minimum income is 120 percent of the median income for the county in which the property is located.

- *Area-driven programs.* These are programs that are available only to people purchasing property in certain designated census tracts or zip codes determined to be deserving of extra attention and assistance.

- *Other programs.* Various other programs from many lenders do not have the preceding restrictions, but lenders will make special allowances for first-time home buyers. At this time, loans requiring only a 5 percent down payment are available on amounts up to $300,000 in a wide assortment of loan programs in addition to the 30-year fixed-rate programs. ✳

QUALIFYING ISSUES

Credit

When buyers have minimal equity to protect the lender, the buyers will be expected to have near-perfect credit. If this is you, I reiterate that it is extremely important to get your credit report to determine whether there are any problems. For further details on credit and solving credit problems, read Chapter 8. Make sure the bureau from which you get your report gives you credit scores from at least two bureaus. This score will be of growing importance in the years to come. FNMA has made FICO (the name comes from Fair, Isaac & Co.) scoring mandatory on all loans sold to them, so you should make sure you have this information *before* it's reported to your lender.

Equity Requirements

Until the mid-1980s, except for FHA and VA programs, a home buyer was typically required to have a 20 percent down payment. The only other hope for the cash-strapped buyer was to find a seller who was willing to finance part of the purchase price to facilitate the purchase. In the early 1980s, some of the banks and S&Ls did a lot of "seconds" behind old low-interest-rate "firsts" that were assumable in that era. (Today, most fixed-rate loans are not assumable, and ARMs are assumable only with the consent of the lender.)

As I mentioned earlier, there are a wide variety of programs available requiring only 10, 5, or even 3 percent down. Naturally, qualifying for these programs means meeting more rigid requirements than those for the buyer with 20 percent down, but some lenders today offer programs to routinely approve loans for buyers with only a 5 percent down payment, even if their qualifying ratios are high. (See Chapter 9.)

Down Payment

I don't know how many people decide to buy a home before they are really financially ready to do so, but it's a whopping big percentage. Once someone decides to purchase a home, it may take two years to accumulate a down payment, and many people do not want to wait that long. Consequently, many rely on help from more established members of their families. Because asking for help is so common, the industry has agreed to consider such assistance if the assistance takes the form of a *gift*—meaning it is not a loan. My guess is that about 75 percent of such "gifts" are not really gifts at all, but loans that are eventually repaid. So why does the industry treat these loans as gifts? Well, family members aren't likely to foreclose in case of a problem. Indeed, if the borrower gets in a financial bind, more often than not the relatives will step in and actually help protect their investment.

If you are the beneficiary of a gift of this nature, there are a few points to be aware of:

- Even when you receive a portion of the down payment from another source, you will be expected to have saved at least 5 percent yourself. To most lenders, this is *non-negotiable,* primarily because it is a PMI requirement. The exception is if the total down payment is more than 20 percent, in which case PMI isn't involved, although many lenders will still not do a loan for people who haven't saved something themselves.

- Most lenders require that the donor have a blood relationship with the recipient. The assumption is that someone not related is simply not going to *give* thousands of dollars to another person without strings attached.

- Get the gift *now!* Don't fiddle around. I have seen deal after deal where someone agrees to help but is reluctant to give the money until two or three days before closing.

That's very shortsighted, because the lender needs ......
to document the gift. That documentation starts with a
gift letter similar to the one shown in Figure 5.1.

It's important to note that just having the gift show up will
not satisfy most lenders. Absent proof that it is really a gift, they
will presume that you are borrowing the down payment, which
is not allowed. The lender will want to see either a Verification
of Deposit on the account the money is coming from or three
months of statements confirming that the donor "owns" the
money and that he or she did not borrow it. The lender will also
want to see a copy of the check from the donor and a copy of the
deposit receipt whereby it was deposited into the buyer's bank
account. You can see how this can be a problem if you wait until
the last minute. Do not underestimate the lender's determination

---

GIFT LETTER

To whom it may concern:

This is to certify that a gift of $_____ is being made
to _____ for the purposes of buying a residence.

No repayment is required or expected.

Relationship of donor to recipient _____

Source of funds _____

Bank _____

Address _____

City _____

Account # _____

As an assistance, you may provide three months of statements on the
above account.

_____   _____
Donor   Date

Address _____   City, State, Zip _____

Phone (___)_____

Figure 5.1   Sample gift letter.

to get the documentation. The lender will hold up funding until the documentation is in hand. It is easy if you start early, almost impossible if you leave it to the last minute.

Co-borrowers

First-time buyers are shocked to learn that when they have a co-borrower, their qualifying problems don't go away. They believe that the problems created by lack of a down payment, nonexistent or poor credit history, or high qualifying ratios will evaporate when a financially strong person agrees to join the picture. Right or wrong, this is not the case. Led by FNMA, the industry will accept "nonoccupying co-borrowers" on loans where the LTV is greater than 80 percent, but there are still some severe restrictions. It is expected that the "occupying co-borrowers" (the principal borrowers) will *almost* qualify on their own and that help from outsiders is merely to *strengthen* the application. That is harsh, I agree. These restrictions are probably justified by the performance history of such loans over a long period of time, because the rules are getting more strict, not less so.

   If, however, you are putting down 20 percent, there are portfolio lenders that have adopted different policies (thank goodness!). They just want to make sure that someone is responsible to ensure the payments are made.

100 PERCENT LTV LOANS

A few years ago, one of the major brokerage houses came out with a unique program. It would provide financing for 100 percent of the sales price of a home. The kicker was that the portion of the loan over 80 percent of the purchase price would be collateralized by the equity in the buyer's stock and bond portfolio at the firm. This shows creative thinking, and I like it—for some people. A newer wrinkle is that the firm will also provide financing to the buyer using an outsider's portfolio, usually the parents', for the additional security. This is a slick program for certain buyers, but it comes at a cost.

   One of the California S&Ls will also do 100 percent financing if you deposit 25 percent of the purchase price into a CD. I suppose that as long as you are a CD investor and you like the loan terms, that would be good, too. Both programs offer flexibility for those people who do not want to make an outright gift to a family member in need of assistance.

Sadly, a number of uninformed buyers pay way too much for these 100 percent LTV loans (remember what I said about "programmitis?"). They had the 20 percent down and they could have gotten much cheaper financing with an 80 percent loan, but their stockbroker sold them on a high-profit loan offered by his or her firm. Again, I caution the buyer to beware of marketing madness. Do the research.

PREAPPROVAL

Earlier in this book, I have encouraged buyers to get preapproved by a lender, not just prequalified. When you are preapproved, you can close the transaction in literally 10 days! All you need to do is give the lender the sales contract, the appraisal, and the preliminary title report. These can be quickly approved, and the lender will draw up the documents. When two buyers are vying for the same property, and the other party needs 45 days to make preparations with a lender, but you are prepared to close in 10 days, *you* will be the one who ends up with the home. You can frequently negotiate a better price, too, because you are willing to close quickly, which means less uncertainty for the seller.

SUMMARY

The lending industry today stands better prepared than ever to offer financing for first-time home buyers and others who would have been considered only marginally qualified just a few years ago. If you are a first-time home buyer, this is good news for you. After reading this book, go out and find someone who will help you avail yourself of a program that is suited to your needs.

6

THE LOWDOWN ON ARMS

For every complex problem, there is a simple solution. And it's wrong!

—H. L. Mencken

KEY POINTS

- They may look similar, but there are important differences between ARMs, and these differences are not usually made clear by the lender.
- The most important factor is the index. Which index is best depends on the current direction of interest rates and the business cycle.
- There are important differences between so-called negative-amortization loans and the no-neg loans.

If, after reading Chapter 4, "How to Choose the Right Loan," you conclude that your risk factors and the current rate environment indicate an ARM is the best loan for you, read on. If you didn't come to that conclusion, skip this chapter.

HOW IMPORTANT ARE ARMS?

ARMs generally account for almost half of all mortgages, so they are very important. However, most people, including many people who have them, have only a fuzzy understanding of them. One reason is that there are as many as 500 different ARM programs offered by lenders today. Industry jargon—such terms as *index, margin, cap,* and *negative amortization*—further confuse the would-be borrower. I am convinced that a large number of consumers are sold an ARM when it is an entirely inappropriate choice. Why? Because the lender has designed the loan with an appealingly low start rate—4, 5, or 6 percent. When rates on fixed-rate loans are at 8 percent, it looks enticing, doesn't it? That's why they call it a *teaser rate.* You might conclude that the rate you're quoted stays fixed for quite a while, but you'd be wrong. As a general rule, the lower the rate, the shorter it will be operative. The *real rate* on an ARM may be higher than the fixed rate, at which time it makes no sense at all. Nevertheless, people still buy them because they do not understand what they are buying—which is why I think ARM disclosure should be reformed, a topic covered in Chapter 21.

Another problem is that, unlike most consumer products, one loan doesn't have unique features compared to similar loans. When shopping for a car, you know whether you want a four-wheel drive or two-wheel drive. You know whether you want two doors or four doors or a hatchback. There may be many models available to choose from and salespeople touting various features, but once you've identified the type of vehicle you want, at least you have a head start.

On the contrary, the sales pitch for every ARM sounds about the same. All lenders say, "My product is the best." Remember that it's mostly just marketing hype! The purpose of this chapter is to separate the hype from the facts and give you a framework for determining whether an ARM is suitable for you and, if so, which one.

All ARM loans have a few things in common. They are tied to an *index* that is independent of the lender's control. A typical index is the yield on one-year Treasury bills, the instruments the Treasury Department auctions off every month. At a specified interval called the *change date,* the lender will add a number, the *margin,* to that index value to get the note rate for the next period. Think of the margin as a profit margin. It is usually between 2.5 and 3 percent. Thus, as interest rates go up and down over the years, you will pay accordingly more or less for your mortgage, but the lender's profit margin remains constant regardless of the rate. That's okay; it's the incentive for banks and S&Ls to provide loans.

All ARMs have a *ceiling rate,* or *cap,* which is a limit on how high the rate can go over the life of the loan. Currently, this cap is about 12 percent. You may hear, "The cap is 5 percent," meaning the cap is 5 percent higher than the start rate. All loans also have a mechanism (I like to call it an *interim cap*) that limits the amount by which the rate or payment can vary in a given period.

All ARMs have these features in common, so if some loan rep brags about them, remember that all competing loans have similar features.

ARM TERMINOLOGY

ARM terminology is confusing to borrowers, so let's begin by defining some terms. First I'll discuss the most difficult concepts: negative amortization and its counterpart, the no-neg loan.

Negative Amortization

A common feature of the COFI loans that have been very popular in some parts of the country are negative-amortization, or *neg-am,* loans. The etymology of the term *amortization* is unpleasant: Its root is the French word *mort,* meaning death. Over time, the balance on an amortized loan is reduced to zero. Thus, as you make the payments, the loan "puts itself to death." In a neg-am loan, it is possible to make payments that are less than the amount necessary to amortize the loan. In fact, sometimes the obligatory payment isn't even enough to pay the interest that is accruing monthly on the loan. During such periods, the loan balance isn't going down (amortizing), but going up! That's why it's called a negative-amortized loan. I prefer the phrase "a loan with the potential for accrued interest," but because everyone else calls it neg-am, so will we. Before we get into the specific mechanism of the neg-am loan, I want to discuss its counterpart, the no-neg loan.

No-Neg Loans

If it weren't for neg-am loans, the expression *no-neg* wouldn't exist. A no-neg is a normally amortizing loan. The change mechanism limits the amount by which the interest rate can change, typically 2 percent per year; you then pay whatever you owe each month. If the rate changes every six months, there is a 1 percent limit on the amount of change. Regardless, within any period during the life of the loan, your monthly payment is sufficient to amortize the loan. The loan balance never increases, so it is always a "positive-amortization" loan, if you will. The term *no-neg* is really a double-negative, but, again, that is what the industry calls it. All no-neg loans have a ceiling rate, frequently 6 percent above the start rate, giving rise to the industry terminology, *2/6 no-neg*. No-neg loans are a favorite of banks and Wall Street. Figure 6.1 shows how the interest rate varies on a no-neg loan during a period of rising rates.

You can see that the rate rose by the 2 percent limit in the first year, from 6 percent to 8 percent. Without the limit, it would have gone up further. In the following years, it moved up and down as index plus margin moved. By comparison, Figure 6.2 shows how the same loan performed in a period of dropping rates. You can see that the 2 percent limit works both ways because, in late 1991, the interest rate on the loan would have dropped more than 2 percent had it not been for the limitation.

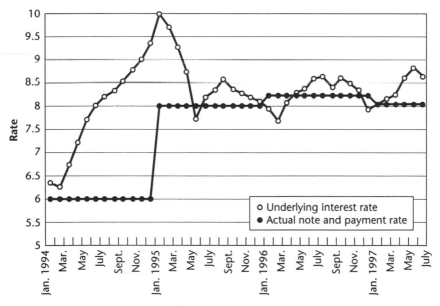

Figure 6.1   No-neg loan during a period of rising rates.

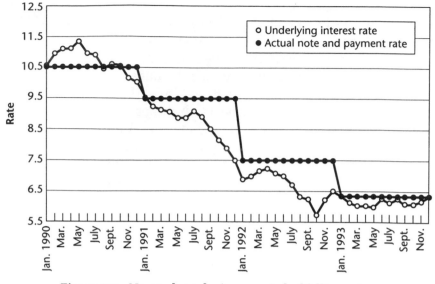

Figure 6.2   No-neg loan during a period of falling rates.

Neg-Am Loans

With a negative-amortization loan, the lender "disconnects" the payment rate from the interest rate. You make a payment that over a long period of time follows interest rate fluctuations but is not directly connected to the rate. Usually, the loan's initial rate is deeply discounted. I've done loans with start rates as low as 2.95 percent. This is the actual interest rate but, take note, only for the first three months. The interest rate adjusts upward to index plus margin (covered later) in the fourth month. For the balance of the loan period, another 357 months, the interest rate is adjusted every month. It is important to realize that regardless of what interest rates do, the annual payment adjustment—whether increasing or decreasing—is limited to a 7.5 percent adjustment from the payment of the previous year.

Thus, if you are paying $1,000 per month in year 1, the most you will have to pay in year 2 is $1,075. That's easy, and it's a very attractive feature, but it is a two-edged sword. We'll get to that in a minute. If interest rates rise, say, from 6 percent to 7 percent, your payment would increase to approximately $1,110. With a neg-am loan, you *may* make a $1,110 payment, but you may also take advantage of the 7.5 percent limit, so your payment would go up to $1,075. What happens to the other $35 per month? The lender tacks it onto the loan balance and says, "Pay me later." Note that when this is happening, you are not paying anything to reduce the principal. In fact, because the lender is adding the unpaid interest to the loan, the balance increases instead of going down. That's what negative amortization describes. The loan gets back onto its normal principal-reduction curve later, when rates are falling. Maybe your payment should fall from $1,000 to $890, but it will go down only $75. Every month, $35 goes back to the lender.

Let's look at neg-am loan performance on a graph. Figure 6.3 shows actual data from the recent past, starting in January 1994.

My assessment is that there are good and bad aspects to the neg-am loan. The bad is that if there is a prolonged period of rising rates, those $35 amounts can add up. Let's say you buy a $200,000 home, put $20,000 down, and get a $180,000 loan. Five years later, you might end up owing, say, $183,000. If your house declines in value to $195,000 and you have to pay a 6 percent commission to sell it, your equity drops from $20,000 to $300. That's devastating! Had you gotten a fully amortized loan, your balance after five years would be less than $170,000 and your equity would still be $14,000 or so. You'd be hurt by falling values, but you wouldn't be wiped out.

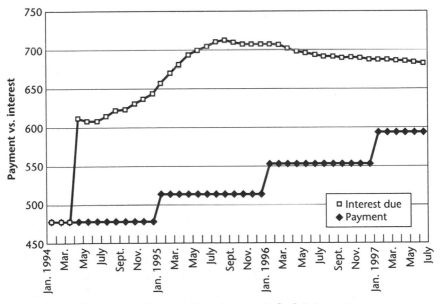

Figure 6.3   Neg-am loan in a period of rising rates.

Some negative-amortization loans that start out with a really low teaser rate can get you into a hole. Let me give you an actual example. A lender I know offered a loan with a 2.95 percent teaser rate. On a $180,000 loan, the initial payment was only $754.04. Attractive, right? Not so fast. In the fourth month, the interest rate jumped to 6.25 percent, at which rate the normal amortizing payment would have been $1,108.29. The interest cost was $937.50, so the borrower was "short" $183.46 per month. A year later, the payment would have gone up by its obligatory limit of 7.5 percent, to $810.59. However, in that year, interest rates went up, so the underlying rate moved up from 6.25 percent to 7.35 percent. Now the interest cost was $1,102.50 and the borrower was going into the hole at the rate of $291.91 per month. In this example, it might take five years to catch up to where the payments and the interest cost are equal; by that time, the loan balance would have grown from $180,000 to $188,000.

| WARNING | The opportunities for borrower abuse are manifold with neg-am loans. Many studies have been done to determine which loan features attract borrowers. Every study shows that a low monthly payment is the most important feature for many people. Obviously, then, any loan that starts out 2 or 3 or 4 percent below the rate for 30-year fixed-rate loans is going to attract a lot of attention. The start rate is good for perhaps only three months, and then it jumps up. Why do people choose such a loan? *Because they don't understand it.*

My belief is that at least half of the people who sign up for neg-am loans are attracted by the low start rate and the low initial payment, but they do not understand what is going to happen in years 3, 4, and 5 and beyond. Review Figure 6.3. The difference between the payment curve and the interest rate curve is the amount of interest that is not being paid currently but that is being added to the principal balance of the loan. Now you can see the other side of the neg-am equation. The attractive features of the neg-am loan—its low introductory rate and low payment cap—make people *think* they are saving money. But they're not. They just defer paying it until some later date. That's not necessarily bad per se, but borrowers should understand what's happening from the outset, and I believe that they don't. The ARM disclosure forms supplied by the lender have this information on them, but they do not show a graph like the one in Figure 6.3. If they did, more people would opt for a different loan. If I had a nickel for every borrower who would have changed his or her mind on seeing such a graph, I'd be rich. Sadly, lenders who offer neg-am loans have a powerful lobby that prevents revision of the loan disclosure forms to better explain the features (dangers) of this loan to unsuspecting borrowers.

I realize that much of what I have said so far may imply that neg-am loans are all bad. That's not so. One good feature of these loans is that some lenders who offer them will allow borrowers to qualify at a lower rate than will fixed-rate lenders. If fixed rates are at 8 percent, a lender might allow you to qualify at a rate of 6 percent. That's a big difference, and the actual payment may be even lower. The lender is betting that you can handle the initial payment plus the 7.5 percent annual payment increase. Often, this is true. Another good feature is that a home buyer with limited cash can use the accrued interest feature to "finance" landscaping or drapes on the new home. The savings in actual payments, say $2,000 to $3,000 in the first year, can be used for other purposes, and then you can increase your payments in later years to pay the loan back down.

In summary, neg-am loans are no better or worse than no-neg loans. It's just important that you, the borrower, understand the potential of a neg-am loan before choosing one. To the extent that you are less disciplined than others, I'd choose a no-neg loan. It has less potential for danger. If you choose a neg-am loan, the important thing is to calculate what's going on every month. My advice is to make whatever payment is required to amortize the loan in 30 years, regardless of what the payment coupon says you can do.

> **WARNING** Most neg-am loans are tied to the 11th District COFI, which may not be the index you want.

THE INDEXES

Index is the name applied to a number that a lender uses as the basis for determining the interest rate of an ARM. The prime rate is an index. It's the rate the big banks charge their best customers, but it is so frequently used that people refer to it as the *prime rate* rather than using the actual number at any given point in time. For example, if your bank granted you a business loan at prime plus 2 percent, you'd know exactly what they were talking about.

If the prime rate were 8 percent, the interest on your loan would be 10 percent.

A lender uses an index the same way, and the rate on its loans during any period is based on the value of the index at the start of the period. Importantly, the index must be one that is beyond the control of the lender. You don't want to pay more just because the head of some loan committee decided to raise rates.

In spite of the hype from lenders, there is no single index that is best all of the time. A loan is a financial instrument. If you own stocks, you know that over a long period of time, sometimes it's better to be more heavily invested in stocks and other times in bonds. There are even times when you should have more cash.

If you own stock, once a year you get a proxy statement from the company. As part of its annual report to you, the Securities and Exchange Commission (SEC) requires the company to show you a graph of the five-year performance of its stock, the performance of the S&P 500, and the performance of other companies in the same industry. As an investor, you can see at a glance how the stock has been performing relative to other companies in the same industry and relative to the rest of the market. That's an extraordinarily useful tool for investors. Borrowers should have a similar tool for comparing ARMs, and I'm going to give you one. Figure 6.4 shows the actual cost to borrowers of loans tied to the common indexes. Following subsections explain the details of each index.

Six-Month CD

This is the rate banks pay on jumbo certificates of deposits greater than $100,000. It is almost always higher than the rate you can get on a CD at your local bank because it is not insured by the FDIC. It is also usually higher than the yield on U.S. Treasury six-month T-bills. This index changes weekly, and loans tied to it usually change every six months. Loans tied to this index are not widely available, but some banks like it because a large portion of their deposit base is from CDs like this. It is also offered by a few large mortgage bankers. Lenders often offer this loan with a low margin, such as 2.125 percent. That's a terrific loan, if you can find it. This is a leading index, and you can get its current value by calling the Federal Reserve Board at 415-

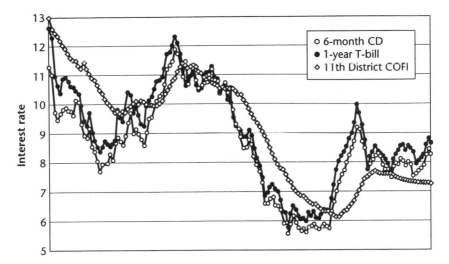

Figure 6.4 Comparison of various ARMs, 1986–1997. Index plus margin equals loan cost.

974-2859. You can also get these data on the Internet. Go to http://www.frbsf.org banking and click on the Statistical Survey. Or check out my Web site at http://www.loan-wolf.com.

One-Year T-Bill

This is the most widely known index and is also known as the Constant Treasury Maturity Index, or CMT. Some lenders call it TCM. It is an average of the current yield on U.S. Treasury securities with a maturity of one year. This is probably the most widely offered ARM in the United States, excepting California, and is favored by the Wall Street lenders. Most loans tied to this index change rates annually and have a 2 percent limit on the amount of the annual change. A few, however, change every six months, and those loans have a lower start rate (teaser) because the lender can change it (read "raise it") 1 percent after six months rather than having to wait a year.

The common T-bill index is the spot index, which is a leading index. There is, however, one uncommon variation on this index, the so-called T-bill Average, which averages the previous 12 months' spot index numbers. Because it is a moving average of 12 different numbers, it lags the spot value index. Think of the average temperature of the last month compared with the temperature today. I am not fond of this index because lenders seem to trot it out only when rates are falling, thus increasing their yields and their customers' costs. You can get the current index value by calling 415-974-2859.

LIBOR

The London Interbank Offered Rate (LIBOR) is the rate European banks charge each other when they lend dollars among themselves. When lenders started selling loans in the secondary market to European investors, they started using this index because the buyers (Europeans) understood it. There are several different LIBOR rates, but the most common is the six-month LIBOR rate. This index acts a lot like the six-month CD and is a leading index. Although 99 percent of LIBOR loans are no-negs, be wary if you see a loan with an exceptionally low start rate because it may be a neg-am loan (discussed earlier in this chapter) and thus not directly comparable with the others. Beware of this loan. A neg-am loan tied to LIBOR is like a hand grenade, and I would avoid it. The index values are available daily in the *Wall Street Journal*.

Prime Rate

This index is commonly used for mortgage loans only by the brokerage houses and other Wall Street sources. Personally, I consider these to be sucker loans, manufactured by companies to give their stockbrokers another product to sell to their customers, thus generating more commissions. The prime rate index should be disqualified from consideration. It may sound like just another index, but with one *huge* difference: The entire management of the banking industry is trying to increase it because it affects bank profits. The other indexes are the result of free-market action and, as a rule, some group of people is trying to keep them as low as they can. Wouldn't you prefer to have your mortgage payment tied to an index people were trying to reduce, not increase?

11th District Cost-of-Funds Index

Commonly called COFI, this index is the weighted average cost of deposits in savings institutions in California, Arizona, and Nevada. It is a loan that is offered primarily in California and is less common in the rest of the country. Because only a small fraction of savers' deposits roll over each month, this index changes very little from month to month. This slow-moving feature makes it a lagging index compared with the other indexes, which is a very attractive feature when rates are rising. It may lag 1 percent or more behind the other types of loans. Obviously, when rates are falling, a borrower with a loan tied to this index may pay 1 percent *more* every year than a neighbor with a T-bill loan. You can get the current index value by calling the Federal Home Loan Bank Board at 415-616-2600.

Index Summary

To give you an idea of the relative index values, here are the approximate values of these indexes as I write this in September 1997.

6-month CD	5.24
1-year T-bill	5.62
6-month LIBOR	5.65
Prime rate	8.25
COFI	4.98

The more important question is, "Which Index is better?" The answer is, "It depends."

From 1983 to 1993, the CD, T-bill, and LIBOR loans were preferable because rates were dropping. In such times, you want to be on a leading index. Conversely, when rates are rising, as they did abruptly in 1994, you want a loan tied to a lagging index, such as the 11th District COFI. Figure 6.5 shows the one-year T-bill index and the 11th District COFI during the 1990s. You can clearly see the difference between a leading index and lagging index. The lagging index was higher when rates were falling and lower when rates were rising. So your choice of index depends on the direction of rates at the time you make your decision.

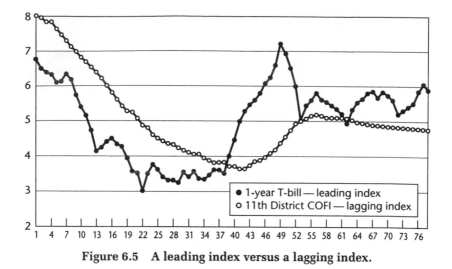

Figure 6.5   A leading index versus a lagging index.

If this seems obvious, to you, it wasn't to millions of people who made the wrong choice because information like this has not been easily available to the public. Consequently, most borrowers are guided largely by sales pitches from loan reps and marketing hype from the big lenders' advertising departments. Choosing the loan that is wrong for the time costs borrowers millions and millions of dollars. If you skipped Chapter 3, "How Lenders Market Loans," you should go back and read it now.

ASSUMABILITY OF ARMS

A feature of almost every ARM is assumability. Simply put, this means someone buying your home could take over your mortgage. Assumability isn't unconditional. The lender has a right to approve the party assuming your loan. It's not an involved process. The buyer makes an application. If his or her credit is good and the down payment is reasonable, and if the value of the property, as evidenced by the escrow instructions, shows sufficient equity, 99 percent of the time the lender will approve the assumption. That has been my experience.

Let's look at assumability from the perspective of lenders. First, they usually like the loan because you have been making payments for years. Second, they liked your property initially, and at the price at which you are selling, they would still grant the loan. Third, the new buyer is okay. Fourth, they don't have to "subsidize" the loan with a teaser rate. Fifth, they usually get an assumption fee, typically 1 percent. Pretty strong advantages.

If the buyer isn't going to get a teaser rate and if he or she has to pay a 1 percent assumption fee, why would anyone do it? Usually it's because the buyer doesn't understand how disadvantageous it is. Consequently, I recommend a loan assumption only if you are marginally qualified or are not sufficiently creditworthy to get your own loan or if the property has a problem such as a leaky new roof, which a lender will demand be corrected before it funds a new loan. Finally, for the original owner, assumability is a highly overrated feature. Unless your loan balance is in the 80 percent LTV range, you're not normally going to find someone with a sufficient down payment to take over your loan. When you shop for loans, therefore, don't pay anything extra for assumability.

COMPARING ARMS

I hope you have come to the conclusion that choosing the right index for the time is the most important objective; that is, choose a lagging index when rates are increasing and a leading index at other times. You can stay on top of this information by making a few phone calls or surfing the Web. You might stop by my Web site at http://www.loan-wolf.com.

The second most important factor is the margin. The margin is the first marketing hook lenders will use to entice you. Obviously, if you are comparing otherwise identical loans, one with an index of 2.5 and the other 2.75, choose the one with the lower margin. However, a COFI loan with a 2.5 margin is not necessarily better than a T-bill loan with a 2.75 margin. Only after you have selected the index most suitable for you should you go margin shopping. You can use the form in Figure 6.6 as an aid to organize your material.

The third important factor is the start rate. Most of the time, the start rate is a few percentage points lower than the current market (index plus margin)—a teaser rate. When borrowers shop, they ask, "What are your rates?," and the lenders tell them the start rate, which might apply for only two or three months in the

LENDER				
Start rate				
No-neg or neg-am				
Changes every				
Limit per change				
Index type				
Margin				
Current index				
Current index + margin				
Life cap				

Figure 6.6   ARM comparison shopping guide. You can make copies of this form to use in your shopping.

case of a neg-am loan and perhaps for only six months for a no-neg. It is important to consider what you pay over an entire 5- or 10-year period, not just what you pay initially. For those interested in a no-neg loan, keep in mind that if the teaser rate is low enough, you are buying the rate down for additional periods as well. If index plus margin is 8.5 percent and the start rate on a six-month adjustable loan is 5.375 percent, your actual rate will increase from 5.375 percent to 6.375 percent to 7.375 percent to 8.375 percent and, finally, to 8.5 percent in the third year if that's where rates are then. Compare that with the neg-am loan, where the actual interest rate goes from, say, 3 percent to index plus margin. Perhaps you'll be paying that same 8.5 percent in the third month, not the third year.

Currently, there isn't much talk about caps or ceiling rates for a very good reason: Since ARMs were introduced in 1983, less than 1 percent of them ever got high enough for their caps to become operative. There are times, however, when lenders will use this as a hook. In 1993 and 1994, I did a number of loans with caps that were 9.5 and 9.875 percent. That looked like a great deal considering that most loans originating between 1983 and 1993 had caps between 13 percent and 16 percent. But given the current low level of inflation we are experiencing, most people will probably move or refinance their loans before they ever hit nine-point-anything. So I wouldn't pay too much attention to this factor.

In conclusion, ARMs are terrific—about half the time. When rates were high and declining, as in the period from 1983 to 1993, I originated a lot of them. When rates are low, as they are as I write this in 1997, fixed-rate loans are better. It's has been almost a year since I originated a pure ARM.

PART
2

CHOOSING
A LENDER
AND
GETTING
APPROVED

QUALIFYING 101

KEY POINTS

- Qualifying is not a totally rational process.
- Qualifying is based not just on facts but upon documentation.
- There are a number of ways to package your income that will help you avoid problems if you know the difficulties ahead of time.

The purpose of this chapter is to give you some background on underwriting, the process through which a lender determines if you are qualified for a loan. I will give you some information that applies to all borrowers and then explain qualifying for borrowers with stable, straightforward income. In Chapter 15, "Qualifying 201," you'll learn how the industry deals with self-employed borrowers and others who have complicated income. In that chapter, I will also discuss EZ Qualifier or no-income documentation loans.

OVERVIEW

Underwriting and qualifying are mysteries to most people. You may have heard comments like, "We do commonsense underwriting." Then, a day later, the person who told you that may call you to say, "We won't approve your loan because your ratios are 40.1 percent and we can't go over 40 percent." That doesn't seem like common sense. And now we have computerized loan underwriting, technology that uses artificial intelligence to evaluate borrowers. My experience with these systems makes me extremely optimistic that these programs will result in faster processing, lower costs, and better service for our customers. I am committed to using them as much as I can. I like them because they tend to look at applications as a whole rather than focusing on trivial details, a fault that sometimes overwhelms people in the traditional underwriting process.

The vast majority, perhaps 90 percent, of applicants are going to deal with traditional loan processing and underwriting systems that are highly bureaucratic, so that's the system I'll discuss in detail, to show you both how it works and how to improve your chances of winning.

The purpose of underwriting is to ascertain whether you are a good risk. The loan application package is designed to answer the three questions an underwriter asks about you:

1. Do you have sufficient, stable income so that you will be able to make all the loan payments on time?
2. Does your credit history reflect that you pay your other bills on time?
3. Does your property provide adequate collateral to protect the lender's interest?

The balance of this chapter will address the first question.

EMPLOYMENT AND INCOME STABILITY

The first task is to evaluate the stability of your income. As a general rule, employment on the same job for more than two years is considered satisfactory. Some people have occupations, such as construction, that offer inherently more volatile, or at least variable, income, in which case you will have to show that you have successfully been able to earn money for a longer period of time and have demonstrated ability to manage your financial affairs. If you have had several jobs in the same field in the last couple of years, you may be asked to provide documentation from your employer that makes a case for future stability. A borrower who has advanced while changing jobs within the same line of work will obtain more favorable consideration than someone who has a record of frequent job changes without obvious advancement—what I call "job-flopping" as opposed to job-hopping.

The key is income stability, and if a borrower has maintained stable income in spite of an unstable employment history, he or she will likely be approved. In addition, a borrower's financial history is important. A borrower who has demonstrated a pattern of consistent saving will have a much better chance of having an application approved than someone who spends all of his or her income.

Exceptions and Additional Documentation

There are a couple of exceptions to the preceding rules. If you are a recent college graduate, obviously you aren't going to meet the two-year rule, so plan on also giving your lender a copy of your degree or transcript to prove that you just graduated. Likewise, if you were away on a long trip, out of work due to prolonged illness, on maternity leave, or have some other reasonable explanation, be straightforward with your lender regarding the circumstances. Don't wait for your loan to be denied before explaining the gap in your employment record. In all of these cases, I suggest that you include a letter from your new employer to show that your future looks stable even if the most recent past does not. This also applies to overtime. For example, if a nurse gets overtime on a regular basis, the lender may not count it because there isn't a two-year history of such earnings. Again, a letter from the employer will help.

A person who has recently retired will be relying on Social Security income, retirement benefits, and income from stocks and bonds, none of which will show up on last year's tax return. You will have to document this income. First, ask the Social Security Administration for an Award Letter, which describes the level of benefits to which you are entitled. Your employer's human resources department or the pension administrator can provide documentation about the level of your retirement pay. Income from a portfolio is more complex, especially if you have money in an IRA, 401(k), or other tax-deferred plan. Your assets may be earning good return, but this income will not yet have shown up on your tax returns. Assuming that you are more than 59½ years old, you are probably entitled to take distributions. Many underwriters have a tough time figuring such income, so you must help them by getting your financial planner or CPA to write a letter explaining your future income. In addition, even though you may have consistently earned a 10 percent return, most underwriters will assume that you will make only what the banks pay on CDs, perhaps 4 or 5 percent. Specifically, if you have $100,000 in your plan, they will give you credit for only $5,000 per year.

| TIP | For conventional (not FHA or VA) loans, lenders use gross income before deductions to calculate your qualification ratios. If you earn $1,000 per month, deductions for Social Security, Medicare, and federal and state taxes will leave you only $700 or $800, but $1,000 is the amount used to determine qualification. Someone who has income that is not taxable is at a disadvantage in the system, so lenders use a procedure referred to as *grossing up,* where the underwriter increases the income figure by 20 to 30 percent to make it equivalent to taxable income. Using this system, a person with $1,000 nontaxable income would be considered to have constructive income of $1,200 to $1,300. If this applies to you, and it is important in qualifying, be sure to go to a lender who will use this procedure. Have your loan rep or processor check with underwriting to determine the factor to be used.

Do You Have Enough Income?

In my experience, people start thinking about buying a home when their income has risen to the point where they feel comfortable with the proposed payment on the home of their choice. The overwhelming majority of such borrowers usually qualify themselves, meaning they have a good comprehension of their financial capabilities and know what housing payment they can afford. That is not to say that these people understand all the components of the qualifying process. Perhaps they don't know much about property taxes, insurance, or homeowners' association dues and how they figure in, but usually when I ask people how much they can afford, they quickly respond with something like, "$1,400 per month." About 90 percent of the time, they are correct. Nonetheless, before parting with $50,000, $100,000, or $500,000, the lender wants to make sure that you have sufficient income according to its own calculations. That's what determining your qualifying ratios is all about.

THE QUALIFYING MODEL

To approve or deny loans based on a comparison of peoples' incomes and housing payments, a line has to be drawn. Above the line, you're approved; below, your loan will be denied. Industry gurus studied a large number of households to try to get a handle on what people could really afford. It is no secret that even on a given income, some households are always in financial trouble and others are always comfortable. With enough data, you can start separating the two groups. Calculations of this kind give lenders a high degree of confidence that when they approve a loan, the borrowers will be comfortable with the payments, and it will be a good loan. You may have heard of the numbers 28/36, the most commonly accepted ratios used by lenders selling loans to FNMA and FHLMC. There are no hard-and-fast rules, and many lenders use ratios more liberal than this, but every lender has a certain comfort zone of ratios. The ratios used by the strictest lenders—*A lenders,* as they are referred to in the trade—will be lower than those of the B lenders, who will approve loans that the A lenders turn down. All lenders, whether class A, B, or C, will calculate the ratios, so let's discuss them. They are at the heart of the process of having your loan approved.

Ratios

The first number an underwriter calculates is called the *top ratio.* It's the ratio of your housing expense to your gross income, which is income before withholding for taxes, Social Security, and Medicare. Your housing expense is the sum of the mortgage loan payment (principal and interest), property taxes, and insurance, hence the acronym, PITI (principal, interest, taxes, insurance). The study we talked about earlier determined that when less than 28 percent of gross income was devoted to housing expense and less than 36 percent of gross income was devoted to housing expense plus recurring obligations, such as car loan and credit card payments, people didn't have trouble making their payments. Conversely, when they devoted more than those percentages of income to those categories, they were more likely to be late on their loan payments and more likely to be candidates for default at some time in the future.

In short, *qualifying* is the process of comparing your income ratios against the target ratios your lender uses to determine whether you are likely to be a trouble-free customer.

If you are an employee of a large company, you are probably paid a fixed hourly wage or a fixed salary every month. No one will have problems determining your income. If your salary is $36,000 per year, you know it, your company knows it, and, subsequently, the lender knows it. No problem. If your rate of pay is $10 per hour, that's clear, too, although a lender will want to confirm that you always work a regular number of hours every week and that any overtime being factored in is consistent and ongoing.

Income is one thing—documenting it is another. No question about it, the mortgage industry's driving need for documentation can drive you mad. Even for people with simple, salaried income, documentation can be horrendous. In a typical case, a lender will ask for the following:

- Verification of Employment (VOE) form sent to your employer will show your date of employment, your current rate of pay, your income for the current year and the previous two years, and the likelihood of continued employment.
- W-2s for the previous two years (should be consistent with the VOE).
- A current paycheck stub.
- If a lender requires a full Residential Mortgage Credit Report, it will include a telephone verification of employment.
- Some lenders require another paycheck stub with 30 days of closing.
- Although not all lenders require it, some even do a pre-funding employment check to make sure that you weren't just fired.

The good news is that the new artificial intelligence underwriting systems promise to make things better. With a clean credit report, you might have to show only last year's W-2 and a current paycheck stub. If your income is simple to understand, ask lenders up front if they use these systems. It might save you a little grief.

If your income is easily determined, you've cleared one big hurdle. However, if you are among the tens of millions of people whose lives are more complicated than that, this is only the beginning, and I'll address your hurdles in Chapter 15.

How the Industry Qualifies Borrowers

To demonstrate how the mortgage industry makes those calculations, I'm going to ask you to complete a worksheet that is a lot like the one a lender uses. If you have a computer, I'd encourage you to re-create this worksheet on a spreadsheet program such as Excel or Lotus 1-2-3. To calculate payments, use the payment function built into your spreadsheet program; or you can purchase a disk from me using the form at the back of the book.

If you do not have a computer available, make copies of Figure 7.1 to fill in by hand. You will also need a tool to calculate payments. I recommend buying one of the handheld calculators that have this capability. Texas Instruments makes one that costs $20 or $30, or you can use the payment tables at the back of this book. These are rounded off to the nearest $1,000, which is close enough for our purposes.

The worksheet in Figure 7.1 is set up to compare several alternatives. For example, you can compare how you qualify for houses of different value. You can also set it up with the same loan amount and then check how your ratios vary with different loan programs and different interest rates. We'll go over this worksheet line by line.

1. Enter the property value of the home you are considering buying.
2. Enter the loan amount, which is the property value minus your down payment.
3. Calculate the loan-to-value (LTV), line 2 divided by line 1.
4. Enter the interest rates of the various alternatives you are considering.
5. Calculate the loan payment (using either the payment function on a computer with a spreadsheet program, a financial calculator with a payment function, or a factor from the appendix).

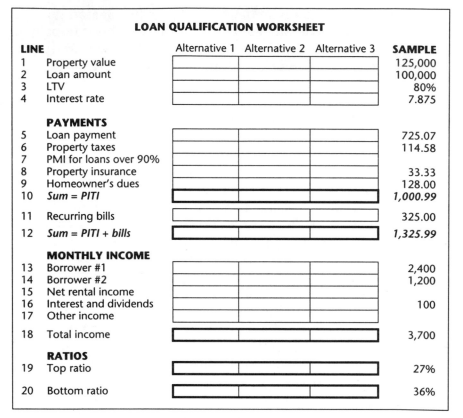

Figure 7.1   Loan qualification worksheet.

6.   Enter one-twelfth of the annual property taxes, fre-quently about 1 percent of the property's value.

7.   Figure the private mortgage insurance (PMI) premium. Use the following table to approximate the amount. (Note, .75 percent is ¾ percent. Divide by 12 and enter.)

LTV	PMI premium	Sample amount on a $100,000 loan
95 percent	0.75 percent	$62.50 per month
90 percent	0.5 percent	$41.67 per month
85 percent	0.3 percent	$25.00 per month

8. Enter the property (fire or casualty) insurance premium; unless you have a quote from an agent, use $400 or $500 and divide by 12.

9. For condos and planned unit developments, enter the monthly homeowners' association dues.

10. Add lines 5 through 9.

11. Insert your car payment(s) plus 5 percent of outstanding credit card balances.

12. Add lines 10 and 11.

13. Enter the first borrower's monthly income.

14. Enter the second borrower's monthly income.

15. Enter interest and dividend income.

16. Enter other income not included above.

17. Calculate your total income by adding lines 13 through 17.

18. Calculate top ratio, line 10 divided by line 18, expressed as a percentage.

19. Calculate bottom ratio, line 12 divided by line 18, expressed as a percentage.

The sample column at the far right of Figure 7.1 shows what a typical borrower's numbers might look like. Completing this worksheet should help you zero in on a range of homes that you could afford. More powerful analytical tools are available for those who have access to a computer, and you might investigate them. Most important, you have the confidence that an underwriter will analyze your application the same way and approve your application quickly.

Ongoing Bills and Other Recurring Obligations

I want to expand on recurring obligations, shown on line 11. If you have outstanding credit card bills, you receive monthly statements showing the minimum payment due, which will sometimes coincide with the amount listed on your credit report and sometimes not. Here's what a portion of a credit report might look like.

Creditor	Balance	Payment
FirstBank Visa	$2,602	Flex $65
SecondBank M/C	$2,468	Flex $52
ThirdBank Visa	$1,780	Flexible
ABC Auto	$12,456	48 * $461
XYZ Auto	$756	36 * $256

Using the information on the report, your lender would calculate the payment on the ThirdBank Visa at 5 percent of the balance of $1,780, or $89 per month, even though the statement may require a minimum payment of only $35. That's another reason to get a credit report now! The 5 percent may sound harsh, but it is not unreasonable; if you foresee a problem here (that is, if you are pushing the bottom ratio and your report shows "flexible" on all of your bills), make copies of your monthly statements showing the *actual* minimum payment due and submit them with your application. You should also do this if you have cards that you pay off in full every month. Creditors report to Experian (formerly TRW), Trans Union, and the others on a monthly basis. If the balance on a card is $1,806 on the fifth of the month when they report, and you pay it in full on the sixth, $1,806 will appear on the credit report and the lender is unaware that you paid it off. Therefore the lender will add 5 percent of $1,806, or $90 per month, to your monthly obligations, which will push up your ratios. To avoid this, submit copies of four or five or six months' worth of statements with your application showing that you pay the card off every month.

There is some good news here, too. Note that the last car payment in the sample credit report had a balance of only $756, reflecting that only three payments remain. The rule is that if you have fewer than 10 months left on an obligation, it will not be counted. (*Hint:* If your ratios are a little high, and you have, say, 15 months left on a high car payment, you can send in six extra payments right now so that the lender's next report to the credit bureaus will show fewer than 10 payments remaining, which won't affect your ratios. This does not apply to car leases because at the end of the lease, you have to give the car back, and, presumably, get another car with another car payment.)

The purpose of doing all of these calculations at home before looking at houses or talking with lenders is to give you a good idea of how mortgage lenders will view your application. For example, if you calculate your ratios to be 40/50, you know that you are reaching for too large a loan. Most people, however, will discover that they are in the ballpark. Remember, most people know what level of housing payment they can afford. That said, after reading this book and coming to a conclusion about the kind of loan that is best for you, have your lender preapprove you for a loan sufficient to purchase the home you want.

SETTING STANDARDS

An A loan from an A lendor is going to have the lowest rates. If that's what you want to qualify for, shoot to keep your numbers under 28/36 and you should have no trouble getting approved. If, however, your ratios are higher than that, don't be discouraged. There are a number of exceptions to these limits, and many lenders will routinely approve higher-ratio loans.

First, there is the issue of loan-to-value (LTV). If you are putting only 5 percent down and want a 95 percent loan, you will have to have all your ducks in a row. There is simply not enough equity in the home to protect a lender in the event of default, so you will have to prove income that is more stable and stronger than average, and you must have an excellent credit history. If you are putting 20 percent down, these criteria are relaxed. If you are putting more than 25 percent down, the lender will be even more tolerant. Let me give you some examples from one lender's manual:

	Acceptable Qualifying Ratios
If LTV is more than 80 percent	28/36
If LTV is less than 80 percent and income is	
More than $75,000	40/40
More than $75,000 but less than $150,000	42/42
More than $150,000	44/44

As you can see, these ratios are more lenient than those previously discussed. In Chapter 5, we learned that some lenders approve high-ratio loans as a result of Community Reinvestment Act programs. It should be clear by now that higher income and a higher down payment can work to your benefit. Here are a couple of other important points:

- If you've gone through the worksheet calculations and your analysis shows that your ratios are high, your search for a lender should concentrate on those with more liberal underwriting policies. The policies dictate *whether* you will be approved and are therefore more important than the rates. That is, you must go ratio shopping *first,* prior to rate shopping. As sure as God made little green apples, some lenders will turn down loans because the ratios are 1 percent higher than some standard they have been told to enforce.

- Any competent employee of a lender will know how flexible the underwriters are, and you need to get them to be honest with you about this. This is another reason why preapproval is important. You can get preapproved either for free or for the cost of a credit report, say $50. If you run up against a problem, you have plenty of time to find another lender who is more flexible.

FHA AND VA

The previous discussion centered on Conventional Financing. But many buyers are interested in FHA loans, those insured by the Federal Housing Administration and, for those in the military and eligible veterans, loans guaranteed by the Veterans Administration. In this section, I want to discuss qualifying for these programs.

First, always keep in mind that anything connected with the government comes with extra paperwork and will therefore be more time-consuming than if handled by private industry. FHA and VA loans used to take as long as 90 days to approve and fund! Even at half that, it is unacceptable from a service standpoint. The good news here is that some lenders have Direct Endorsement authority, which means they can approve your loan without submitting it to the FHA or VA. If you are going to get an FHA or VA loan, I strongly suggest that you deal with such a lender. When shopping, that is the first question to ask. If you do not get a straight answer immediately, hang up and move on to the next one.

Traditionally, FHA and VA loans (the industry calls them "Govies") have been the hope for those with minimal down payments. Today, eligible buyers can still get a VA loan with no down payment at all; FHA offers programs to accommodate 3 and 5 percent down payments. In addition, both agencies have dozens of special programs to assist various special groups—from those with disabilities to Native Americans. For example, FHA's 203(k) rehabilitation loan program will provide funds to purchase *and* rehabilitate a property, which is just great for the borrower who wants to purchase a fixer-upper.

In addition, FHA and VA are almost universally more lenient about both qualifying ratios and credit. Currently, their published ratios are 29/41 compared with FNMA's 28/36. So why doesn't everyone get one of these loans instead of conventional financing?

First, VA loans are available only to those who have qualified by virtue of their military service. Second, maximum loan amounts, while close to FNMA/FHLMC limits, are less. In the case of FHA, the limits vary by county, depending on HUD's determination of housing costs in that area. FHA limits may be $100,000 less than the FNMA/FHLMC limits. (For up-to-date information, check out your local FHA office in the phone book, or go to the following Internet site, which lists the loan limits for all areas: http://www.hud.gov/fha/sfh/sfhhicos.html.) Third, although this is a moving target, the mortgage insurance premium (MIP) on Government loans is currently slightly higher than the PMI premiums on Conventional loans. This difference becomes more dramatic as the down payment amount increases. Fourth, pricing on Government loans has recently been substantially deregulated. Formerly, HUD established a fixed interest rate that was below Conventional rates, and the seller of the property had to make up the difference (sometimes many thousands of dollars). Builders didn't care because, frankly, they factored in this probable expense when they determined the cost of their homes. Sellers in the resale market frequently would not accept offers from FHA or VA buyers because they did not want to pay the points required to bring the rates up to competitive levels. Today, the market rates are influenced largely by the same forces that determine the pricing on Conventional loans, except that FHA and VA loans are more expensive. As I write this, the difference is about ¼ percent in rate or 1 point in fee, a huge amount in my mind.

If that isn't enough, let me add one more tawdry reason. Although no one wants to talk about this, I believe that some borrowers choose Conventional financing first and switch to a Govie if they get turned down. This means that the FHA and VA borrowers, as a group, are regarded as somewhat "impaired." Sadly, this has led to a situation whereby the lenders will take advantage of their customers who just aren't qualified for other, more competitive programs. My funding sources confirm that the commission income to brokers on government loans averages about one point higher than on Conventional loans. Remember that Government loans are also priced about one point higher, so the total difference is two points, or $2,000 on a $100,000 loan. No doubt HUD and VA assume that market forces will act to keep things fair, but I do not see that happening. This is yet another reason to heed my advice about searching for a trustworthy lender. If you want an FHA or VA loan, you need to be especially wary.

SUMMARY

In spite of the fact that the industry has become more rigid in some ways, it stands more ready today than ever before to accommodate borrowers with almost any profile. Your goal should be to get qualified by a lender with the best programs and rates. If you meet A standards, go to an A lender. You should also be wary if you are told that you don't qualify for an A loan. Standards for A loans are stricter today, but a B/C lender (one that specializes in loans for borrowers who do not meet the stricter standards of A lenders) told me recently that almost 50 percent of its clients could have qualified for A rates if the loans had been packaged by someone who knew what he or she was doing. The clients just chose an incompetent lender. In Chapter 9, we'll discuss how to find competent people to help you.

CREDIT

KEY POINTS

- Your credit rating is an important factor in determining whether you are approved for a loan.
- The better your credit rating, the better the pricing.
- Lenders may view the slightest amount of derogatory information as an excuse to downgrade you to a B/C loan, which is more profitable to them.
- There are a number of ways you can clean up your credit and improve your credit rating.

A cornerstone of the mortgage underwriting process is the assumption that people will act in the future as they have in the past. Their past income is an indicator of their future income, with allowances made for raises and promotions. If they paid their bills in a timely manner in the past, they will probably continue to do so. There is ample justification for this belief; my experience is that people with an excellent credit history will maintain it 99 percent of the time. The flip side of that coin—that those who were flakes before will be flakes in the future—is just not true. Many responsible people have professional, health, or financial problems that thrust them into a period of financial difficulties; after they solve those problems, they often return to financial health and resume their responsibilities. Of course, some people really *are* flakes, and they do not understand the words, "I hereby promise to pay . . ." It is difficult to differentiate between the two because the flakes try hard to masquerade as responsible citizens.

The mortgage industry tries to answer the question of credit-worthiness by running credit checks. There are two types of credit reports: a merged credit report and the full Residential Mortgage Credit Report. A merged report is prepared after a local agency checks with three credit-reporting bureaus, such as Experian (formerly TRW), Trans Union, and Equifax. This report typically costs about $20. The Residential Mortgage Credit Report is more inclusive because the agency also conducts a telephone verification of the applicant's employment and a public-records check for judgments or liens filed against the borrower. The additional work increases the cost to about $50.

As a borrower, you want the opportunity to check the report first to confirm its accuracy before a lender sees it. This is essential, because I would estimate that about 60 percent of the reports contain some inaccuracies. Therefore, as soon as you even think about buying a home or applying for refinancing, get your credit report from one of the bureaus, or better yet, spend $20 and get a merged report. It takes time to correct errors, and you'll need as much time as you can get.

Figures 8.1 and 8.2 show samples of the reports my agency prepares. Study them carefully. Figure 8.1 shows page 1 of a full report. Figure 8.2 shows a life-size portion of that page in greater detail.

WHAT'S IN THE REPORT?

The bureaus retain records on consumer accounts for 7 years and on bankruptcies and other legal claims for 10 years. That's a long time, considering most of us can't remember what we did last week. A common response of people when they see their report is, "I can't believe that they keep track of that stuff!" Well, they do, so you have to deal with any error that pops up years later.

My reports are divided into the following categories: Open Accounts, Closed Accounts, Derogatory Accounts, and Credit Score. Some agencies include residences and employment history as well. The first category shows all accounts on which you currently maintain a balance; this is used to determine the amount you pay on your bills when the qualifying ratios are calculated. A lender will compare this list with your application to determine if you have disclosed all open accounts—obviously, they should correlate. Lenders get upset if you neglect to mention important accounts. This section also shows any account that a creditor reports as open, even though you may not have used it for years.

Member
Associated Credit Bureaus Inc. MEMBER

MBA

CONFIDENTIAL REPORT FOR:	ACCOUNT NO
ANY MORTGAGE COMPANY 1234 W MAIN ST NEWPORT BEACH, CA 92662	005005

TYPE OF REPORT		PROPERTY ADDRESS AND/OR LOAN IDENTIFICATION	
RESIDENTIAL MORTGAGE CREDIT REPORT		123 RUE CHAT ROYALE / 123456	
ORDERED BY	DATE ORDERED	DATE COMPLETED	SUPPLEMENT DATE	JOINT OR INDIVIDUAL	TYPE OF LOAN
	05-12-97	05-12-97		JOINT	CONVENTIONAL

BORROWER	CO-BORROWER
RICH, JOHN BEVERLY PALMS HOTEL BEVERLY HILLS, CA 90210 SINCE 2 YEARS PREVIOUS ADDRESS 623 E 68TH ST #3D NEW YORK, NY 10027 SINCE 01-78	MARY BEVERLY PALMS HOTEL BEVERLY HILLS, CA 90210 SINCE 2 YEARS PREVIOUS ADDRESS 623 E 68TH ST #3D NEW YORK, NY 10027 SINCE 01-78

AGE	SOCIAL SECURITY #	MAR STATUS/DEPS	RENT/BUY/OWN	AGE	SOCIAL SECURITY #	MAR STATUS/DEPS	RENT/BUY/OWN
35	123-45-6789	MARRIED /1	OWN	35	234-56-7890	MARRIED /1	

PRESENT EMPLOYER	VER	POSITION	PRESENT EMPLOYER	VER	POSITION
CLUB LOOLOO	N	SELF EMPLOYED	---	N	HOMEMAKER
SINCE	EST. INCOME	VER	VERIFIED BY	DATE	SINCE	EST. INCOME	VER	VERIFIED BY	DATE
01-94	---	N	SEE FINANCIALS	---		---	N	---	

PREVIOUS EMPLOYER	VER	POSITION	PREVIOUS EMPLOYER	VER	POSITION
TROPICAL CLUB	N	ENTERTAINER	---	N	---
SINCE	EST. INCOME	VER	VERIFIED BY	DATE	SINCE	EST. INCOME	VER	VERIFIED BY	DATE
01-86	---	N	LIZ R.		---	N	---	

CREDIT HISTORY REPOSITORY SOURCE(S): TRW AND TU   INTERVIEW: NOT OBTAINED
PUBLIC RECORDS: YES

CREDITOR AND ACCOUNT NUMBER	F/N O/T/E	DATE OPENED	DATE REPORTED	HIGH CREDIT OR LIMIT	PRESENT BALANCE	TERMS MIN. PAYMENT OR 5% OF BALANCE	MANNER OF PAYMENT	# OF MOS. REV.	AMOUNT PAST DUE	TIMES PAST DUE 30-59 DAYS	60-89 DAYS	90 & OVER	DATE LAST PAST DUE	ECOA
					***** OPEN ACCOUNTS *****									
MERCEDES BENZ CO 938485738	-	3-94	4-97	58,000	12,000	60X$1000	SATIS	34	-0-	0	0	0	0	---	I
B OF A AUTO 0384848393	4	5-93	4-97	30,000	5,900	60X$502E	SATIS	48	-0-	0	0	0	0	---	J
BLOOMINGDALES 93857857387373	2	3-80	4-97	2,500	500	FLEX$30	SATIS	99	-0-	0	0	0	0	---	I
LORD AND TAYLOR 884625173	-	7-83	5-97	2,500	200	FLEXIBLE	SATIS	99	-0-	0	0	0	0	---	J
					***** CLOSED ACCOUNTS *****									
DICK/JANE SMITH N/S	1	7-85	5-94	10,000	-0-	12X$950	PD SATIS	99	-0-	0	0	0	0	---	J
HOT SHOT HAT SHOP 93726123	5	2-80	5-93	100	-0-	$15/MO	PD SATIS	99	-0-	0	0	0	0	---	I
					***** DEROGATORY ACCOUNTS *****									
BEV HILLS S&L I999929992	-	4-95	5-97	900,000	825,000	360X$8500	PAST DUE	99	8500	1	1	0	0	5-97	J
MACYS 93847587393	-	6-82	5-97	1,000	300	FLEXIBLE	CURRENT	99	-0-	0	1	0	0	4-94	J
5TH AVE COLL 937847	3	11-90	5-97	200	173	COLL ACCT	UNPAID	79	173	0	0	0	0	---	J
CHEVRON 99384375	-	1-92	4-97	200	124	FLEXIBLE	CURRENT	64	-0-	0	1	0	0	5-95	J

CERTIFICATION

1. Classified Credit Data, Inc. [ ] certifies [ ] does not certify that this report meets the underwriting requirements of FNMA, FMHC, FHLMC, VA and FHA. The report is provided to assist in the decision to grant credit and is compiled from various sources in good faith. The accuracy of the report is in no way guaranteed and the information is strictly confidential.
2. CCDI certifies that public records have been checked for judgments, foreclosures, bankruptcies, and liens involving the borrower(s) or equivalent information has been obtained through a public records repository or secondary reporting service.
3. CCDI certifies that the borrower(s) credit history has been checked through accumulated credit records maintained by repository sources covering the community in which the borrower(s) reside.

COMPLETED BY:		LOG	AN	QC	SUPP
ANY MORTGAGE COMPANY , 1234 W MAIN ST , NEWPORT BEACH, CA 926		JK	DC	DC	

SECURITY CONTROL	AND MUST	SECURITY CODES ARE:	
IMAGE IS → [ ]{ }{ }	MATCH → [ ]{ }{ }	8596591	15 005005 00 043789
Copyright CCDI 10/89 06-30 14:49 06-30 18:13 D			PAGE 1 OF 2

Figure 8.1 Page 1 of a credit report.

MBA

CONFIDENTIAL REPORT FOR:	ACCOUNT NO
ANY MORTGAGE COMPANY 1234 W MAIN ST NEWPORT BEACH, CA 92662	005005

TYPE OF REPORT				PROPERTY ADDRESS AND/OR LOAN IDENTIFICATION		
RESIDENTIAL MORTGAGE CREDIT REPORT				123 RUE CHAT ROYALE / 123456		
ORDERED BY	DATE ORDERED	DATE COMPLETED	SUPPLEMENT DATE	JOINT OR INDIVIDUAL		TYPE OF LOAN
	05-12-97	05-12-97		JOINT		CONVENTIONAL

BORROWER	CO-BORROWER
RICH, JOHN SEE PAGE 1 SINCE PREVIOUS ADDRESS SINCE	MARY SEE PAGE 1 SINCE PREVIOUS ADDRESS SINCE

AGE	SOCIAL SECURITY #	MAR STATUS/DEP'S	RENT/BUY/OWN	AGE	SOCIAL SECURITY #	MAR STATUS/DEP'S	RENT/BUY/OWN

PRESENT EMPLOYER	VER	POSITION	PRESENT EMPLOYER	VER	POSITION

SINCE	EST. INCOME	VER	VERIFIED BY	DATE	SINCE	EST. INCOME	VER	VERIFIED BY	DATE

PREVIOUS EMPLOYER	VER	POSITION	PREVIOUS EMPLOYER	VER	POSITION

SINCE	EST. INCOME	VER	VERIFIED BY	DATE	SINCE	EST. INCOME	VER	VERIFIED BY	DATE

CREDIT HISTORY	REPOSITORY SOURCE(S): TRW AND TU	INTERVIEW: NOT OBTAINED
	PUBLIC RECORDS: YES	

CREDITOR AND ACCOUNT NUMBER	F/O/N/O/T/E	DATE OPENED	DATE REPORTED	HIGH CREDIT OR LIMIT	PRESENT BALANCE	TERMS MIN. PAYMENT OR 5% OF BALANCE	MANNER OF PAYMENT	# OF MOS. REV.	AMOUNT PAST DUE	TIMES PAST DUE 30-59 DAYS	60-89 DAYS	90 & OVER	DATE LAST PAST DUE	E/C/O/A

INQUIRIES:

MERCEDES BENZ, 3-2-97, AUTO DEALERSHIP

FOOTNOTES:
1. PRIVATE PARTY ACCOUNT IS A PAID REAL ESTATE 2ND TRUST DEED LOAN.
2. CREDIT FOUND IN THE NAME OF MARY JONES.
3. COLLECTING FOR AT & T PER ANN (202)555-1234.
4. APPLICANT IS CO-SIGNER ON ACCOUNT, PRIMARY HOLDER OF ACCOUNT
   IS JOHN RICH JR.
5. CREDIT FOUND IN THE NAME OF MARY RICH.
CREDIT ALSO CHECKED UNDER THE NAME OF MARY JONES

PUBLIC RECORDS:
1. CIVIL JUDGEMENT FILED 9-95 MAGISTRATE COURT #96006800
   SMITH MANAGEMENT FOR $509.
TRW REPORTS FAIR, ISAAC CREDIT RISK SCORE = 599 (BOR)
   SCORE FACTOR: ACCOUNT(S) NOT PAID AS AGREED AND/OR LEGAL ITEM FILED
   SCORE FACTOR: LENGTH OF TIME ACCOUNTS HAVE BEEN ESTABLISHED
   SCORE FACTOR: LENGTH OF TIME (OR UNKNOWN TIME) SINCE ACCOUNT
                 DELINQUENT
   SCORE FACTOR: DELINQUENCY REPORTED ON ACCOUNTS
TRW REPORTS FAIR, ISAAC CREDIT RISK SCORE = 720 (COB)
   SCORE FACTOR: ACCOUNT(S) NOT PAID AS AGREED AND/OR LEGAL ITEM FILED
   SCORE FACTOR: DELINQUENCY REPORTED ON ACCOUNTS
   SCORE FACTOR: PROPORTION OF BALANCE TO HIGH CREDIT ON BANK REVOLVING
                 OR ALL REVOLVING ACCOUNTS
   SCORE FACTOR: LENGTH OF TIME ACCOUNTS HAVE BEEN ESTABLISHED

CERTIFICATION

1. Classified Credit Data, Inc. ☑ certifies ☐ does not certify that this report meets the underwriting requirements of FNMA, FMHC, FHLMC, VA and FHA. The report is provided to assist in the decision to grant credit and is compiled from various sources in good faith. The accuracy of the report is in no way guaranteed and the information is strictly confidential.
2. CCDI certifies that public records have been checked for judgments, foreclosures, bankruptcies, and liens involving the borrower(s) or equivalent information has been obtained through a public records repository or secondary reporting service.
3. CCDI certifies that the borrower(s) credit history has been checked through accumulated credit records maintained by repository sources covering the community in which the borrower(s) reside.

COMPLETED BY:

	LOG	AN	QC	SUPP
ANY MORTGAGE COMPANY , 1234 W MAIN ST , NEWPORT BEACH, CA 926	JK	DC	DC	

SECURITY CONTROL	AND MUST	SECURITY CODES ARE:	
IMAGE IS → { }{ }{ }	MATCH → { }{ }{ }	8596591	15 005005 00 043789
Copyright CCDI 10/93 06-30 14:49	06-30 18:13 D		PAGE 2 OF 2

Figure 8.1 *(Continued)*

				************ OPEN ACCOUNTS ************								
MERCEDES BENZ CO 938485738	-	3-94	4-97	58,000	12,000	60X$1000	SATIS	34	-0-	0 0 0 0	---	I
B OF A AUTO 0384848393	4	5-93	4-97	30,000	5,900	60X$502E	SATIS	48	-0-	0 0 0 0	---	J
BLOOMINGDALES 93857857387373	2	3-80	4-97	2,500	500	FLEX$30	SATIS	99	-0-	0 0 0 0	---	I
LORD AND TAYLOR 884625173	-	7-83	5-97	2,500	200	FLEXIBLE	SATIS	99	-0-	0 0 0 0	---	J
			************ CLOSED ACCOUNTS ************									
DICK/JANE SMITH N/S	1	7-85	5-94	10,000	-0-	12X$950	PD SATIS	99	-0-	0 0 0 0	---	J
HOT SHOT HAT SHOP 93726123	5	2-80	5-93	100	-0-	$15/MO	PD SATIS	99	-0-	0 0 0 0	---	I
			************ DEROGATORY ACCOUNTS ************									
BEV HILLS S&L I999929992	-	4-95	5-97	900,000	825,000	360X$8500	PAST DUE	99	8500	1 1 0 0	5-97	J
MACYS 93847587393	-	6-82	5-97	1,000	300	FLEXIBLE	CURRENT	99	-0-	0 1 0 0	4-94	J
5TH AVE COLL 937847	3	11-90	5-97	200	173	COLL ACCT	UNPAID	79	173	0 0 0 0	---	J
CHEVRON 99384375	-	1-92	4-97	200	124	FLEXIBLE	CURRENT	64	-0-	0 1 0 0	5-95	J

Figure 8.2   Detail of a credit report.

The Closed Account category is not important. After discussing credit scoring, I will devote the rest of this chapter to derogatory accounts, called "derogs" in the industry, and actions you can take to eliminate erroneous information and improve your rating.

CREDIT-SCORING SYSTEMS

Credit scores will be of growing importance in the coming years. Several lenders have been using these systems for years, and FNMA now requires that all loans sold to them include credit reports with FICO scores, a score developed by Fair, Isaac and Co. When you look at 100,000 people, I'm sure there is a strong correlation between these scores and the rate of foreclosures, but I am not happy about the potential impact on consumers. My experience is that it gives a lender a new excuse to deny a perfectly good loan. If that's going to be the case, then you better learn which factors lead to lower scores and actions you can take to improve your credit score.

Each of the major bureaus has its own scoring system, but the most common is the FICO score, so that's the one I'll discuss. We are already seeing lenders develop criteria similar to the following:

- If the FICO score is above 680, the loan will qualify for special, or streamlined, processing. Translated, this means the lender is happy with the borrower and won't ask as many questions, so approval will be faster.
- If the FICO score is between 620 and 680, the lender will evaluate the borrower further.
- If the FICO score is less than 620, an A lender may want to see offsetting strong factors that will justify approving the loan.

FICO scores may be a blessing to some borrowers, but they will be a curse to others. Streamlining the process for squeaky-clean borrowers is laudable, but I also know the bureaucratic mind tends to focus on what is wrong rather than what is right. Therefore, I caution you: Do not underestimate the anguish this mentality can cause.

Furthermore, the FICO scoring process is purposely mysterious because industry professionals think that if the public knows their system, someone will figure out a way to beat it, thus making it meaningless. I have seen a lot of credit reports since this system was introduced, and I have come to the following conclusion: At a basic level, the system works, but like all other rule-driven systems, it is sometimes unduly harsh on certain individuals. I have seen some credit reports that I thought were more satisfactory than some others with higher FICO scores.

The following factors will reduce your FICO score:

- A number of open accounts (the weight they give to unused accounts is not clear)
- A number of open accounts with balances
- A number of accounts with balances close to or at the limit
- A number of inquiries from other creditors
- A number of accounts with derogatory information
- A number of collection accounts, tax liens, or judgments

At first glance, most of these criteria make sense, but they don't account for lifestyle differences due to income. Just three credit cards may be too many for one person, while for another, three more cards wouldn't adversely affect his or her financial situation. Perhaps more important, the FICO system does not take into account those people who use credit cards for convenience and pay them off every month. Even worse, an executive who travels extensively and routinely runs up as much as $10,000 on a credit card but pays it off when he or she receives the expense check is still penalized under this system.

Another problem with scoring is the time it takes to change a score. Under the old system, if you had an error on your report, you could get the creditor to send you a letter deleting it, show it to your lender, and the lender would ignore the derog. Under the new system, even though you obtain error-apology letters from a creditor, it will take some time, perhaps several months, before your FICO score is recalculated—not desirable when you are under a deadline to buy a house.

Although FICO scoring has been in common use now for less than a year, I have already heard lenders make comments such as, "I can't do that loan because the FICO score is less than 700," or "If the score is less than 660, we won't consider it." One major lender turned down an 80 percent LTV loan for a borrower with $25,000 in the bank, $131,000 in his pension plan, a 15-year history in his own company, and ratios of 23/24. His sin? He prefers to pay cash for things and had just a few cards that showed a short history of usage. This borrower scored low on the lender's internal credit-scoring system due to his brief credit history, and no one—not even the chief underwriter—would override the computer, despite the fact that this customer's overall financial strength was greater than 90 percent of the company's borrowers.

The point is that if your FICO score is lower than the lender's limit, you may be in for a disappointment. Get your credit report early in the process so you have time to correct errors. If your FICO score seems lower than your credit warrants, don't deal with a lender that places emphasis on FICO scores. As I write this, about half of the lenders I know don't seem to use them, but the other half do, so your loan shopping should include another question: How does your underwriting department use FICO scores in evaluating loans?

CREDIT PROBLEMS

This section is intended to demonstrate how underwriters in general view credit reports. We'll pinpoint some problems you may encounter and discuss ways to take care of those problems.

I like to divide credit problems into three categories: insignificant, minor, and major. Insignificant, for example, refers to a small number, say three or four sporadic 30-day late payments on revolving debts such as a Visa card. Minor problems include a regular pattern of late credit card payments or late car payments, especially within the last 12 months. Major problems reflect late payments on real estate loans, foreclosure notices on a mortgage, repossession of a car, and personal bankruptcy. Other serious problems are collection accounts, judgments, and tax liens. Strangely, these problems can arise in the most innocent ways. Let me give you a few common examples.

You check into your local hospital and rack up a $5,000 bill. At discharge, you pay $1,000, or 20 percent of the bill. The hospital then sends a $4,000 bill to your insurance company, which subsequently pays only $3,965. The hospital does not call to alert you that you still owe $35. It sends the unpaid bill to a collection agency. That agency notifies Experian that you didn't pay a bill. Although it is required by law, the hospital may even fail to write you a letter. For the cost of a postage stamp, the hospital may end up collecting only $10 of the $35 balance. Bingo! You have a derog on your credit report and your FICO score drops a notch.

You hire a painter to paint your house for $3,750. He destroys some plantings that cost you $250 to replace. You pay $3,250 and tell him you'll pay the other $250 when he acknowledges that $3,500 is all you owe. He takes you to small-claims court for $500. You show up with pictures of the ruined plants and tell the judge you're willing to pay the $3,750 less $250. The judge finds in your favor and you write out a check for $250—which you were willing to pay in the first place. Unfortunately, this shows up on the public record as a judgment filed against you and later satisfied—in other words, it appears exactly as though you'd lost and are the kind of person creditors must take to court. When you write the check, have the painter sign a Notice of Release of Lien and file it with the court. Otherwise, it will show up years later as an unsatisfied judgment.

You co-own a boat with your neighbor. You finally tire of the boat, and when your partner calls one day and says, "I just sold the boat to Harry," you're elated. He sends you a check for your half, $4,400. However, if your county collects taxes on personal property like boats, failure to submit a bill of sale with the new owner's address will find you presented with another tax bill next year. If you say to yourself, "This isn't my bill, we sold the boat," and don't pay it, the county will file a tax lien against you for the amount due, maybe $76.45. Voilà! Another derog on your credit report: an unsatisfied tax lien. Not only will you have to explain this, you may be required to pay it as well.

No doubt you have credit cards with payments due on various days of the month. If you're like me, you probably pay them in batches. Sometimes this results in payments received by creditors *after* they send you the next bill. Well, technically, that payment is late. Whether creditors report such delinquent payments to the credit bureaus is up to them. My experience is that some do and some don't. It is not at all uncommon for credit reports to reveal some kind of derogatory information on people who are actually quite scrupulous with their finances. Frequently, this occurs on seldom-used accounts like the department stores, which, incidentally, seem to be the fastest on the trigger in reporting delinquent payments. Most of the time, people are totally unaware that a late payment made years ago is still sullying their record. Remember, *get a credit report early.*

Believe it or not, even more innocuous behavior can result in a less-than-perfect credit report. Illegible handwriting on credit applications may result in information being misread or misreported. Keyboarding errors when data are entered into a computer may go undetected until someone requests your credit report years later.

HINTS ON REPAIRING CREDIT

Let's use the example of a credit card to demonstrate how to undo a damaging entry on your report. First, and most important, remember that you have every right to get this corrected. Assume the company reports that you have few 30-day lates. The first step is to call the company and calmly say, "*I just got my credit report and found that you reported that I made late payments. I believe that I have never been late with my account.*" In my experience, many creditors are happy to remove this blight from their reports as a matter of accommodation and convenience to the customer—even though you may actually have been late once or twice. Frequently, when you call, the computer screen may not show any lates, in which case it really is an error. In other cases, if only minor lates show up, the first-line people you talk with are authorized to delete them. You might be asked to send in the portion of the report with the offending entry to show exactly how it is entered before the creditor can correct it.

If, however, the customer service rep tells you that he or she has to check with someone else, request a callback in 15 minutes to confirm the adjustment. If you get some waffling from the representative, it may mean that only a supervisor has the authority to make the change you are asking for. If that happens, don't waste time; just ask nicely but firmly, "May I please speak with your supervisor?" Then explain your problem again to the supervisor.

In general, you'll find that credit card companies, especially the banks, are a little tougher to deal with than department stores, although, as with any business, some are better than others. If you find that you get an unfriendly reception, consider canceling your card and finding a friendlier bank.

Usually, "affiliation" credit card issuers are the easiest to deal with. For example, many trade groups, professional associations, charitable organizations, and alumni groups offer credit cards where a portion of every dollar you charge is donated to the organization. At one such bank where I have a card, you talk with a person called a "customer satisfaction representative," which is just that. A company that is willing to describe its employees that way is going to be a lot easier to deal with than the average bank.

Getting Action

When the creditor agrees to correct your report, don't hang up the phone thinking that you're home free. It will probably take 45 to 60 days for the change to work through the system—too long if you're trying to get your mortgage approved. Ask the creditor to write you a letter clearing the report and have it faxed to you immediately. Be sure to get the name of the person you are talking with. If the letter doesn't arrive within 24 hours, call that person; you don't want to start from scratch with someone new. Figure 8.3 shows a sample "clearing-your-report" apology letter.

The creditor may send a notice directly to the bureau and to you, which is even better. When you have all the proof you can get your hands on, take it to the agency that generated your credit report so it can eliminate the derogatory items. Be sure your report is retyped; don't settle for a *supplement* to the original report. You want to ensure that the underwriter sees a squeaky-clean report.

FIRST BANK

Regarding account 372 555 1212

Dear Mrs. Wilson,

We have reviewed the history of this account and find that all payments were made on time. Our report of late payments is incorrect. We will forward our correction of our report to the bureaus.

We apologize for any inconvenience this may have caused you.

Sincerely,

Mary Bostwick
Credit Supervisor

Figure 8.3   Sample letter clearing a report.

WARNING Creditors are notorious for "forgetting" to follow through on correction commitments, even though they are legally required to do so. To ensure that Experian (formerly TRW), Trans Union, Equifax, and the other reporting bureaus get this update, order another credit report 90 days later to verify that the changes you instituted have been carried out.

Paying Off Credit Cards with a Refinance

Many lenders have a rule that states, "The payoff of revolving debt by a refinance will not improve your ratios." The obvious assumption is that you'll go out and run up your cards again. If you decide to pay off your bills with a refinance, believing that zero balances on your cards will improve your ratios, you may be unpleasantly surprised. My advice is to add yet another question to your loan-shopping list to be asked right up front, even before filling out the application: How does your underwriting department treat the payoff of consumer debt with a refinance?

TIP If you run into this problem and you find no other way around it, there is a solution, albeit a cumbersome one. Oddly, many banks with this onerous policy do not use it in their equity-line department. That means you can apply for an equity line, pay off your bills, and then ask for a new underlying loan. The lender views such an action in a different light and will approve your loan.

A kinder, gentler lender's policy manual might say, "In order not to count the payment, you must also close the account." Others don't care at all.

Additional Pitfalls

Credit reports also list any recent inquiries to the bureaus. Invariably, these result from new applications for credit that you have made or perhaps requests for increases in the limit of existing accounts. Nevertheless, you will be asked to explain these because the lender may assume you are running up credit balances that will mean additional payments beyond what is shown on your credit report, and that would affect your qualifying ratios. And unless you are highly qualified, do not buy a car while you are looking for houses or are in escrow. There is no more sure way to ruin your deal. If you are highly qualified and want to buy a new car, first sit down with your lender and ask, "How would an additional $485 monthly payment affect my qualifying ratios?"

Letters of Explanation

Most lenders ask the borrowers for letters explaining any derogatory items or recent inquiries, regardless of how insignificant. However, if you have a high credit score (for example, a FICO score over 680), some lenders are now waiving this requirement, although there are individual exceptions to this. One lender adopted a policy of not requiring letters on minor consumer credit derogs more than two years old. Can you remember why you made a late payment five years ago on an infrequently used card? No one else can either, so why bother to ask? I applaud this practice and recommend it to other lenders.

More serious derogs still require an explanation letter, especially if they've occurred within the past 24 months. These include 60- or 90-day lates on credit cards, lates on installment debt like car loans, collection accounts, repossessed cars, judgments, tax liens, and bankruptcy. These are important, and underwriters pay attention to them, so you should devote sufficient energy to crafting the letter to achieve the result you want: loan approval. Sample letters are shown in Figures 8.4 through 8.7 to give you an idea of what lenders like to see. Your loan officer should also be able to help you write these letters.

The most important point regarding credit problems is that lenders want to help you clear your recent history. They are therefore likely to be understanding about problems that were confined to one particular period of time or that had a distinct, definable cause. Loss of a job or severe health problems can happen to anyone and can cause finances to become strained to the point where payments are missed. If this has happened to you, tell your lender what happened. That will help to classify you as a person who *had* a problem rather than someone who still *has* a problem.

To whom it may concern:

I wish to respond to the items on my credit report.

My family and I spend a month vacationing in Japan every year. Because of the duration of our stay, it is possible a bill that arrives shortly after we leave won't be paid until the 32nd or 33rd day or 34th day. I'm sure that this is the source of the late payments shown on the report.

Also, I moved my office twice in 1991, once to temporary quarters and then to the office condominium I purchased. As a result of two consecutive moves, some of our mail was delayed and did not get to us promptly. I own my office now and do not plan to move.

As to the collection account, the landlord of the building where I maintained offices in 1990 and 1991 attempted to collect noncontractual charges from his tenants. We refused to pay, and he harassed all of the tenants, including referring the matter to a collection agency. The report says that the account was paid, but that is not true. Because the charges were not proper, the matter was ultimately dropped.

We have always paid our creditors, and I appreciate the privilege of having good credit. I hope that this response will reassure you as to my record and my determination to maintain my good credit standing.

Figure 8.4   Sample borrower letter of explanation.

To whom it may concern:

I wish to respond to the items on my credit report.

_____ card—One company sold its accounts to another. It sent me a bill for the annual fee but I did not renew the card. Its charge-off is merely an internal reversal on the company's books of a charge for which I am not liable.

M_____ Department Store—This bill came when we were on a trip to Europe. We have been current with the account for 14 years.

ABC Motors—I bought a new BMW. I paid cash for the car and did not finance it.

Figure 8.5   Sample borrower letter of explanation. (*Note:* If you apply for a mortgage shortly after purchasing a car for cash, be prepared to provide a copy of the title to the lender to prove you don't have a car loan. When you finance a car, the lender keeps the title until you pay off the loan.)

Late Payments on Real Estate Loans

In the past, mortgage lenders didn't report mortgage credit histories to the credit bureaus, but now almost all do, which could cause problems for you. Here's how. You are obligated to make your payment on the first of the month, but almost universally, lenders give you a 15-day grace period. (Sometimes it's 10 days! When you sign loan documents, check this out.) If you don't make your payment until the seventeenth of the month, you will owe the lender a penalty, typically 5 percent of the amount of the payment due. You probably already know this, but here's some-

To whom it may concern:

Regarding our credit report, we do not have an account at S_____ C_____ and have never bought anything there. I called the company and it had us confused with someone in Lawndale. They said they will correct the error.

I have no recollection of the other items, all of which happened between two and seven years ago.

Figure 8.6   Sample borrower letter of explanation.

To whom it may concern:

We applied to both ABC Savings and XYZ Savings for this same loan. I canceled both applications, although it appears that XYZ ignored my request.

The B_____ Bank inquiry was in response to our application for a check guarantee/debit card. This card was issued to us and is the first item listed on our credit report.

Figure 8.7   Sample borrower letter of explanation.

thing you may not be aware of: Credit reports are set up to report 30-, 60-, and 90-day lates. There isn't a column for payments received *after* the grace period but *before* 30 days. Therefore, the lender frequently reports them as a 30-day lates. Ironically, when *granting* credit, lenders don't worry about 15-day lates, but the underwriting manual tells them to worry about payments made more than 30 days late. You see the problem.

There's more. Some lenders keep detailed records for only 24 months. Say you were 18 days late (not 30 days late) on your March 1993 payment. After March 1995, the lender reports it as follows: "Number of times 30 days late = 1; Date of late payment = N/S." (N/S means "not stated," which the lender uses because it didn't keep records and doesn't remember the date.) When you apply for a new loan, the new lender looks at your credit report and assumes that you were late last month. If you have such an entry on your credit report, have your loan rep immediately send a verification-of-mortgage form to that lender to get a more detailed loan history. Then go back through your records, dig out the most recent 12 months of canceled checks, and make copies—front and back—to show the lender that you haven't been late in the last 12 months, which is the only period they usually care about.

After you've purchased your home, I urge you to be scrupulous about making your mortgage payments on time. Mortgage lenders hate late payments on mortgages. If you get into a financial bind someday, let the Visa card slide, but do whatever you have to do to make your mortgage payment on time. Failure to do so can be very expensive as it can instantly turn you into a B/C borrower.

Delinquent Property Taxes

If you are engaged in a refinance transaction, the preliminary title report shows the status of payment of property taxes. I once received a prelim showing that a borrower was delinquent not only on his current tax payment, but also on tax payments for the prior two years. The bottom line is that underwriters hate it when you don't pay your taxes. They consider it a grave offense. If you are about to refinance your home and haven't paid your taxes, pay them. Your lender will demand that you pay them before the transaction closes. When you pay, do so in person with a cashier's check. Get a receipt and give this to your loan rep to pass on to the title company. Make sure that the preliminary title report shows all taxes have been paid. If it does not, have it retyped. If an underwriter sees the delinquency, even with the subsequent payment, you'll have to write a convincing letter of explanation, but if you have the prelim retyped, the lender will never know it happened.

The same is true for other tax liens or judgments that may have been filed against your property. The lender will require that they be paid prior to closing anyway, so you might as well get it taken care of up front.

MAINTAINING GOOD CREDIT

 $\boxed{\textit{HINT}}$ If you own a new or one-year-old car, even if you paid cash for it, the lender is going to assume that you have a car loan, even if you are a person of substantial wealth.

The lender's way of confirming ownership is to require you to show the pink slip, title, or whatever your state uses to prove ownership. If there is a loan on the vehicle, the lien holder will keep this until the loan is paid. I think that it is at least annoying, and perhaps even insulting, to have to show that you have clear title to a car. To avoid the issue, when you fill out the application, omit the year your car was manufactured and state its value conservatively. I will quickly add that you should *not* lie, about this or anything else, especially if you actually have a loan on the car that doesn't show up on the credit report. Sometimes these car loans show up on the backup credit reports that lenders get.

WARNING I don't know why more family lawyers don't suggest this, but if you are going through a divorce or have gone through one, my advice would be to make sure you and your ex-spouse split up the credit cards. Take the cards you want and have your ex-spouse expunged from the accounts. If necessary, get a new card. As part of the divorce proceedings, demand that your ex-spouse do the same.

I have seen too many cases where, three or four years later, the spouse creates problems. If your ex-spouse uses these cards, the balances show up on *your* credit report. If your spouse forgets to make some payments, this shows up on *your* credit report. It is very hard to prove that these aren't really yours.

ADVICE You take some of the cards and let your spouse take the others. You should cancel all joint accounts. You are both liable for cards with existing balances because the credit was granted on the assumption that you would both be responsible for debts. You can, however, close the account to new purchases so that when the balance is paid, the account will be closed. You can then get an individual account in your own name.

HINT Instead of being a cosigner with your child on a car loan, ask the bank if you can guarantee the loan. If you are a cosigner, the bank will report the loan to the credit bureaus as *yours,* under your Social Security number (SSN) as well as the SSN of your child. Banks are not used to doing this, so you will almost certainly have to talk with a manager before you can find someone who even remembers what a guarantee is! You're just as liable as a cosigner this way, but the loan is reported only on your child's SSN, not yours.

HINT In a "rolling late," you miss a payment, make the next five on time, and then make up the missed payment. The creditor may report this as five 30-day lates, four 60-day lates, and three 90-day lates even though only one payment was actually late. The lender probably has the contractual and probably the legal right to apply any payment received to the *oldest* outstanding payment, so the report is not technically incorrect. However, your lender will be a lot more understanding if you have canceled checks and monthly statements from the creditor to show what went wrong.

HINT I have seen innumerable situations where people pay off a car loan early, and late-payment reports show up later. It is as if banks have two computers, one to keep track of balances and the other to keep track of payments due. When you pay off the loan, computer 1 doesn't tell computer 2, so computer 2 still expects a payment from you. When it doesn't get one, it calls the credit bureau and reports you as late. When you pay off the loan, do so in person if you can, and get a dated receipt.

HINT This may sound silly, but it happens all too frequently. Let's say you are selling or refinancing your home. The settlement agent gets the legal Demand for Payoff from the lender being paid off. It's the legally binding document that says, "They owe us $135,357.54 plus interest at the rate of $28.50 per day from 03/01/97." Your escrow is supposed to close on April 10. The settlement agent will collect from you the balance plus 40 days' interest, 30 days in March that *would* have been paid with the April 1 payment and 10 days in April, plus maybe one additional day to make sure the lender gets it.

You don't make the payment on April 1, assuming that the escrow company or settlement agent will just make the payment when the old loan is paid off. However, if escrow is delayed until April 15 and the lender doesn't get the payment until the next day, the loan payment becomes delinquent. In addition to the extra five days' interest, you'll also incur a late fee, and probably a derog on your credit report as well. To satisfy the lender you aren't a flake, you'll have to show the closing statement on that transaction, and it'll be trouble enough just finding it two years later.

ADVICE When you are refinancing, make your regular monthly payment to the lender on the first of the month or earlier (yes, you can pay early, too!). That way the lender will have time to update its Demand for Payoff, so interest will be collected only from April 1 and you won't be late.

HINT If you hold too many credit cards and have a problem making purchases you really cannot afford, I recommend the following solution. It's called the "310 trick." You take all your credit cards, put a rubber band around them, set your oven for 300 degrees, and put the cards in there for 10 minutes. Bingo. No more temptation! It is a very useful hint for some people.

HINT Some people and companies advise getting your credit report annually, just as you replace the batteries in your smoke alarm. I don't think that is necessary, but I sure wouldn't let it go until you need a clean report. Check it every two years, perhaps, just to see what's on there and to make sure that if some erroneous information has crept in, you can correct it at that time.

HINT If you do not have many accounts or if they have been newly established (for example, you recently graduated from school and are just entering the labor market), lenders want you to show some history of handling credit responsibly. It may even be that your FICO score is low because of this. You can cure this by going to your parents and saying, "Please add me as a cardholder on a couple of your clean credit accounts, presumably ones with zero balances." The bank or department store will send you an application and add you. When they send their next reports to Experian and the other bureaus, these accounts will also be reported as your accounts. Bingo, instant credit history. If they are hesitant about keeping you on the account, have them close it and open up another one. Then it shows up as a closed account with satisfactory payment history. If someone says that this isn't fair, I'd respond that a lot of this credit stuff is game playing, and it's okay to play back!

CREDIT-REPAIR AGENCIES

Credit-repair agencies are in the business of removing derogatory data from credit reports. This is a complex, time-consuming issue and many people find it difficult to go through these steps on their own. Credit-repair companies, which promise glowing results, have a bad reputation, so bad that the Federal Trade Commission has determined many of them are scams. Therefore, I would recommend that you use one only after very careful investigation, including calling their past customers. Another reason not to use one is that you can do most of the work yourself if you will just devote the time to it, and, believe me, it is worth it. You have a lot of rights under the law. But creditors are often difficult to bring to the table, so persistence counts.

Other information on how to repair your credit is published by the Federal Trade Commission. You can access it on the Internet at http://ftc.gov. Also, the Consumer Credit Counseling Service, a nonprofit agency, offers assistance through over 850 offices in every state. Check your telephone directory, or call 1-800-388-2227. You may also write or call the following:

National Foundation for Consumer Credit
8611 Second Avenue, Suite 100
Silver Spring, MD 20910
301-589-5600

Now that we've covered the preparatory phases of the process—choosing the right loan, qualifying, and credit—we're ready to discuss making a loan application. You must first choose the kind of lender you want. We'll cover that in the next chapter.

BANK, S&L, OR BROKER?

There is very little difference between one man and another, but what difference there is, is very important.

—Winston Churchill

KEY POINTS

- There are many retail places to get a mortgage.
- In certain circumstances, it is better to deal with a mortgage broker or mortgage banker. In other markets, at other times, and under other circumstances, it is best to deal directly with the lender itself, whether bank, S&L, or credit union.
- You will get better results when you find the most competent person you can, *regardless* of the employer, and put him or her to work for you.
- The best people in the industry treat their clients like family. They will be proud to work for someone who trusts them, and you'll like it, too.

In this day and age, you are likely to find a reasonably broad product selection at most lenders. Rather than simply listing the functions of banks, S&Ls, and mortgage brokers, I want to focus on organizational behavior and how you can interact with organizations to your advantage. You're going to have to deal with your lender for 30 to 60 days, so a wise choice is paramount—even more important than rates, which will take care of themselves if you choose your lender with care.

INDEPENDENT BROKER VERSUS EMPLOYEE LOAN REP

Good

Before launching this discussion, I must admit to a bias, because I have spent the last 17 years as a mortgage broker. Brokers offer what no employee of any lender can offer: independence. As a broker in California, I am *legally* an agent for my clients, a relationship that confers on me an obligation no employee of a company has to any customer. Note that not all brokers feel the way I do, and various states allow different relationships between borrower and broker. I think that an agency relationship with a mortgage broker offers many advantages for borrowers.   *BAD*

Contrast brokers with loan reps, who are employees of banks or S&Ls or even one of the mortgage megacorporations. Loan reps are expected to pursue clients and get loan applications. If the underwriting department denies the application, the rep is not expected to go to bat for the client. This may come as a surprise to you, but in many large companies, the underwriting department reports through its own chain of command; specifically, the loan rep and his or her boss have no authority over the underwriting department. At companies like this, your loan rep may be a nice person, but he or she has virtually no power to help you if your file gets in trouble; to the contrary, the loan rep may even get in trouble trying to buck the system. I think borrowers need an advocate, but in many organizations, that's not part of the loan rep's job description.

In many large banks, the system is wrapped in even more red tape. Many of them use a central processing facility where all loan applications are processed and underwritten. The loan officer you deal with in your branch could be a trainee making $7 to $9 per hour. His or her job is to act as a conduit through whom information is sent. If the processor wants more info, he or she calls the loan officer, who then calls you. If your loan is denied, that friendly little loan officer won't be so friendly any more. He or she may even get upset if you ask why your loan was denied. At my bank, the loan officer isn't even allowed to call the processor and ask, "What's the status of the Jones file?"

bad

There is a very credible reason for the hierarchical processing systems. Large institutions such as the big banks may have hundreds, perhaps over a thousand, branches. They are not going to be able to find 1,000 competent loan officers. Any bank employee who likes the business and is competent can probably triple his or her income on the outside, working as an independent broker.

All this is not to say that you shouldn't do business with a bank or S&L. Just understand what you can expect from these people, and be realistic about what they cannot and will not do for you. Remember what I've said before and will say again: The kind of loan you want will dictate which lender you should talk with first. You should certainly talk with the bank or S&L where you have a deposit relationship. If it doesn't do mortgages, ask someone in the commercial banking department for a referral.

THE DENIAL RATE

A few years ago, the *Los Angeles Times* investigated bias in lending. This study showed that African-Americans and Hispanics were denied loans at a slightly higher rate than white applicants. However, the conclusions that everyone seemed to miss was that regardless of your color, ethnicity, or gender, you still had no better than about a 70 percent chance of getting your loan approved. In other words, one out of every three loans is rejected. What are the implications of this statistic?

First, put another way, approximately one-third of the people employed in the mortgage industry do nothing but turn down loans. Second, someone has to pay the salaries and overhead of the staff who work on these denials—and that someone is you. That's right, you pay for approval your own loan and about half the cost of processing the loan of someone who was denied. I'd estimate that this adds from $300 to $500 to the cost of processing your loan.

There are a couple of reasons for this. A rational one is that lenders such as banks are subject to federal regulation and must abide by the Equal Credit Opportunity Act provisions. One provision requires them to accept a loan application from any person who applies. They are legally obligated to process fully all applications, even those that don't have a prayer of being approved. This has nothing to do with race, creed, or color. Some people are simply not qualified for a loan as large as they want. [Another reason mortgage brokers are more efficient than the big banks is that we are more adept at targeting people toward a loan that will be approved and for which we will get paid.] go to mortgage broker

It's perfectly true that there are many fine banks and large lenders. They hire the best people they can, run their organizations with integrity, and treat their customers honestly and fairly.

Others can be sloppy and cumbersome, mistakenly rejecting your perfectly good loan application. The point is that you as a borrower must assess the various institutions before you apply for a loan. How big are they? What are the qualifications of the people you will be dealing with? Can you meet the manager? Where is your loan processed—at your local branch or at some centralized office hundreds of miles away? The choices will be different in every community. If you decide to pursue a loan on the Internet, a topic covered in Chapter 20, your choices are even broader, but the issues and questions are the same.

BAD-APPLE BROKERS

Lest the preceding discussion be interpreted as a blanket indictment of large lenders and an unqualified endorsement of brokers, this section is intended to balance the scales. While for obvious reasons, I favor independent mortgage brokers, I'm not naive and do not for a moment believe that all brokers are either competent or honest. You need to be aware that a small mortgage brokerage company is not bound by any rules about pricing other than what the market lets it get away with. A large bank with hundreds of branches is simply too cumbersome an organization to allow anyone to fool with pricing. Conversely, a small operation is more focused on wringing every penny out of every deal. With such an ability to control pricing and profit, there are brokers who, shall we say, are unhampered by the constraints imposed by ethical standards of conduct. Regulators don't concern themselves with pricing; they assume free-market forces protect consumers. Again, make sure you know who you're dealing with and that you fully understand your agreement. This topic is more fully explored later in this chapter, when I discuss competence, and again in Chapter 13, "How Lenders Can Cheat Their Customers."

CREDIT UNIONS

Credit unions stand out in my experience as notable exceptions to some of the harsher points I make about banks and S&Ls. Members of a credit union do not have an adversarial relationship with the organization. That relationship precludes an employee from taking advantage of a fellow member. In my area, many credit unions originate and sell mortgages through a central organization set up for that purpose. If that organization makes a profit as a result of its activities, it rebates the excess back to the originators, and thus the members. With that kind of system, there is no incentive for overcharging the customer. If you are a credit union member, certainly consider it as a loan source.   FANNIE MAY

That said, you should realize that most credit unions are best at FNMA/FHLMC-conforming loans because of the demographics of their membership—usually employees of large industries or trade groups. Therefore, they focus on providing fair pricing on plain-vanilla products rather than a full spectrum of loans. Also, you should be aware that while their pricing may be fair, it isn't going to be very aggressive. And I wouldn't expect a lot of hand-holding, either. At a larger credit union, there may be a trained mortgage specialist, but the smaller ones may not have anyone who does anything more than help you fill out the forms.

If your loan is uncomplicated and you prefer to deal with your credit union, you should take considerable comfort in knowing that you are at least on a level playing field, which in my view is more than adequate compensation for whatever modest shortcomings they might have.

SELECTING A COMPETENT LOAN REP

Competence is a bit like the weather: Everyone talks about it but no one does anything about it. Like the weather, competence is elusive, hard to predict, and undependable. Of course, everyone would like to believe that he or she is dealing with a competent professional, but half the consumers end up dealing with someone who is worse than average, by definition. The truth is that lenders can train almost anyone—perhaps even the waiter who served you last night at a restaurant—to look and sound like a loan rep during the day. The reason so many home buyers are dissatisfied with the service lenders provide today is that they are fooled into dealing with someone who is not competent enough to handle their transaction smoothly and efficiently. Incompetence can lead to expensive, if not horrendous, consequences. It's so important that I have included this special section devoted to helping you find a competent person.

Bureaucracy and Advocacy

The mortgage business is organized to do simple loans. The average loan in this country is only $68,000. If this sounds low to you, remember that the average home is worth $105,000. Approximately 85 percent of people work for someone else, and their income is pretty well described on their W-2s and their paycheck stubs. Writing straightforward mortgages for the average person is the easiest part of the business. That's why underwriters are expected to process four or five files every day. When they get to a file that has, as I like to say, "lots of moving parts," it is difficult for them to justify spending the time to work through the problems to approve it. It's easier to deny it and move on to the next one. I've actually had underwriters say to me, "I've spent too much time on this file already." It requires perseverance to overcome bureaucratic lethargy, and that's where a competent loan rep comes in. A trainee won't do it, but the veteran knows the ins and outs of his or her organization, and the best ones will go to bat for you, using a combination of experience and persistence.

The goal is to get the most competent person you can working for you. Remember, half of all agents are better than average, and the other half are worse. Ten percent of loan reps are in the top 10 percent. Your goal is to find one of those.

Questions You Should Ask

No one, including you, can judge or assess character or competence just by looking at someone or by talking with that person on the phone. That said, let me assure you that there are ways of determining who is competent and who isn't. Here's how I recommend doing it.

1. As in every other service business, the first step is to ask for recommendations from as many respected and responsible people as you can.

2. Make appointments to meet with these people. *That's what a phone is for.*

3. If you're calling a bank, an S&L, or a large mortgage company, ask for the manager and find out how many loan reps are working there.

4. Ask about the qualifications and experience of those reps.

5. If you like what you hear, request that the manager assign you to the best person on the team.

If the manager says you can be assigned only to the person who handles your territory, consider it a red flag. The territory rep may have been hired last week. As a customer, if you've done enough research to be asking these questions, it is only fair that you be assigned the most competent person. The manager's first priority should be the customer. When you have that issue worked out, I would also ask the manager to become personally involved in and committed to the success of funding your loan. This helps clarify that you are someone who has the determination to be *part of* the process, not a *victim* of it.

While you have the manager's attention, ask about the company's strengths. Be specific. Ask which types of loans the company does best and which loans it prices aggressively. If you get a we-do-everything-well response, consider it another red flag. Conduct this same interview at each lender recommended to you. You will find that some will turn you off and others will attract you—and for good reason. You're beginning to make real progress.

When you are finally face-to-face with your agent, interview that person, too. In a nonconfrontational tone, ask about background, education, and experience. You should ask how many loans the agent has funded in his or her career and, in particular, within the last year or so. Another purpose of this process is to enable you to determine the communication skills of your agent or rep. Success in getting your loan is dependent, in part, upon your ability to communicate well with one another. The most competent reps will be pleased you are asking such essential questions and will tell you about themselves with pride.

Finally, there are a couple of more delicate questions you should ask. One is, "How many of your loans are approved and how many are denied?" A good agent will have an approval rating of 90 percent or higher. It's high because that person has learned how to solve problems.

Once you have determined that your agent is knowledgeable and comfortable to work with, you should also ask, "How are you compensated?" Many mortgage brokers feel this is not your concern. If they dodge the question, a red flag is waving. In many states, a broker is legally the agent of the borrower, just as a real estate broker is. My clients are entitled to full disclosure about how I'm compensated. In states where that is not the case, the better loan reps will feel comfortable sharing this information with their clients and will have no problem discussing the topic of compensation forthrightly. After all, the Real Estate Settlement Procedures Act (RESPA) requires that compensation to brokers be disclosed on the final loan documents, so why wouldn't they be willing to discuss it up front? Indeed! If the method of compensation is left intentionally vague at the beginning, you may be in for an unpleasant surprise at closing. Keep in mind that you cannot negotiate something if you do not know the facts. Commissions are negotiable, but you cannot negotiate if the other party is keeping secrets.

If you are dealing with an employee of a bank, your rep may be salaried, particularly if he or she is in the bank's training program. S&L employees are more likely to be on commission, which is fine, but it means you need to ask a further question: "Do you get paid extra commissions depending upon pricing (overages), or do you get a higher commission rate for certain programs?" Some institutions pay their people a fixed commission rate and do not allow them to make more by gouging customers. Others train their people how to gouge! You want to know which kind you're dealing with.

If these questions make you uncomfortable because they sound too personal, remember that it's *your* money we're talking about. You pay your barber or hairdresser, you pay your CPA or tax preparer, and you have a right to decide if their pay is reasonable or not. Why is a loan rep any different? My feeling is that the better agents will respect you for asking these questions. Speaking for myself, I'd much rather deal with knowledgeable buyers; I'm perfectly willing to negotiate and fix my commission for someone who respects my ability to help him or her. My income is tied to my ability to create value. All good professionals, if they are really good, will save you more than they cost you.

Your Relationship with the Loan Rep

Let's assume that you have used my suggestions to find an expert, and that expert gave you the benefit of his or her experience and saved you a lot of money. Be sure to reward that person appropriately by following through and giving him or her your business. It is unfair, and in my view unethical, to take advantage of a person's expertise and then go to some other lender and say, "This is the best deal I have found. Can you beat it?" Professional behavior goes both ways. Consider this: Would you want to be sitting across the desk from a lender who would treat you that way?

SUMMARY

You will notice that I did not mention *pricing* in this chapter. My profoundly held belief is that when you get the right person, the pricing will work itself out to your benefit. I also want to keep you from asking questions that will elicit sleight-of-hand discussions about pricing from unethical people. *Do not underestimate the emotional power that can be exerted by someone who lies about rates.* Incompetent loan reps are at a tremendous competitive disadvantage because they haven't been in the business long enough to establish competence. What are they to do? They lie about rates, and not just a little bit, because they have to appeal to your sense of greed to draw you away from the demonstrably better lenders. Ultimately, an unethical agent will be unable to deliver as promised, and the borrower will end up paying more than if he or she had chosen the honest, competent lender.

Let's move on to some specific tactics you can use to negotiate a killer deal with your lender.

SHOPPING FOR A LOAN AND NEGOTIATING WITH A LENDER

KEY POINTS

- Most people do a poor job of shopping for a loan because they use ineffective tactics.
- The rate differences between lenders on so-called A programs is much less than you think.
- Getting the best deal begins with developing the correct relationship with your lender.
- Be careful and deliberate before locking in your loan. You can usually save more money by locking at the right time than you can by using the right lender.

We are a nation of shoppers. We learn early. By the time you are six years old, you have learned that candy isn't really free—your mom *pays* the grocer for it. When you're a little older and get an allowance and run out of money too soon, you become a shopper too. When you think of the enormous financial implications of buying a home, you'd think that people would spend at least as much energy shopping for a loan as they do for a VCR. Unfortunately, that is not usually the case. People become bewildered when they realize there's a difference and they do not know how to shop for a mortgage. Let me ask you if you think the following assumptions are reasonable.

1. There is a big difference between the prices of one lender and another.

2. If a lender's quote is the lowest today, it will be the lowest on the day you lock in your rate.

3. If a lender is lowest on one program, it will also be lowest on the others.

4. Lenders will tell you the truth when you ask them questions about rates.

Guess what? Every single statement is *wrong*. Let's review them in more detail.

First, I want to talk about the pricing on A programs, because I think most readers are interested in those programs. These are the loans with the lowest rates, the loans that are sold to FNMA and FHLMC or to the Wall Street conduits through the secondary market. It is very competitive because, as we've discussed, most lenders are selling loans to the same sources. To demonstrate this point, I called 30 national lenders who do the lion's share of business in the country and asked them their rates and points on a 30-year fixed-rate loan. Every lender has as many as a dozen different rate-versus-fee alternatives, so to make it easier to compare, I requested their points at a specific rate, 7.625 percent. The answers I received are shown graphically in Figure 10.1. As the graph shows, at an interest rate of 7.625 percent, 24 of the lenders quoted 1 point, 1.125 points, or 1.25 points. In other words, most of the lenders were within one-eighth of a point of each other in

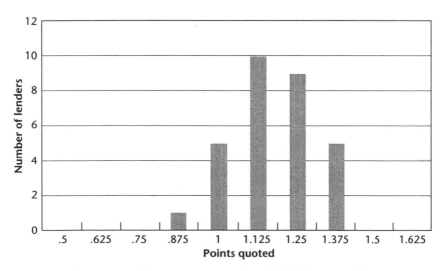

Figure 10.1 The mortgage market is highly competitive.

pricing. On a $100,000 loan, that's the average: plus or minus $125. If you were thinking of savings thousands, it's just not in the cards. We'll get back to this a little later, but it is important to note that for similar loans, there isn't as much difference in pricing as you might think. Remember that the definition of a commodity—such as wheat or pork bellies—is that the pricing is uniform. The same is true with loans.

Second, let's say that you did your shopping on one day and then repeated those steps the next day. You'd find some similarities—and differences, too. The lowest price on day 1 would probably not be lowest on day 2. Rates move daily, and although lenders can tie down commitments with their source of funds, most of them price to market on a daily basis. Let's demonstrate this with another graph (Figure 10.2), this time showing one national lender's pricing over a two-month period of time.

The lender is taking the market yield on various types of mortgage-backed securities, including FNMA and FHLMC securities, and adding a markup to that. Its pricing is determined after the bond market opens in New York, and its retail price on any given day reflects the yields of that day plus a factor that reflects the lender's assessment of *risk* (that is, whether the market will move higher or lower). With 100 lenders, you will find 100 different estimates of those factors, which are reflected in their pricing for that day. Those factors change from day to day just as prices in the stock market, which isn't all that different from this. My point is that dealing with a dynamic equation and making

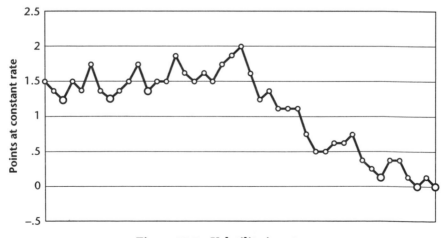

Figure 10.2   Volatility in rates.

rigid assumptions about lender behavior is a prescription for disappointment.

Third, because you don't look at these data every day as I do, you cannot see the dynamics of the market here. Refer to the appendix, where I have shown one lender's wholesale rate sheet. This lender is no different than the other national lenders. It has over a dozen programs, and it is probably selling loans to five or six different companies. Why is it reasonable to think that all of these sources, which are also buying loans from many other lenders, would choose to reserve their best prices for this particular lender? It *isn't* reasonable, which is why the assumption is wrong. As I do loans for my customers, I will go to lender A for FNMA loans, lender B for 5/1 ARMs under $350,000, lender C for 15-year loans of $500,000, lender D for COFI ARMs, and so forth. The market is constantly changing, and you need to account for that in your strategy.

I want to explore assumption 4 in greater detail. Let's go through the shopping process many people use. They take out the phone book and make a bunch of phone calls to people they do not know at companies they may never have heard of and request rate quotes—most likely on programs that aren't even right for them. People rate-shop in an "exclusionary" manner; that is, they exclude from further consideration the lenders that quote higher rates. Such shoppers do not realize how rarely they get either the full or straight story. Lenders who are honest and aboveboard always lose in this process, discarded by borrowers chasing lenders who have exaggerated their rates. *This poor shopping strategy accounts for the single most common complaint about the industry.* Have you ever heard someone say, "They quoted us one rate but when we went to sign loan docs, the rate was higher"? The truth is that the lender probably never did have good rates. . . . The rep just lied to the borrower, the borrower believed the rep, and reality finally caught up with the borrower too late to do anything about it. Fortunately, there is a better way.

SHOPPING FOR A MORTGAGE

People often misjudge how to save the most money on their mortgage. We discussed earlier that you can save the most money by getting the right type of loan. Assuming you have done this and have selected a particular loan program, let's say a 5/1 ARM, how much are you likely to save? Refer back to Figure 10.1. Remember that on a $100,000 loan, one-eighth of a point (the amount by which most lenders differ on pricing) is only $125. Let's assume that you made a half-dozen phone calls and you found four lenders quoting 7.625 percent and 1 or 1.125 points. In my opinion, almost any aspect of competent service—compared with lousy service—is worth far more than saving $125. Consequently, I would choose any one of the four lenders based upon how well you communicate with the loan rep or some other service-based factor.

If you are wondering why I didn't mention the one lender that is at only seven-eighths of a point, let's do that now. First, assuming you can find that lender, it will save you only another $125 (one-eighth of a point), so you must ask yourself just how much time you're willing to spend on the search. Consider this: If you've made six phone calls already, statistically you have to make another nine calls just to have a 50 percent chance of tracking down the lower-priced lender. If you figure your time is worth, say, $5 per call, those nine calls are going to cost another $45. You have to make *24 calls* to have a 100 percent chance of finding that hot lender, and 24 times $5 per call is $120. It cost you $120 to save $125, a net profit from your efforts of $5. Probably not a good use of your time. My point is—shopping around is important, but its value lies in finding a constructive middle ground.

This brings the discussion back to where we broke off in the last chapter, *competence*. To repeat myself, shopping isn't just about rates. Rates are important, but they are the result of a process that starts with finding the *right person* with the *right company,* one you like and trust. It also goes back to what I said earlier about loans being a commodity—when the prices are the same, shop for service!

HOW TO NEGOTIATE

If you've done your work in the preceding chapters, you should be pretty well along the road to determining your needs. Let's say that you are prepared to make your application. You can deal with a broker or a direct lender, so let's discuss how to deal with both.

Negotiating with a Mortgage Broker

If you are dealing with a broker, and you've settled on a program and made your application, ask him or her to reveal the source of funds for your program. If the lender is hesitant to do so, make this statement: "You are my agent, and I expect you to act in a fiduciary capacity. You owe me your loyalty, and perhaps you or your manager can explain how secrecy is consistent with that responsibility." You probably won't have any difficulty in getting this information if you've done all the preliminary work of finding a competent and honorable lender. You have a right to reasonable service in return for reasonable compensation.

Once you've gotten past that issue, ask the next question, "May I see the rate sheet of the source you have selected for me, and may I have your commitment to show me the rate sheet on the day I lock in my rate?" (See the appendix for a sample rate sheet.) If you get some resistance at this point, it will be because borrowers do not usually request this, but you have a right to know. Of course, it wouldn't hurt to reassure your lender by saying, "Look, I'm not going to go around you; I just want to know what the base rate is."

With this information in hand, it's time to negotiate. Here's one good way to begin: "I know this isn't actually *your* rate, but the source's rate, which is nonnegotiable. What is negotiable is what *you* make, whether points, commission, servicing-release premium, or yield-spread premium. What is your method of compensation?"

Brokers are not used to such questions. In fact, some may riposte, "What do you care what I make as long as you're happy with the rate?" The fact is that you want your broker to act as your agent, and an agent's compensation is disclosed to you as the principal. This isn't any different than the commission your real estate broker makes. So let's assume that the broker says, "Well, normally we make 2 points [over the source's base rate] on transactions like this." If you're applying for a $150,000 loan, 2 points is $3,000.

Negotiation in this case means getting the broker to cut his or her commission. If you have an easy loan—meaning you have stable employment, are well qualified, and have clean credit—you have every reason to expect a better-than-average deal. You probably qualify for one of the automated loan underwriting systems (FNMA's Desktop Underwriter or FHLMC's Loan Prospector), which allows your broker to get credit approval in less than an hour. Second, this is usually the loan rep's decision because it's largely his or her commission you're negotiating, not the company's. You can say, "My loan is going to be one of the easiest you do this year, so you should charge me less. How about one and one-half points?" (That would save you $750.) First, the rep looks at you and thinks, *I've almost got this loan, I've prequalified them, all the paperwork is here and in order, they're happy with everything else, so the rest is going to be easy.* Second, the rep will still make $1,500 out of the company's $2,250 commission. Third, he or she sees that you are a shrewd shopper and that the next lender you visit will probably agree to your proposal. The smart broker will agree to your terms and try to sign you up right away. When you come to an agreement, state, "When we have the final documents, I want confirmation that your compensation is what we have just agreed to." What you've just done is to make an agreement in advance with the provider of a service. If you can't get this assurance, perhaps you should reconsider your choice of lender. When it comes time to lock in your rate, be sure to ask the broker to fax or deliver the lender's wholesale rate sheet for that day.

Note that probably only 5 percent of mortgage shoppers engage in this kind of negotiating, so most lenders will initially be taken aback. Stand your ground, and the good lenders will appreciate your professionalism and respect you for it.

Finally, as a further confirmation that you are being dealt with fairly, if you have Internet access, go on-line to one of the sources of current rate information. The best site is FreddieMac's site at http://www.freddiemac.com. Check out Chapter 20 for more details.

Negotiating with a Bank or Other Direct Lender

If you're dealing with a bank or an S&L, remember that, unlike a broker, these companies are under no legal obligation to tell you their profit margin. Usually, they have a printed rate sheet, which, presumably, is the same one they hand out to everyone. Look for your program, and if the rate sheet lists only a couple of rates and fees, ask for more information.

When you meet with your loan officer, ask, "How are you compensated?" If the answer is "commission," ask, "Does your company have certain programs or pricing options on which you get a premium or extra commission?" (For example, the rep may get a bonus for loans with a prepayment penalty.) If so, have the rep identify those programs; then make it very clear you don't want one of those premium programs. Your ability to negotiate terms with a direct lender is more limited because the rep may simply not have the power to change anything. It is not at all uncommon for the company's computers to lock out any other pricing to keep its employees from changing anything. Assuming that your transaction is easier than average, that you are well prepared, and that you have demonstrated your seriousness, you should ask to speak with the manager. In many institutions, managers may not be able to change the rates, but they can waive some of their garbage fees, such as the underwriting fee or document fee. This can amount to $500. In my opinion, once they see you are both knowledgeable and serious, you have a pretty good chance of getting what you ask for.

On the day you lock in, you'll probably get rates verbally from the lender. Ask to see a current rate sheet. If your lender hesitates, call another branch of the same institution and ask for the rate of the program you chose. *The rate should be the same as what you were quoted by your loan officer.* If it isn't, you're being bamboozled! Insist on speaking with the manager at your branch, and be *very firm* about getting the lower rate.

FILLING IN THE BLANKS: FORMS AND APPLICATIONS

Once you've chosen a program and successfully negotiated an agreement with your lender, fill out the application. The loan rep should help you with this. I can do one in 20 minutes. It may take you two hours without help. When the lender receives your application, it is legally obligated under RESPA to send you the Regulation Z, Good Faith Estimate of Closing Costs, the Truth in Lending form, and the HUD booklet, *Buying Your Home.* Samples of these forms are in the appendix, so you can familiarize yourself with them. Technically, lenders have three days after application to do this, but with the widespread use of computers, there is no excuse for not doing it while you are there. *Insist on this.* Get all the forms they are required to give you. Read them and ask questions. These forms itemize the costs and fees of the program on the date you applied. Of course, the numbers on these forms are not binding on the lenders, but they are supposed to be making reasonably accurate estimates. If the final figure is very far off from the estimate, the lender is, in my opinion, in an indefensible position. You should be able to get a refund for any significant difference.

| WARNING | Some lenders use a worst-case assumption when preparing the Good Faith Estimate. Others strive for accuracy. Be sure to ask your lender's policy.

When you get these forms, use the glossary in the back of the book to understand each term. Then decide whether the charge listed is appropriate. Also study Chapter 14, which discusses closing costs and fees. Ask your lender to explain anything you don't understand.

When they get these forms, many people think that they are locked in at the rate shown. *This is not the case! That is a separate issue. You need to find out your lender's lock policy.*

LOCKING IN YOUR LOAN

Locking in a rate on a loan is the cause of many communication problems between borrowers and lenders. Very frequently, borrowers think it means one thing and lenders another. It is what the lender thinks that counts, so you should understand this process. I'll give you some background and some specifics here, but it is important to ask and get *very specific details* from your lender about its lock policy. Almost every lender has internal lock forms. Get as much in writing as you can. Second, most lenders have different lock-in policies for purchases than for refinance transactions. The reason is that in the case of refinance transactions, some borrowers will apply to two lenders, locking in one and floating the other. For that reason, many lenders will not lock in a refinance unless they have approved the loan.

Locking In a Fixed-Rate Loan

When you lock more than 15 days in advance of closing, you are asking the lender to guarantee the rate at closing. Refer to Figure

10.2, which shows the volatility of the market on a daily basis. Locking poses special risks for lenders because the variation in rates, even over a short period, may actually be more than their profit margin. As a means of clarifying this, let's use the analogy of buying stock. Assume you call a stockbroker to ask the price of IBM today, and you find out it's $98 per share. You can buy stock immediately at $98, but you can't place an order for 100 shares at $98 per share and offer to pay next month. That's not what brokers do. If you want to do that, the broker will sell you a call option to buy the stock at $98 in the future, and that option may cost $4 per share.

As with stockbrokers, lenders don't want to accept the risk. If you want to lock in your loan at, say, 8 percent, they want some guarantee they can sell your loan to their source at 8 percent. They do that by *hedging,* in effect buying an option to sell your loan at that yield. It costs them money to do that, but unless you want a lock of longer than 60 days, they do not usually ask you to put up any money.

Let's look at this more closely. Here's what one line on a lender's rate sheet might look like:

Points

Rate	15 days	30 days	60 days
8.125%	1	1.125	1.5

As you can see, the longer the lock guarantee period, the more money it costs you. Let's say you are 60 days away from closing, your loan has been approved, and you are worried about rates going up. If you lock today at 8.125 percent, at closing you'll pay 1.5 points, or $1,500, on a $100,000 loan. If rates go up between now and closing, say to 8.5 percent, you were smart to lock. Had you waited until 15 days before closing to lock, you would have paid only 1 point, or $1,000, but your loan would have been at 8.5 percent, not 8.125 percent. In locking early, you paid an extra half point, or $500, for rate protection, which saves you $375 per year over the life of the loan, a good deal.

But what happens if rates go down? Let's say you lock for 60 days, as previously, and after 45 days, rates fall to 7.625 percent, a full ½ percent below your lock. You look at your lender and say, "I want the current rate of 7.625 percent," and they look at you and say, "A deal is a deal; you locked in at 8.125 percent." Sure, you can go to another lender and pay the current rate of 7.625 percent, but can you get approved and funded in 15 days? Probably not. You're stuck with your lender. You can see the problem. And there's no easy answer. Some lenders won't negotiate at all; others will meet you halfway—for example, at 7.875 percent. The long and short of it is that you just have to work it out.

| HINT | The more vociferous and persistent you are, the more likely you are to be successful.

Locking In an Adjustable Rate Mortgage

Most frequently, lenders have more liberal lock-in policies if you have applied for an ARM, especially on purchase transactions. With ARMs, you frequently can lock for as long as 60 days on a *float-down basis,* which means you are guaranteed the lower of (1) the price at application or (2) the price at closing. That's a good option. Be sure to ask for and get *very specific details* of their policies. Otherwise, you'll be surprised at some point down the line. The reason lenders are more willing to offer long lockins on ARMs for free is because they are guaranteeing the rate for only the first six months or the first year, depending on the type of ARM. Say you lock in a start rate of 5.5 percent. At the end of the first year, your loan's rate will jump up to the fully indexed rate, say 7.25 percent. Whether your loan started out at 5.5, 5.75, or 6 percent isn't a big deal because it was only for the first year. You see the point.

THE VALUE OF TIMING

The most effective way to demonstrate the importance of timing is to go back and review Figure 10.2, which shows the lender's points at the same rate during a two-month period of time. No other 60-day period will be exactly like this, but every period will demonstrate volatility similar to this. When you look at these numbers, keep in mind the following:

- Regardless of the time frame, there are periods, perhaps only a day or two, during which the rates are better than average. You want to lock in on one of these favorable

days. You and your lender are not in an adversarial relationship; your rep is not trying to get you to lock in when
rates are high. Lenders don't care because they are just
selling your loan anyway.

- No one can predict the future; however, you can be very
  sensitive to the market—by charting interest rate information every day, for example, and keeping abreast of
  fluctuations and trends.

- If the volatility is greater than you anticipated, consider
  your effort rewarded. We learned from Figure 10.1 that
  the variation in rates between lenders was minuscule,
  plus or minus only one-eighth of a point. By comparison, the variation in rates over *time,* in this case only 60
  days, was *2 points.*

I will repeat: It is more important to know when to lock than
which lender to choose. To that end, I offer the following advice:

- Do not bug your lender every day about the current rate
  unless the rep will fax it to you. An easier way is to
  track the yield on 30-year Treasury bonds, which moves
  almost in parallel with rates on 30-year mortgages. It is
  reported daily in newspapers and frequently on radio
  and TV business programs. You can also get it from
  stockbrokerage companies or on the Internet. Keep track
  of the data and develop a chart similar to the one in Figure 10.2.

- Do not lock in on an uptick. Except in the case of a major
  market move, you probably have a better-than-even
  chance of rates going back down a day or two later.

- After rates have made a downward move and have been
  steady for a few days, be very careful about your next
  move. At some point in time, the rates will start to rise
  again instead of falling even further. Do not get greedy.
  More often than not, if you try to squeeze too much out
  of the market, it'll turn around and squeeze you back.

This chapter may contain some thoughts that sound bizarre
to you. My recommendations come from my years of experience
in dealing with over 1,000 clients, as well as the experience of
many of my friends in the mortgage industry. I recommend these

strategies because they have worked for others. They will work for you, too.

RELATIONSHIPS WITH REAL ESTATE AGENTS

This is a book about mortgages, but in purchase transactions, mortgages are just part of a larger picture. Accordingly, I want to discuss the relationship with your other business partner: your Realtor. Many buyers are just as confused about their relationships with real estate agents as they are about mortgages. As a lender, I've had a front-row seat on about 1,000 purchase transactions, and I'd like to share what I've learned so your relationship with your real estate agent can be as productive as the one with your lender. I am also married to a Realtor, so day in and day out I'm able to observe how she puts deals together—behaviors and strategies that work and those that do not.

The good real estate agents I know put forth immense effort on behalf of their clients. But there are always a few morons out there. Others are trying to do a good job but just haven't had enough experience yet to avoid making mistakes. The agent representing the seller can take advantage of a weak agent—and, by extension, *you*—if you're not careful. You want a competent agent who will work hard for you. Here are some tips on finding a good agent and working with one.

1.   Be sure you understand who is representing whom. In many states, your agent is legally the subagent of the seller, and if you tell something in confidence to "your" agent (for example, "I'm willing to pay $100,000, but let's offer $95,000") that agent *should* go to the seller and say, "My client's offering $95,000, but he's willing to pay $100,000." That makes it awfully hard to negotiate. If you are located in a state that acknowledges dual agency or allows buyer's agents, I would confirm that your Realtor is really *your* agent!

2.   When you find an agent, demand and expect loyalty, and be sure to give it in return. Working with more than one agent simultaneously is *not* to the buyer's advantage. In a hot market with little inventory, success in purchasing a home is dependent on an agent calling

you—not someone less loyal—when the right property comes on the market.

3. Use whatever means you can to get information about potential Realtors, and seek referrals from friends. This is better than calling a real estate office and taking the next available agent. You may find yourself with a yo-yo.

4. When you make an offer to purchase, be sure to specify terms for disposition of the earnest money you give to the real estate agent. Most states use a deposit receipt or purchase-offer form, which gives you the right to specify the terms under which your money is returned if the deal blows up.

5. An honest agent will make sure you know as much about a property as possible. The problem is that the agent may not know some vital information. You are not relieved of the responsibility of doing you own due diligence; it's your house and your money. If you find a home you like, go back to the neighborhood alone when you have time, and knock on the doors of a few neighbors. In most cases, you'll just be meeting new friends a few days early. But you *might* uncover something that will curl your hair and cause you to cancel the deal.

6. Ask for written list of comparable sales when discussing values with your agent. Most of the time, this list will include a lot of valuable information. You ought to drive around and look at the comps. They are the best indicator of value of the property you are interested in.

7. When the professional home inspection is done (usually with a warranty paid for by the seller), plan to meet the inspector at the property. Don't just rely on the report, because you'll probably get bored reading it and you might miss something important. Be sure to check the property *again* the day before closing to make sure that it's all still there. Sometimes, things that you thought were going to be yours "get legs" and disappear in the night. You'll get better results if you delay the transaction until everything is as promised rather than suing the seller after the fact.

8. Good Realtors work hard and don't like to compromise their commissions any more than you would. But they

don't earn anything until the buyer and seller agree and the deal closes. It's a fact of life that sometimes agents have to cut their commissions. If you and the seller are at loggerheads but close to an agreement, now is the time to say to the agent, "My spouse and I are going back to the motel now. Why don't you two have a little discussion to see how we might make this deal work." If it is reasonable to do so, they will, and if it isn't, they won't.

9. Every once in a while I see clients get their way just because they stonewall. To say, "That's my best and final offer," and walk away from the table is sometimes a very smart negotiating strategy. *But you have to make it look as if you really are walking.* You'd be surprised what sometimes happens the next morning.

10. You should strive to have your agent become a friend, worthy of trust and mutual respect. After all, you and your agent have developed a closer connection than is common in most business relationships—one worth maintaining.

APR, BUY-DOWNS, AND DISCOUNT POINTS

Streams are for wise men to ponder and for fools to pass by.

—ISAAC WALTON

KEY POINTS

- The government-mandated approach to interest rates, the annual percentage rate (APR), is not useful for consumers.
- Every lender has a target net yield for every loan program. A large number of different rate-versus-fee options have the same net yield, so the lender doesn't care which one you choose. However, from your perspective as a borrower, some of these choices are better than others.
- Choosing the best rate-versus-fee alternative is going to save you a bundle over time, and there is a simple method of organizing the information to make this choice easier.

I'm a fisherman, and as I grow older, I see more and more parallels between fishing and life. As we've discussed earlier, many of the opinions borrowers have about lenders and mortgages are based on platitudes. The lenders hope you will be foolish enough to believe these clichés because it will be more profitable for them if you do. I take a different approach: I want you to ponder the process, just as the wise angler ponders the stream. The good news is that analysis is not that difficult once you learn the process. The techniques you will learn in this chapter will save you thousands of dollars.

TRUTH OR CONSEQUENCES

Historically, purveyors of credit have confused people about interest rates. Someone would buy a $300 TV and the salesperson would say, "Do you want to finance it? We only charge 10 percent interest." That rate sounded reasonable, so the consumer would say yes and the salesperson would do the following calculation.

$300 × 10 percent = $30

$30 × 3 years = $90 total interest

$300 for the TV + $90 interest = $390 divided by 36 months = $10.83/month

This looks reasonable—but it isn't. The annual percentage rate on this transaction is actually almost 18 percent, not 10 percent. The interest rate calculation, 3 × $30, assumes that the entire principal is repaid at the end of the third year. Because the consumer is making payments and reducing the principal every month, the average loan balance in this transaction is only $150, not $300. If the *real* rate were only 10 percent, the total interest due would be only $48, not $90. The actual payment at 10 percent is only $9.68, a difference of only $1.15 per month. That may not sound like much, but if the store earned an extra $1.15 on every TV, every month, the money made from misleading their customers would really add up. Think about this as it applies to mortgages. Clearly, getting a mortgage is a much more complex process than financing a TV set, and there is a huge difference between a three-year consumer finance loan and a 30-year mortgage.

To correct such abuses, Congress passed laws that were intended to ensure truth in lending, requiring, among other things, lenders to give consumers information disclosing the annual percentage rate on any proposed loan. Although these laws have done much to improve consumers' understanding of the cost of financing TV sets, they have done almost nothing to correct similar problems in the mortgage industry. Simply put, mortgage financing is different from and more complex than common consumer finance. If someone offered you an APR of 18 percent, and someone else offered 10 percent, it would be easy—10 percent is a lot less than 18 percent—but with mortgages, it's never that simple.

In calculating the APR on mortgages, the lender must factor in certain costs affiliated with the loan, called *prepaid finance charges.* First, the lender keeps the interest accrued between the date of funding and the end of the month so that the first payment isn't due for at least 30 days. That means if you were to borrow $100,000 at 10 percent and zero points on the first day of the month, the lender keeps 30 days' interest, or $833.33. Throw in processing fees, underwriting fees, document fees, and so on, and your lender will fund only $98,500, not $100,000.

The APR is then calculated based on your paying interest on the amount financed, which is only $98,500 (the loan amount less those prepaid finance charges). Obviously, the APR is always going to be higher than the note rate. The APR in our 10 percent, no-point loan turns out to be 10.185 percent.

If the difference between 10 percent and 10.185 percent is lost on you, let me share a secret with you. Almost no one in the mortgage industry understands APR very well, either. Lenders hire computer programmers, give them the regulations from the Federal Reserve Bank, and tell them to program the computers to calculate APR on the forms they give to customers. Ninety-nine percent of the lenders don't even know how to calculate it themselves.

The greater flaw in the APR calculation is not mathematical, but behavioral, because it assumes that the borrower will keep the loan for the entire period of the loan, say 30 years. In reality, however, 95 percent of loans are paid back far sooner, and that means the APR calculation is wrong 95 percent of the time.

Here's another way of expressing the problem that gets to the heart of the way many people shop for loans. Let's assume that Bob and Becky Phillips are buying a new home and they are making the rounds of local lenders. They come into my office and ask, "What is your APR?" Being a little coy, I ask what they have already been quoted and they say, "10.185 percent." Then I quickly calculate that I can get an APR of 10.185 percent if I have a 10 percent loan with zero points (from the example above). I also know that my lenders offer this same loan in as many as a dozen other rate-versus-fee combinations, one of which is 9.75 percent and 1 point. Let's look at these two choices this way:

	Rate	Points	APR
Alternative 1	10%	0	10.185%
Alternative 2	9.75%	1	10.051%

So I say to them, "I've got that beat; my APR is only 10.051 percent." The Phillips are happy because I quoted an APR of 10.051 percent, which is lower than 10.185 percent—the best rate they had found before. The government agrees with them; my loan is better. So the Phillips and I agree to do business. But did they get a better loan? The entire mortgage industry says, "No, these two pricing alternatives loans are just two different ways of looking at the same loan." When lenders do their calculations, both loans have the same net yield. I used the APR calculation to "sell" the Phillips, and, as we'll see later in the chapter, if they stay in their home longer than four years, my loan *is* better for them.

The heart of the issue is to find a more realistic calculation to help borrowers analyze alternatives. What you want is not some esoteric calculation, not even your neighbor's APR. What you want to know is, "What is my APR?" To determine that, you should amortize the points and other costs over the period you'll actually own the home. Let me demonstrate this simply. Assume you choose a 10 percent loan with exactly 1 percent in prepaid finance charges. Here are the calculated *effective interest rates,* amortizing the costs over the time you have the loan.

Period of ownership	Effective interest rate
1	11%
2	10.5%
3	10.33%
4	10.25%
5	10.2%
30	10.123% (= APR)

As you can see, the actual APR becomes a valid number only if you keep the loan for 30 years. But as I said earlier, you are probably not going to keep either your home or your loan for 30 years.

In the upcoming section on buy-downs and discount points, you'll learn that the mortgage industry offers many rate-versus-fee alternatives that are based on a formula that hits a target yield figure. To understand the difference between the reality of the market on the one hand and APR on the other, refer to Figure 11.1, where I have charted the rates one lender offered and then calculated the APR on each alternative. You can see that there is very little in common between the two lines.

Let me put this another way. Consider your reaction if the government instructed car dealers to give buyers a disclosure statement showing the price per pound of the cars they offered and advised consumers to compare the value of cars by comparing the price per pound. Of course, there is *some* relationship between a car's weight and its value; common sense tells you that a small car like a Geo isn't going to cost as much as a Cadillac, but obviously this method of comparing car prices is silly. Similarly, the graph in Figure 11.1 demonstrates the fallacy of using APR as a means of comparing loans.

Let's go back to the Phillips. They were analyzing my answer using the APR line on the graph, while I was using the market line. In using the government's method, they failed to analyze the situation in the most meaningful way. Most impor-

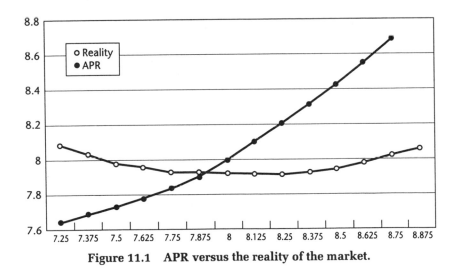

Figure 11.1   APR versus the reality of the market.

tant, they may have failed to get the best loan. In summary, I think the financial markets know more about yields than does Congress, which is why no one I know of looks at APR to make decisions. I don't think that consumers should, either.

APR AND ADJUSTABLE RATE MORTGAGES

When it comes to adjustable rate mortgages (ARMs), it's even more complicated. In Chapter 6, I showed how home buyers need to compare one ARM's index's historical performance with the performance of an ARM tied to other indexes for the same period. In calculating the APR on an ARM, however, the government-mandated method throws that out the window. It does the calculations for the teaser-rate period and assumes that once it gets to the currently calculated value of index plus margin, say in year two, it stays there for the life of the loan. Ladies and gentlemen, I am here to tell you that this is a patently absurd assumption. The actual rate in years 2 through 30 is going to vary widely—maybe even wildly—but it is *not* going to stay at today's rate. Whatever the differences between one index and another—sometimes one is better, sometimes the other—the government's approach makes it appear that whichever loan has the lower index plus margin *today* is the better loan. Again, that's just plain wrong. I repeat, comparing APR is not the best way to shop.

No doubt the folks at Housing and Urban Development would ask, "What other number do you want us to use?" The answer is that there is no way of knowing today how the interest rates are going to vary over the next 30 years, so there *isn't* an appropriate number. It's not the number, it's the method itself that is flawed. Again, consumers need an ARM disclosure that graphically compares one index's performance against the performance of other available loan indexes. With that in mind, we'll move on to take a more in-depth look at rate-versus-fee alternatives.

UNDERSTANDING RATE-VERSUS-FEE ALTERNATIVES

To begin this section, we're going to go back to the two loan alternatives we discussed in the APR section. We compared a loan at 10 percent for 0 points and one at 9.75 percent and 1 point.

Because this trade-off confuses most people, I'm going to demystify it right now. Let's go through this example using my method and assuming we are borrowing $200,000.

	Loan 1	Loan 2	Difference
1. Establish the loan balance.	$200,000	$200,000	
2. Determine the rates.	10%	9.75%	
3. Determine the points.	0	1	
4. Calculate the annual interest.	$20,000	$19,500	$500 savings per year
5. Express the points as dollars.	$0	$2,000	$2,000 up front
6. Divide cost by savings.	$2,000 ÷ $500 = 4 years		

This process proves that if you pay an extra $2,000 now, you'll save $500 every year in interest. After the fourth year, you'll get back your $2,000 and still save $500 every year thereafter. What do we learn from this? If we are going to be in the house for more than four years, we should pay the point and collect the savings. Most people find this method much more meaningful than trying to decipher the difference between 10.185 percent APR and 10.051 percent APR. I hope you agree. Actually, almost all lenders offer many more than just two alternatives, and this method works well in analyzing them, as we'll see later in the chapter.

I can just hear someone with a calculator saying, "The difference between the payments is $36.83 . . . and that gives a different answer." Using the payment instead of the interest brings reduction of the principal into the equation and skews the answer; thus we use interest, not the payments, in making these calculations.

How far should we carry this? What if we had a 10-year breakeven? You might ask, "If I'm going to be in this property for 10 years, why isn't it a good deal?" The answer is that rates might come down even more, so it might be advantageous to refinance in year 5. If you do, you'd have recouped only half of your up-front costs. That's a mistake because you would have wasted money. *Hint:* I recommend one-, two-, and three-year break-even deals. I'm not in favor of four-year deals unless the borrower is very risk averse or it is the last loan on their last house.

My method forces you to ask questions about how long you are going to be in the home, what interest rates might do, and so forth. As difficult as this might be, it's a lot better than assuming you will be there for 30 years. You should not assume rates are as low as they're going to get, because you don't know that, and neither do I. Rather than worry about the hazards of predicting the long-term future, make decisions that you are going to be happy with for the next few years. When you get a loan, you aren't going to consider refinancing unless there's a major rate change. Beyond that, it's anyone's guess.

The Importance of Alternatives to You

Let's delve into this a little deeper, keeping in mind that while the lender may be indifferent to pricing alternatives, for you there are some that are better than others. The numbers I'm going to show you are eight actual rates and fee alternatives from a lender's rate sheet. Some lenders have even more than this. Check out the wholesale rate sheets I have included in the appendix.

| TIP | The day you meet your loan rep and the day you lock in your loan, you should get all the applicable numbers from your lender and analyze them according to the method shown here.

In column 1, note that there is a ⅛ percent difference among the rates. Column 2 shows the points associated with each rate. Column 3 shows the difference between the points at this rate and the points associated with the rate on the previous line. Next, we are going to divide the difference between points in column 3 by one-eighth to determine how quickly you get your money back. Look at column 4. It shows the break-even time in years.

Rate	Points	Difference	Breakeven
7.875	0		
7.75	0.125	0.125	1 year
7.625	0.375	0.25	2 years
7.5	0.75	0.375	3 years
7.375	1.125	0.375	3 years
7.25	1.75	0.625	5 years
7.125	2.25	0.5	4 years
7	2.75	0.5	4 years

Let's say that initially you were considering a zero-point loan at a rate of 7.875 percent. Now it's time to lock in. You have all these numbers from the lender and you want to figure out if there are better alternatives. You can get 7.75 percent by paying .125 point (or ⅛, expressed as a fraction). You'd pay ⅛ point to get down to 7.75 percent; you'd get back that ⅛ percent in the first year and every additional year you have the loan. You can see that has a one-year breakeven. If you have the loan 10 years, you'd get ¹⁰⁄₈ back for ⅛ cost. That's terrific. Look at the next one. It costs .375 (⅜ point) to get a rate of 7.625 percent. That's .25 (¼ point) more than .125 points associated with 7.75 percent. That's good, too, a two-year breakeven. Does that make sense? It does to lenders, because they all say, "You can have a lower rate if you just pay a little more up front. Pay me now or pay me later."

The next two loans offer a three-year breakeven, also attractive for most people. But when you get to 7.25 percent, it would take five years to break even, and that's not a good deal in my opinion. So the ideal rate would be either 7.625 or 7.375 percent. Again, I can make no rational case for the 7.25 percent option, and thus none for either 7.125 or 7 percent.

In order to get the 7.375 percent rate, you as the borrower would probably be perfectly willing to pay the 1.125 points, because it's such a good deal. Many experts say that zero-point loans are the best, and sometimes they are, but with *this particular—and most other—rate-versus-fee offerings* it makes more sense to pay some points and get a better rate. Compared with the zero-point alternative of 7.875 percent, you'll get a rate that's ½ percent lower and that costs only 1.125 points—your breakeven is just over two years.

I know this methodology is tough for people to grasp until they work a few examples for themselves. Recently, I did a loan for a professor of physics who can probably solve differential equations in his head, but even he struggled with this at first. However, this concept is important, and I recommend that you play with some examples from the wholesale rate sheets in the Appendix. It will become clear after a few tries. Remember, if you don't choose an alternative that's best for you, the lender will choose what's best for itself.

‎⎢TIP⎟ If you are computer proficient, you can set up a spreadsheet to do these calculations and output them graphically. That's what I do for my customers. You can order a computer

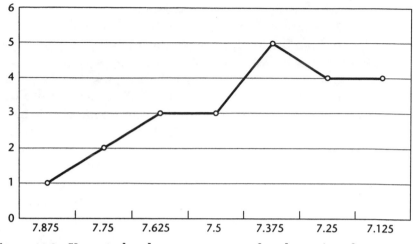

Figure 11.2   Years to breakeven: rate-versus-fee alternatives for a 30-year fixed-rate loan.

disk with a worksheet designed for this purpose by using the coupon in the back of the book. If you don't have a computer, not to worry, you can still do it very easily on paper. After a few examples, it will become easy; soon you will be able to look at a schedule and quickly calculate the breakevens.

To illustrate this further, I've tried to simplify this concept by portraying the data graphically, as shown in Figure 11.2. In the figure, you can see that there are two common characteristics. First, it is obvious that as the rate gets lower, the buy-downs become more expensive. The implications are clear: Although you consider some of these, as the cost goes up, the loan will reach a point where it's too expensive. Second, the numbers usually bounce all around. Look at the same lender's pricing options for 15-year loans in the following table; then view its graphical representation in Figure 11.3.

Rate	Points	Difference	Breakeven
7.5	−1		
7.375	−0.875	0.125	1 year
7.25	−0.5	0.375	3 years
7.125	−0.125	0.375	3 years
7	0.25	0.375	3 years

6.875	0.25	0	0
6.75	0.75	0.5	4 years
6.625	1.125	0.375	3 years
6.5	1.625	0.5	4 years
6.375	1.625	0	0
6.25	2.125	0.5	4 years
6.125	2.625	0.5	4 years
6	3.125	0.5	4 years

Note that two of the break-even years are zero. Who in the world would take 7 percent if he or she could get 6.875 percent for the same points? Well, more than a few people did exactly that, either because they didn't know how to get this information or because their lenders wouldn't give it to them. You, on the other hand, will be well armed and very knowledgeable and will get the most advantageous deal.

TIP Remember that the rate-versus-fee trade-offs are not orderly; if they were, there wouldn't be much point to going through the process. Because lenders have to round off to the nearest ⅛ percent, the results aren't rational. Some will be slightly in your favor and others will be in the lender's favor. That's why it is so valuable for you to go through this exercise.

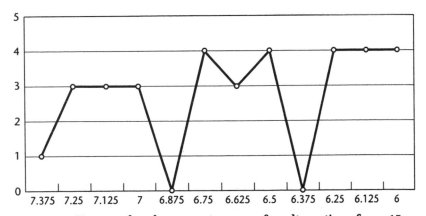

Figure 11.3 Years to breakeven: rate-versus-fee alternatives for a 15-year fixed-rate loan.

RATES VERSUS FEES ON ARMS

The entire process is different for ARMs. A loan may start at 5 or 6 percent, but after its first adjustment in a year or two, the real interest rate is going to be at index plus margin. Thus the period of variability of rate-versus-fee options is so short that the lender has only a very short period in which to recoup its costs. Therefore the differences between alternatives are typically less than for fixed-rate loans. To compare ARMs, I know of no other way than to just sit down and do a period-by-period analysis. Using a computer spreadsheet, it's more tedious than difficult. The table that follows is extracted from one page of a lender's three-page wholesale rate sheet. It shows the lender's pricing alternatives on one ARM program. (The lender offers four more programs that are slightly different.) As you can see, there are 96 alternatives. I include them here to show you how complex this process can become.

Here's how to read the table. Let's say you want your loan to have an initial rate of 3.7 percent—the start rate. In the case of this particular loan, that initial rate is valid for only three months; then it goes to index plus margin. You can get a 2.45 margin and pay .25 discount point plus, say, another point origination fee, for a total of 1.25 points. If you want a lower margin of 2.255, you have to pay 1.375 discount points. Add the loan origination fee for a total of 2.375 points. (See circled numbers below.)

If you want a zero-point loan, you have to choose one with points equal to minus 1 so that when you add the loan origination fee, it equals zero. One of those is a start rate of 3.7 percent with a higher margin—2.8 instead of 2.225. Another zero-point alternative is a start rate of 5.7 percent and a margin of 2.6. Although this may seem pretty confusing, more choices are better than fewer.

Margin	2.225	2.35	2.45	2.6	2.8	3
Start rate						
2.95	1.5625	0.9375	0.4375	−0.3125	−0.8125	−1.3125
3.2	1.5	0.875	0.375	−0.375	−0.875	−1.375
3.45	1.4375	0.8125	0.3125	−0.4375	−0.9375	−1.4375
3.7	(1.375)	0.75	(0.25)	−0.5	−1	−1.5
3.95	1.3125	0.6875	0.1875	−0.5625	−1.0625	−1.5625

4.25	1.25	0.625	0.125	−0.625	−1.125	−1.625
4.45	1.1875	0.5625	0.0625	−0.6875	−1.1875	−1.6875
4.7	1.125	0.5	0	−0.75	−1.25	−1.75
4.95	1.0625	0.4375	−0.625	−0.8125	−1.3125	−1.8125
5.2	1	0.375	−0.125	−0.875	−1.375	−1.875
5.45	0.9375	0.3125	−0.1875	−0.9375	−1.4375	−1.875
5.7	0.875	0.5	−0.25	−1	−1.5	−1.875
5.95	0.8125	0.1875	−0.3125	−1.0625	−1.5625	−1.875
6.2	0.75	0.125	−0.375	−1.125	−1.625	−1.875
6.45	0.6875	0.0625	−0.04375	−1.1875	1.6875	−1.875
6.7	0.625	0	−0.5	−1.25	−1.75	−1.875

In summary, whether you choose a fixed-rate loan or an ARM, you're going to have to do some work to find the loan-pricing alternative that is best for you. You should be encouraged by the prospect that the result will be well worth the effort.

WHAT TO DO WHEN YOU RUN INTO A PROBLEM

Our company is like a log train going down a mountain. If one of the logs falls off, we don't stop the train and go back for it.
—REPRESENTATIVE OF A MAJOR LENDER

The opening quotation is a very accurate description of how many large lending institutions operate. Typically, at such firms the underwriters are paid to evaluate four or five files every day. If an underwriter can't underwrite and approve your file in the allotted time, he or she really doesn't like to set it aside and work on it later. He or she will want to deny the loan and go on to the next one in the stack. This may sound heartless, but that's the way it is. I do not want to condemn underwriters, because I know that when the industry gets superbusy, many will take files home and work on them in the evenings and on weekends. But, as a general rule, management pressures underwriters for *volume,* and I have never seen companies give much of an incentive to their underwriters to spend a lot of time with an individual file, even a large, highly profitable one.

Speaking very practically, there is only one reason an underwriter can't approve a loan: There is a problem. There are only two types of problems: solvable and unsolvable. Successful mortgage professionals are those who have learned how to solve the solvable problems and quickly identify the unsolvable ones. With that in mind, let's talk about the types of problems that might confront you.

QUALIFYING PROBLEMS

Without a doubt, qualifying is a major problem for many borrowers. Let me quickly say that from an income standpoint, almost everyone qualifies for some-size loan. That is why getting preapproved is so important. Once you know the largest loan you are qualified for, you won't be tempted to waste time looking for a home that requires a larger loan.

Essentially, there are only three questions in determining qualification:

- Is the borrower's employment stable?
- How much is the income?
- How do the borrower's qualifying ratios compare with the lender's allowable limits?

Many people have no problem in determining their income. They are on a wage or salary paid by an employer, and they have been working long enough to be considered stable (usually more than two years). For many other borrowers, however, determining income is more complex. Although the specifics of these borrowers' dilemmas are covered in Chapter 15, I summarize them here for the purposes of this discussion. In brief, most qualifying problems come when an underwriter won't count income that is actually being received, such as the following:

A recent increase in salary

Bonus or overtime income that has no historical precedent

Recent commission or self-employment income higher than a two-year average

Income from recent self-employment

A second job

Income received as a result of transition from employee to independent subcontractor

If approval of your loan will depend on income from such a source, identify it when you begin working with a lender. If you just got a raise, ask your boss to write a short letter to that effect and include your most recent paycheck stub showing the increase. If you have a part-time job, document the income. However, do not expect your lender to count any income you receive "off the books." Compensation not reported to the IRS won't be considered by lenders.

Fortunately, there are some lenders who are a little more courageous in looking at income. Frequently, portfolio lenders will not apply FNMA rules to qualifying, especially if other factors such as LTV, credit, and liquidity are good. They are also more likely to approve a loan with higher ratios. Many, many lenders have programs, particularly for first-time home buyers, that allow more liberal underwriting. These include the Community Reinvestment Act and Community Homebuyer programs.

You will recall from the discussion of qualifying that lenders calculate expense-to-income ratios to determine whether a candidate qualifies. Let's assume that the top ratio, housing expense to income, is acceptable, but that you have too much outstanding debt, causing the bottom ratio to be high. You can solve that by paying off credit card debt or by paying down a car loan to get the remaining number of payments under 10 months, at which point the debt won't be counted. If you are getting a gift from parents that will comprise part of the down payment, you might consider allocating a portion of those funds to pay off debts instead—the positive impact on your ratio may be advantageous. You might be better off with a 95 percent LTV loan and no debt rather than a 90 percent loan with too much debt.

Finally, if your lender says that your ratio is too high, say 30/40, and its standard is 28/36, your problem is a little easier. What you need to do is find a lender with more liberal standards. They are certainly out there. You might have to settle for an ARM, but you will be able to buy the home. Just to let you know what is possible, I recently did a 95 percent LTV loan for an Air Force pilot whose ratios were 35/40.

DOWN-PAYMENT PROBLEMS

For a variety of reasons, lenders are particularly paranoid about the source of a down payment and will go to great lengths to make you document where your money came from. The following are ways to document the sources of typical down payments. Some have been discussed previously but bear repeating here.

- If you have sold another house, the settlement agent or escrow company will have given you a closing statement (HUD-1) on that transaction disclosing the amount you received. Show this to your new lender to verify the source of down payment.

- If you are first-time home buyer and are putting less than 20 percent down, you'll need to show that you have saved at least 5 percent of the purchase price yourself. The balance can be gift funds. Your lender will ask you for three months of bank statements or a Verification of Deposit form showing how much money is in your account and the average balance over the last 60 days. If you currently have $17,000, but the 60-day average shows only $7,000, you won't get a loan unless you can explain where the extra $10,000 came from.

- If you sold your boat, provide the bill of sale and a copy of the check. If you sold some stock, show your brokerage statement and confirmation of the sale. If your brother repaid a loan, show that you had the money two years ago and that you declared the interest income on your tax return. If you inherited money from your grandmother, show a copy of the probate ruling and a copy of the check from the lawyer or court. You get the picture.

EMPLOYEE TRANSFERS

Many companies that transfer employees have generous relocation packages. In addition to paying moving costs, they may pay all or most of the closing costs on a new home, offer to buy the employee's former residence, and/or pay for the costs of sale of the former residence. The company will have a written policy that you should provide to the lender.

| TIP | Keep a copy of every check and every piece of documentation you receive during the transaction of selling and buying a home.

Caution: If your employer's relocation policy is to loan you the amount of equity in your former house for the down payment on the new home, this is *not* the same as if an employer agrees to actually *buy* your former home. You are still responsible for the new loan, the old loan, and the equity loan. Almost no one can qualify under these circumstances, so if your employer has this policy, anticipate a problem. You will need to find a receptive lender—perhaps the bank with which your employer has its main banking relationship.

CREDIT PROBLEMS

In Chapter 8, I itemized and explained the impact of credit problems on obtaining a loan, so I won't repeat them here. Suffice it to say that if you have done all you can to clean up your credit and you still can't get a loan from a FNMA-type lender, try a portfolio lender, especially if your problems are ancient history. You may find a sympathetic ear, particularly if the LTV is low enough—lower than 80 percent.

As a last resort, most B and C lenders will still do business with you. But be warned that it's expensive to do business with them, typically about 2 points and 2 percent higher than A-mortgage rates. In addition, you'll have a prepayment penalty clause.

__ADVICE__ A prepayment penalty is expensive, so try to buy out of it, usually for an additional point up front. Then go to work putting your credit problems behind you. When they are straightened out, you can refinance with a lower-rate A loan.

New Credit and No Credit

Credit that has been only recently established doesn't carry much weight with a lender. If, for example, you are still in school or have just graduated, I recommend that you open up a couple of accounts now and use them, even if for small amounts. You want to establish a credit history, and history means a couple of years, not a couple of weeks.

__TRICK__ You can have your parents add you to old, seldom-used accounts. These accounts will then get reported on *your* credit report, too, giving the impression you have had accounts for several years.

APPRAISAL PROBLEMS

Appraisal problems arise when the requested or agreed-upon selling price of a home exceeds the appraised value. At this point, the agents should come into the picture and be very realistic about the value of the property. In most marketing situations, the buyer and seller going through the negotiating process with accurate information only rarely settle on an above-market price (that is, unsupported by the appraisal). However, it can happen between a stubborn seller and a buyer who has become entranced with a property, in which case, the parties involved will simply have to work it out. If the seller is unwilling to reduce the price and the buyer is willing to pay a premium, then the lender will base the loan amount on the appraised value. The buyer will have to make up the difference with additional down payment.

With the widespread decline in real estate values in the early 1990s, borrowers have had a lot of problems with refinance transactions. In certain areas, the value of entire neighborhoods may be worth less than the collective value of the loans on the properties. That's a problem. Before embarking on a refinance, contact a local real estate agent who can give you recent sales data on homes in your area so you can anticipate the outcome of the appraisal. If an identical house two doors away sold a month ago for $192,500, it is not realistic to think that an appraiser is going to come up with a $205,000 value on your house.

If you know that the loan amount you are requesting is likely going to be higher than, say, 80 percent LTV, I would work with a mortgage broker who can select his or her own appraiser instead of relying on a direct lender's in-house appraiser. An independent appraiser will be able to evaluate your property realistically and objectively. It is no secret to those in the industry that many lenders tell their appraisal staff to be conservative. That means if they think a house is worth between $175,000 and $185,000, they will use the lower range of value, $175,000, even if it kills the deal.

Furthermore, it is not uncommon for lenders to send out appraisers who are unfamiliar with the town, much less the neighborhood, in which they are appraising. This causes no end of problems for borrowers. Here's a little anecdote from my own experience: I once did a deal with a bank that required me to use its own appraiser. When I met her at a $950,000 home, she admitted that not only had she never even been in my city before, but that she had just started with the bank! The bank should have sent this green appraiser to new tracts where comparable sales data are easier to find, not to a large executive mansion in an unfamiliar area. You can imagine the results. She came in $75,000 low and it took me two weeks of arm wrestling to get the value up to where it should have been.

OTHER PROBLEMS: BUGS AND RUGS

Most real estate brokers will not allow the transfer of a property without a termite inspection because they don't want a lawsuit a few years later. If the sales agreement calls for a termite report, the lender has a right to the report. In my area, there is termite infestation of some magnitude in about 50 percent of transactions. After all, termites have been around for 100 million years and do not much care that their food supply has been usurped to build houses.

So, you say, just tent the house to get rid of the infestation—no problem. Not so fast. Some sellers want to wait until after they have vacated. The buyers might even agree. Unfortunately, many lenders will not fund the loan until the work has actually been done and a clear report has been issued. There are other lenders who will allow tenting or repair after closing, but they require that one and one-half times the amount of the bill be left in escrow. If the treatment for termites is going to cost $1,000, they want the seller to leave $1,500 with the settlement agent, to be paid when the house has passed inspection. If this applies to your deal, make sure you understand the lender's policy. Work this out ahead of time.

Believe it or not, carpeting can be a problem, too. Strangely, these rules still apply even in the case of a 50 percent LTV loan. I wonder if lenders really think that someone would live in a home without carpets. Regardless, 90 percent of all lenders will not fund loans unless the flooring—whether carpeting, vinyl, stone, tile, marble, or hardwood—has been installed. These policies are rigidly enforced. In the case of new construction, when the home is finished, the appraiser issues a final report declaring that the home has been completed in accordance with the plans and specifications—and that includes flooring. A lender will require the appraiser to include photos of the interior of the home to show that the carpeting really was installed.

Here's the problem for some people: Builders traditionally paint the walls white. Often, the homeowner wants to paint them another color and doesn't want to install the carpeting until the painting is completed. Or perhaps a homeowner wants to deal with a private carpet company rather than the builder's carpet company. These may be reasonable situations, but lenders normally won't fund the loan until the flooring is in, whereas builders won't let someone else's subcontractor in the house until the title is transferred. The good news is that some lenders are large enough not to have to sell every loan immediately, so they'll agree to fund the loan and then give you 30 days to complete the work, although the one-and-one-half-times-cost rule will apply here as well. If you know ahead of time that you will ask for this concession, make sure your lender already has this policy, because a lender that doesn't will not start one just for you.

CONCLUSION

Throughout this book, I have reiterated the lending industry's practice to deny perfectly acceptable loans—in fact, the industry routinely denies about 30 percent of loan applications. You can avoid being one of them by working harder at it, enlisting the help of a knowledgeable professional, and being better prepared when you start the process. If you suspect you are among the 30 percent who may have difficulty qualifying, you can still get a loan, but it will help if you introduce yourself to the manager at whichever lender you choose. Identify your allies up front so they will already know you to be a reasonable person and will want to help you.

PART 3

LOCKING
AND
CLOSING

HOW LENDERS CAN CHEAT
THEIR CUSTOMERS

*There is no product that some man cannot make a
little worse and sell a little cheaper, and the buyers
who consider only price are this man's lawful prey.*
— JOHN RUSKIN

KEY POINTS

- Many borrowers and lenders view their relationship as adversarial.
- In spite of numerous disclosure laws, borrowers never have as much price information as lenders.
- Breaking through the professionals' secrecy barrier—getting lenders to share information with you—is the key to getting the best pricing.
- If you can't find a lender who will share information willingly, there are other steps you can take to gain the knowledge you need.

The mortgage business is different from other types of businesses. Consider this: In a typical commercial transaction, you may see an ad for a shirt in the newspaper; you go to the store and buy the shirt for the price at which it was advertised. Americans expect commerce to be conducted in this manner. But in the mortgage business, the consumer makes the decision to buy shortly after the home goes into escrow. However, the price isn't established until the buyer is ready to close, perhaps 30 or 60 days later. In the case of new construction, six months may elapse. During that period, the borrower is at the mercy of the lender. It's not bad to be at someone's mercy as long as the person, or in this case the lender, is trustworthy! The question is, are lenders trustworthy?

Various laws require lenders to disclose rates, fees, and costs to consumers. These include Truth in Lending, Itemization of Amount Financed, and Good Faith Estimate of Closing Costs, forms mandated by RESPA, and the Real Estate Settlement Procedures Act—all designed to give the borrower information about the costs associated with the loan. The totally incorrect assumption is that once customers have the information, it'll be hard for the lender to change terms later to the borrower's detriment.

WHOM DO YOU TRUST?

Lenders are in business to make money. They like to project the image that they are highly regulated, but the bank examiners and regulators from the Office of Thrift Supervision concentrate on the financial viability of institutions. Occasionally they may check to see if the Equal Credit Opportunity Act forms are signed, but they do not look into pricing to see if a bank is bamboozling its customers. Enforcement of disclosure laws mandated by RESPA is not the job of the people who visit lenders regularly. It is up to HUD, which has only a couple of dozen investigators nationwide—far too few to do an adequate job of investigating the millions of transactions that occur annually. Naively, people assume that the market will take care of pricing and that customers wouldn't agree to pricing unless it were reasonable. I see no evidence to support that contention. If you want to be treated fairly, don't count on some regulator; it's up to you.

The mortgage market is volatile, changing from day to day. Unless you lock in immediately, you are at the mercy of the market. That's the way most of the American economy works. But a lender can use this volatility to disguise methods of improving its profits on your transaction. Most of the time this goes on at a level that is invisible to consumers, and this gives lenders, with their greater knowledge of the market, the opportunity unfairly to take advantage of their customers' ignorance. Let's see how this can happen.

Remember that there is no correlation between the rates quoted on the initial disclosure forms (those given you at the time of application) and the rate you eventually get. The actual rate isn't determined until you lock in. This loophole in the law creates an opening that allows lenders to abuse customers if they think they can get away with it. To demonstrate the amount of volatility, Figure 13.1 charts one lender's points at the same interest rate for a two-month period. As you can see, it's common for pricing to change from one day to another.

Let me elaborate on this pricing situation. I can already hear someone saying, "If you are doing business with a trustworthy lender, you don't have to worry about this." Indeed, a theme you have heard me repeat throughout this book is that you should search for your own advocate, a lender you can trust. Happily, many lenders do not let their employees change pricing from one customer to another, and the larger the institution, the less likely they are to fool around with pricing—their bureaucracies are just too cumbersome and inflexible. Other companies who operate from an ethical foundation would consider it a violation of ethics to allow their employees to control pricing. Still other lenders dictate only a *minimum level* at which loans must be priced on any given day. The employees in those companies have the authority, in fact are encouraged, to charge the customer higher rates if they can get away with it.

In a multibranch operation, an individual branch's profit is directly dependent on pricing, and the branch manager's bonus is almost surely based on the profit. Furthermore, the usual com-

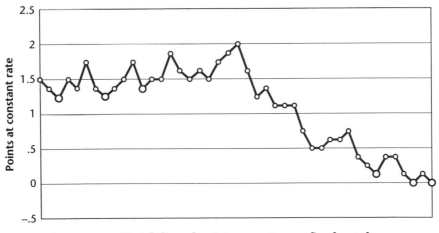

Figure 13.1   Variability of points on a 30-year fixed-rate loan.

pensation arrangement is to split excess commissions with its loan reps. It's called *incentive compensation.* My question is, incentive to do what? The answer: to create additional profit by charging higher-than-market prices. What we have here is a conspiracy between management and employees to squeeze more money from you.

Of course, profit-making organizations have the right to generate extra profit, but they should do so by creating extra value, not by taking advantage of customers' ignorance. There are even lenders that conduct training sessions to teach loan reps how to finesse more money out of the buyers. They regard market volatility as an ally because it creates a situation whereby the true price becomes elusive to the customer, and thus they have a better chance of charging more and increasing profits at the expense of their unknowing customers. Let me make the point this way: Suppose that the market weren't volatile, that during the 60-day period between application and locking in, the rates were absolutely flat and unchanging at 8 percent. Obviously, your rate would be 8 percent. If there is volatility, however, the situation changes. Let's say that during the same time span rates move from 8 percent to 7.75 percent, back up to 8 percent, then to 8.25 percent, and back down to 7.875 percent. Which rate are you going to get now? Lenders know the rates on a minute-by-minute basis because that's their business. If your lender is being fair with you, any change, up or down, will be passed on to you. However, you may not have known about this volatility, and even though you do now, where do you find the information you need? It's almost impossible without help from an insider. Those with Internet access have a greater ability to check rates, and I encourage you to read that chapter.

LENDERS PROFIT AT YOUR EXPENSE

For this discussion, we're going to return to the topic of rate-versus-fee alternatives, which we discussed in the last chapter. We'll examine how they work at the wholesale level—the lender's cost of funds. Keep in mind that most borrowers are not aware of the choices available to them. To begin, let's assume you and I own a mortgage company and that the company to which we sell loans sends us a rate sheet every day. It works the same way in a bank.

Recall from Chapter 11 a matrix of rate-versus-fee alternatives. The same type of matrix is shown here.

Rate	Retail Points
7.875	0
7.75	0.125
7.625	0.375
7.5	0.75
7.375	1.125
7.25	1.75
7.125	2.25

For this example, as lenders we propose to charge 1.5 points over the cost as our markup. We'll take the price list from our money sources and add 1.5 points to the wholesale price to determine the retail pricing on the retail daily rate sheet we give to the loan reps. The customers don't see anything shown in boldface type.

Rate	Retail Points	Wholesale
8.25	**N/S**	**−2.25**
8.125	**N/S**	**−2**
8	**N/S**	**−1.75**
7.875	0	**−1.5**
7.75	0.125	**−1.375**
7.625	0.375	**−1.125**
7.5	0.75	**−0.75**
7.375	1.125	**−0.375**
7.25	1.75	**0.25**
7.125	2.25	**0.75**

Our analysis in Chapter 11 proved that a borrower could pay extra points and get a lower rate. But yield works the other way, too, meaning a loan with a higher yield—a higher rate—is worth more. It provides greater income to the lender, so it's worth more. That value is reflected as a *negative* number in the matrix. It's negative because, as we will see, it represents what our source for funds will pay us, not what the customer pays.

Let's work through an example. If the customer chooses 7.25 percent, we can see from the rate sheet that he or she will pay us 1.75 points. When we sell the loan, we will have to pay .25 points to our source, keeping the 1.5 point difference, our planned profit. If the customer chooses 7.625 percent, he or she would pay us only .375 point. When we sell the loan, the source will *pay us* 1.125 points, called a *rebate.* That 1.125 plus the .375 we received from the customer yields our planned profit of 1.5 points. Our money source will pay us, as the broker, the rebate of 1.125 points because we have delivered a loan that yields more, 7.625 percent instead of 7.25 percent. You can see why it's worth more.

Look at the matrix again, especially the top rates with the *negative* numbers in the third column. Remember, the lender *pays us* those points. What are we going to do with the money? The customer *could* benefit if we, as lender, were willing to pass it on. Or we can keep the money as an incentive to sell the customer a higher-rate mortgage.

Let's see how this can affect the borrower. Let's say that we've approved a borrower when the market is as shown on preceding rate sheet. We know that whatever rate-versus-fee alternative the customer chooses, we will make 1.5 points, the spread we created between wholesale and retail rate sheets. Our customer has been thinking about 7.875 percent and zero points. (Remember, it doesn't make any difference which one he or she chooses because this situation works for all of them.) Then, a month or two later when we're ready to close, the market has improved, and rates are .375 percent lower. Our source sends us a new rate sheet in which the entire matrix shifts downward by .375 percent, but the relationship between rates and fees stays the same. Here's a portion of that rate sheet, along with the previous rate sheet numbers.

Rate	Old retail points	New	Old wholesale	New wholesale
7.875	0	−0.75	−1.5	−2.25
7.75	0.125	−0.625	−1.375	**−2.125**
7.625	0.375	−0.375	−1.125	−1.875
7.5	0.75	0	−0.75	−1.5
7.375	1.125	0.375	−0.375	−1.125
7.25	1.75	1	0.25	−0.5
7.125	2.25	1.5	0.75	0

Note that the rates are .375 percent lower. At a specific rate, the points are .75 point higher than before. I've shown last rate we showed the customer, 7.875 percent at zero points, in bold. I've also shown a new zero-points option, 7.5 percent, also in boldface.

The question confronting us, the lender, is, "What do we tell the borrower?" If we run an honest company, we call the borrower and say, "Good news. Rates have improved and your loan will cost you only 7.5 percent, an even better rate than the 7.875 percent you were expecting." As I said, many lenders instruct their employees to follow the rate sheet. But others look upon situations like this as unique profit opportunities. Here's how.

The branch manager calls the loan rep into the office and says, "We're going to lock in the Smith loan today. What do you plan to charge?" The loan rep knows that the borrower was quoted 7.875 percent and may still be expecting 7.875 percent. He also knows that we, as lender, will make an extra .75 point if the customer still thinks that 7.875 percent is a fair rate. We're not talking chicken feed here. On a $200,000 loan, .75 point amounts to $1,500. So the rep calls the borrower with the "good news" that their mortgage was approved as originally quoted. If the borrower agrees, we fund the loan, pocket an extra $1,500, and nobody's the wiser.

If the borrower objects because he or she has heard that rates have dropped, the loan rep says, "I'll have to see what I can work out for you," and hangs up. The rep may still try to finagle extra profit by calling back a little bit later and saying, "I managed to get you 7.75 percent." If the customer okays that, the lender still makes a bonus. If we look at the rate sheet, we can see that when we sell this 7.75 percent loan, we get paid 2.125 points (also shown in boldface). We've made our planned profit of 1.5 points plus an extra .625 point, an extra $1,250. I can hear someone asking, "Is this legal?" Yes, it is perfectly legal as long as the compensation is disclosed in the RESPA forms that accompany the loan documents. If you, the borrower, don't read or don't understand all those forms you sign at settlement, it's your problem, not the lender's.

REGULATOR PROTECTION

I said previously that regulators weren't going to be much help. There are exceptions. In my state, one is the Department of Real

Estate, which supervises mortgage brokers. It recently publicized the following case: "The broker failed to inform the borrower of a drop in the interest rates and by delivering a loan at the originally quoted rate, the broker received a four-point rebate in addition to the one point that was actually disclosed to the borrowers. This broker collected nearly $7,000 in undisclosed fees for arranging an 'A' paper loan [a prime quality loan] of $175,000."

The problem is that this warning was contained in the department's regular notices to the real estate and mortgage brokers, not to consumers—people like you who really need this information. That extra 4 points is exceptional and probably earned the loan rep the "shark of the month" award at his or her company. More common are charges in the range of ½ to 1 point. On a $200,000 loan, that's $1,000 or $2,000, and this kind of thing goes on all the time.

It can get worse. If a lender has a customer with a problem, one less likely to be desirable to competitors, they call the borrower and say, "Your loan is approved, but we couldn't get it approved on the 7.875 percent program. We could only get you approved on a program that is at 8.125 percent." (That loan will give the lender a rebate of 3 points, or twice the normal profit.) The borrower may grouse a bit, but if it's five days before the scheduled closing date, what can he or she do about it? Not much.

Do not believe that the marketplace will keep this from happening. Remember that the borrower doesn't have as much information about the market as lenders, because the lenders seldom divulge what they have to pay for the money. As the time draws near to close the sale, the seller of the property becomes the lender's unwilling coconspirator, because he or she won't give you enough time to get a loan from another lender.

SERVICING RELEASED FEES AND YIELD-SPREAD PREMIUMS

A number of class-action lawsuits have been filed against some large lenders alleging abuse of the customers. Specifically, the borrowers allege that the practice of money sources paying rebates to brokers is illegal. Such terms as *servicing released fees* and *yield-spread premiums* are used to describe compensation paid by a lender to a broker. In my mind, the lender has to pay its own employees in its retail division, so paying a broker to do the same thing—originate loans—isn't any different. If the broker and the lender have agreed to a commission of 1.5 points, the customer pays something less than 1.5 points, and the balance of the broker's commission will be paid by the lender to the broker as a rebate.

Elimination of servicing released fees and yield-spread premiums would eliminate the ability of the broker's customers to take advantage of low-point pricing. That's clearly unrealistic. As we discussed in Chapter 11, making these choices is a very important part of your rights as a borrower. Clearly, the courts, HUD, and Congress will have the last word on this, but I am always concerned when the government attempts to regulate economics. With any luck, brokers will retain the ability to earn part of their compensation this way, but the disclosure requirements will be strengthened to curb unethical practices.

If you are working with a broker, you want to be aware of and negotiate total compensation paid to the broker, not just the rate and points you pay. Refer to the pricing matrix we used earlier and you will note a number of alternatives in which the broker's compensation was made up partly from fees paid by the borrower and partly from those paid by the source of funds. If you have agreed that your broker will earn a fee of 1.5 points, then it doesn't make any difference which alternative you choose. Let's say you are getting a $200,000 loan; when you get your closing statement with the loan documents, it will show the fees like this:

Loan origination	$1,500	(equals ¾ point)
Yield-spread premium (POC)	$1,500	(the other ¾ point)

The acronym POC stands for paid outside of closing, and it means that the lender has paid a rebate to the broker. In this example, that's all right, because that was our agreement. But you should *always* check this and add up the numbers to make sure the compensation conforms to your agreement.

INSTITUTIONALIZED CHEATING

Although price gouging in the mortgage industry is sporadic, some lenders do this as a matter of policy, even to the extent of teaching their loan reps how to practice it. Let me explain why it is important that you understand this. If a lender's normal price sheet is set up so that it makes a standard loan origination fee, say

1.5 points, that's $3,000 on a $200,000 loan—in my view, reasonable compensation for the work. Let's say that the salesperson gets half of that, or $1,500, and the company keeps $1,500. Out of that, the company has to pay for advertising, marketing, rent, overhead, loan processing, and so forth. Of the $1,500 it received, perhaps there is a profit of $300, which is reasonable.

Let's go back to the example we used earlier. The market moved .375 percent, and we still talked the customer into taking 7.875 percent at zero points. As a result, we made a total rebate of 2.25 points, an extra .75 points, or $1,500 on top of the planned loan-origination fee of 1.5 points. That increases the total revenue from $3,000 to $4,500. The customer still thinks it's a great deal because he or she got a zero-point loan, but to the lender, that extra $1,500 seems almost like free money!

Lenders have so much fun doing this that they are even more generous with their loan reps to encourage them to engage in such practices. They offer the reps a better split, maybe two-thirds of any extra earnings they generate. The industry even has a term for it: *overages*. In our example, the loan rep made $2,500, or $1,500 as a normal commission plus another $1,000 in overages. The lender's gross profit after paying the salesperson increased to $2,000—its original $1,500 plus an additional $500 (its one-third share of the overage). Because its costs didn't increase, the *net* profit increased from $300 to $800. One way lenders attract high-performance sales reps is by offering them better opportunities for overages, and it works.

Collusion and Kickbacks

Some practices are downright nefarious. No doubt our loan rep really likes making $2,500 on every deal, especially if he or she could close 50 deals a year, over $100,000 income. But suppose the real estate agent or tract salesperson tells the rep, "I'm really having trouble getting loans for you. The buyers already have their own lenders." The loan rep offers a solution to this problem: "Why don't I give you a little incentive to get me more loans, say $250 for every loan you refer to me?" Without question, most people in the real estate and mortgage industry are honest, and the practice I just described is illegal. But forewarned is forearmed. If you feel pressured by your rep to use a certain lender, be wary.

Prepayment Penalties

One final shabby practice must be brought to your attention. Some lenders have two price lists: one for loans with a prepayment penalty and another one without the penalty. The penalty is hefty, too: If you pay off the loan within the first three years, you have to pay a penalty of 2 or 3 percent of the loan balance. On a $200,000 loan, that's $4,000 to $6,000, a huge charge to incur if you decide to sell or refinance your house.

Here's the insidious part: If the loan rep delivers a loan with a prepayment penalty, he or she gets an extra half-point commission, $1,000 on the $200,000 loan! Obviously, an honest agent would give you the choice, saying, "You can save an extra half-point if you're willing to accept the prepayment penalty period." That way, you can make an informed choice. It is totally inappropriate for the broker or loan officer to make the decision for you because, he or she stands to gain an extra $1,000. Customers typically don't see this happening until they are signing loan docs—and sometimes they don't even catch it then. If the customer does notice, the loan rep might suggest that *all* lenders have prepayment penalties today. Not true. Alternatively, the rep might say, "You're not going to be refinancing anytime soon, so it won't hurt you." Maybe, maybe not. The point is, it ought to be *your* decision, not theirs.

CONCLUSION

It is not my intention to have you finish this chapter with a jaundiced view of the mortgage industry. Most of the professionals I know are honest, hardworking people who always try to get the best results for their customers. But there are some smooth-talking salespeople out there who not only won't bat an eye while doing these things, it's the very reason they are in the mortgage business.

We're talking about the single most expensive purchase most people will make in their lives, so it is important to know what to *look for* and what to *look out for* when evaluating the people you choose to work on your team.

CLOSING COSTS, LENDER FEES, AND OTHER FEES

KEY POINT

- In addition to points, the appraisal fee, and the credit report fee, lenders charge a number of other closing costs. These items appear on the Good Faith Estimate of Closing Costs and the closing statement (HUD-1 form) that you'll get from the escrow company or other settlement agent. You have a right to know and understand these charges.

A typical closing statement today lists an appalling number of fees and charges. To the uninformed customer, it seems as though everyone in the extended industry wants—and is getting—a piece of the action, which you pay for. Many of these fees will be charged by firms you will never have heard of, and you won't know what they did for you, so it will be unclear why you have to pay them. The U.S. Department of Housing and Urban Development (HUD) instructs lenders to give borrowers a little guide entitled, optimistically, *Buying Your Home: Settlement Costs and Helpful Information.* Unfortunately, it's printed in small type, doesn't read like a novel, and few people seem to get around to reading it. The purpose of this chapter is to make this information more accessible and comprehensible.

The fees and costs are divided into two separate categories: legitimate and garbage. We'll address the legitimate fees first.

LEGITIMATE FEES

Loan origination fee. The loan origination fee encompasses that portion of the points paid to the lender (or broker) for marketing, counseling customers, taking applications, processing, underwriting, coordinating, and funding loans. With brokers, this fee is negotiable; it's their income. If you are well prepared, cooperative, and make their job as easy as you can, you will find it easier to negotiate at the lower end of the schedule. If you have a lot of problems requiring extra work, expect to pay a little more. Most brokers have their own fee schedules, perhaps similar to this one, which I think is reasonable under most circumstances.

Loan amount	Points
Less than $100,000	1.5 to 2
$100,000 to $200,000	1.25 to 1.5
$200,000 to $300,000	1 to 1.25
More than $300,000	1

Loan discount. This portion of the points is the trade-off of rate versus fee, as discussed in Chapter 11. You can lower the rate on your loan by increasing the loan discount. On a closing statement, if you are dealing with a broker these fees will be shown as follows:

Loan origination fee	$1,500
Loan discount	$1,000

However, if you are dealing with a bank or other direct lender, it probably will not separate these fees but will lump them together.

Appraisal fee. This is the money you pay to an appraiser for evaluating the property and preparing a formal report of its value for the lender. In many areas, this fee will range from $250 for a tract home to over $500 for a luxury home. If you qualify for Fannie Mae's or Freddie Mac's automated underwriting, you may be approved for a "drive-by" appraisal, which will cost less than a normal appraisal.

An appraisal is necessary because 99 percent of the time lenders are forbidden, either by state law or their regulators, from funding real estate loans without an appraisal; thus the lenders have no choice. Second, an honest appraisal is one of the most important protections against fraud. If you are buying a home and have negotiated hard with the seller, no doubt you are paying the fair market price for the property. Thus your appraisal won't provide the lender with any important information other than to confirm that the price was reasonable. In a larger sense, however, you can see that not everyone is like you, and the industry would be in shambles in about four minutes if it started doing loans without appraisals.

Credit report. This is the fee (usually varying from $20 to $60) paid to a credit reporting agency to develop your report. Some lenders will accept a "merged report," which costs about $20. However, many lenders still require a Standard Factual Data Report, a more complete report that includes the merged report plus a public-records check for bankruptcy filings, liens, judgments, and so forth, plus a phone verification of the borrower's employment.

Self-employed borrowers should be aware that some lenders will also obtain a business credit report to assure the lender that your business, as the source of ongoing income, is financially healthy.

Flood certification. Federal law requires that borrowers in "federally related transactions" (which means darn near everybody) buy National Flood Insurance if they are in a designated flood zone. The flood certification fee is paid to a company to determine if your property is in such a flood zone. The charge varies from $10 to $30. Even if your property is on the top of a hill or in the desert, lenders still require this certification.

Tax service. Because a local taxing authority can take your house away from you if you don't pay your property taxes, your lender wants to make sure you pay them promptly. This one-time fee, usually $60 or $70, is paid to a tax-service company, which will get the report of tax payments every year from the county tax collector's office after taxes are due, note who hasn't paid their taxes, and then report this information to their lenders, who in turn will send out reminder notices to affected customers.

Settlement fee. This is known as the *escrow fee* in some states. (In many parts of the country, the term *escrow account* is used interchangeably with *impound account,* described later in this chapter.) In California, transactions are handled through escrow companies. Other states may use title companies or attorneys. Settlement agents handle the details of the property transfer, preparing deeds, ordering title insurance, holding the buyer's deposit and down payment, assuring that other requirements of the transaction are completed in a timely fashion, handling the funding of the new loan and payoff of the old loan, allocating taxes and insurance, and, finally, paying the seller the proceeds of sale. Who pays the settlement fee is a matter of custom. If it is customary for the buyer and seller to split this 50-50, that's what the instructions will say. There is no reason you cannot say in your offer to purchase, "Seller to pay settlement fee."

As for refinance transactions, a special deal can usually be negotiated with a settlement agent, because refinances are easier than purchase transactions. Ask your lender to negotiate such a rate for you, perhaps in the $400 range. Sometimes the title company's settlement department will charge less, although you should ask your lender about the level of service to expect.

Title insurance. When you buy a home, the seller pays for a title insurance policy that protects your interest as the new owner. I recommend that every purchaser demand such a policy and not close the transaction without one. Mortgage loans are *secured transactions,* meaning the lender has additional security over and above your promise to pay. Title insurance assures the lender that the collateral for its loan (that is, your home) is free of defects of title, such as encumbrances, liens, or claims by others. You pay for a policy that is issued concurrently to the one the seller paid for. If the lender has to foreclose, it is protected by the equity in the property without consideration of other claims. When you refinance, however, you have to pay for the whole policy, usually between $500 and $1,000. This is one of the largest expenses in a refinance.

I'd like to see the title insurance industry adopt a strategy whereby once you pay for a policy, you can obtain coverage for refinances at a discounted rate, because insurers have less checking to do since the last time they insured it and don't have to pay a sales commission to a rep. Unfortunately, that's not the way they do it.

Sub-escrow fee. Settlement agents used to handle receipt of the proceeds of your loan and handle the payoff to the old lender. But many lenders today do not want to send a $100,000 cashier's check to an escrow company or settlement agent they have never heard of. They prefer to fund through a title company, and you will pay for this. This $75 or $100 compensates for the additional risk involved in handling large sums of money. <u>Sometimes, if the premium you pay on your title policy is high enough, your lender may be willing to waive this fee. Ask.</u>

POC. This is an acronym for "paid outside of closing," meaning the settlement agent or escrow company didn't handle the funds. It can signify nothing more than the money you pay to your lender for the appraisal. That is legitimate. But POC could also mean a rebate, yield-spread premium, servicing release fee, or something similar, referring to extra income paid by the lender to the broker over and above the loan-origination fee.

Let's say you agreed that your loan broker was to make $1,600 on the transaction. The closing statement might show the following:

Loan-origination fee	$800
POC—Lender rebate	$800
POC—Appraisal fee	$275
POC—Credit report	$ 50

Because the loan origination fee and lender rebate add up to the agreed compensation, this is legitimate. However, POC may disguise secret compensation, as we discussed in the previous chapter. It may mean that the lender has paid the broker extra money for delivering a loan at "over market yield," meaning you are going to pay an over-market payment each month. When you ask about it, it is not uncommon for a settlement agent to say, "Don't worry; that's not something you pay." Well, you *should* worry, because it *is* something you pay, but not through escrow.

GARBAGE FEES

I am somewhat sympathetic with lenders because it is expensive to acquire and service customers today. Mortgage lending may seem like a profitable business, but it is highly competitive and margins are thin. It may seem simple to you, but the average loan transaction may involve 100 phone calls and a lot of other work to assemble a file that contains several hundred pages of documents. Sadly, only about 70 percent of all loans initiated are

actually funded. Who pays for the cost of processing
cent that are denied or canceled? Well, if your loan is
you do. It isn't fair, but it won't change until the industry starts
charging applicants an up-front deposit, refundable when the
loan funds but otherwise forfeited. That appalls customers and
the press, so it isn't likely to happen any time soon. We are stuck
with a system whereby lenders do a lot of work for free and then
charge various fees to offset the ever increasing costs of servicing
customers and meeting all the regulatory requirements. Right or
wrong, every lender charges these fees, and there is a reason
behind every one.

Processing fee. As the paperwork has multiplied in this
business, most lenders and brokers have started collecting $200
to $400 to pay for handling costs, courier fees, and long-distance
calls because they're dealing with lenders who are thousands of
miles away. You might say that this is just part of overhead, but
it has become part of every lender's price structure.

Underwriting fee. Like the processing fee, this is another
contribution to overhead, because the actual cost of underwriting a file is only $100 to $200. The typical charge is from $250 to
$500, the excess paying for the cost of those people in the 30 per-
cent who's loans were denied or canceled.

Document fee. There are from 40 to 50 different documents
in a typical loan package today. These used to be typed by hand
on to preprinted forms. Today, they are generated by laser print-
ers. Most lenders have an in-house department that prepares
them and then charges you $150 or $200 for this service. After
you sign, the lender packages your file for shipment to head-
quarters and, probably, to the secondary market. Up through this
chain, there are people who are absolute tyrants about correct-
ness, totally unforgiving about mistakes, so the penalty for error
is high. In fairness, someone has to make sure that every single
one of those papers is signed properly and the file is complete—
and *you* have to pay for ensuring accuracy.

Wire transfer fee. Lenders charge this fee, typically about
$50, because their banks charge them $10 to wire money to the
escrow or title company. Charging $50 for a service that costs
them $10 is the reason these are called garbage fees. This one
isn't actually all that bad: Because a wire is instantaneous, the
lender can fund your loan more quickly than if it had to prepare
a cashier's check and physically send it. The interest you save
may be worth more than the $50 wire fee.

OTHER SETTLEMENT ITEMS

Interest. Interest on mortgage loans is paid in arrears. On the first of every month, you pay the interest that accrued the previous month. If you purchase your home on the twentieth day of the month, you will pay the lender the 10 days of interest owed until the first of the next month, but then you will not have to make a payment until the first of the following month—in this case, 40 days after the loan funds. If you are short on cash, schedule closing until the end of the month.

P M I   *Mortgage insurance premium.* If you put less than 20 percent down, you pay PMI. These days, it seems as if most people choose to pay the premium on a monthly, as-you-go basis. Typically you will have to pay two months' premiums to start out.

Hazard or casualty insurance. Both you and your lender want assurance that your financial interests are protected in case your house should be damaged or destroyed by fire or other hazard. Your lender is named as an additionally insured party on your policy. If you haven't already paid for a policy, you are required to pay the first year's coverage at closing. Most lenders accept a "full-cost-replacement" policy.

Escrow or impound accounts. In cases where the down payment is less than 20 percent, there is less equity to protect lenders in the event of default. A lender doesn't want to foreclose and find that you are also $2,000 behind on your property tax and insurance payments. To protect its interest, the lender may require you to pay one-twelfth of the annual tax and insurance into a special account called an *escrow* or *impound* account. The lender then makes the required payments when they come due. Depending on when your transaction closes and when tax payments are due, you may have to make a sizable deposit to start the account. Be sure to ask your lender the amount it will require. Unless Congress passes new legislation superseding state law, check with your lender to see if impounds are required in your case. In some states, if your LTV ratio is less than 90 percent, the lender may not require such an account. In others, the limit is 80 percent.

CONCLUSION

As a customer, you have a right to know the meaning and purpose of every charge you incur. RESPA gives you the right to a

Good Faith Estimate of Settlement Charges within three days of application and again at closing. Unfortunately, there are few remedies in the event a lender's estimates deviate significantly from reality. If you really get bamboozled, I'd complain first to the lender's president and, if that isn't effective, to HUD, but I wouldn't hold my breath. Just be wary and ask questions. Ask them at the beginning, ask them in the middle, and ask them at the end. Although garbage fees may be incredibly annoying, concentrating on saving an eighth of a percent or a quarter point in fees by going to the best lender is a lot more important.

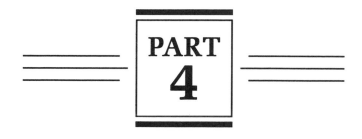

PART
4

ADVANCED
TOPICS

QUALIFYING 201

KEY POINTS

- Borrowers with more complicated income streams, such as those who are self-employed, have greater difficulty getting loans.
- Borrowers with income from an S corporation or who are divorced will confront special problems in qualifying.
- EZ Qual loans, no-income qualifier loans, and stated-income loans are appropriate for some such borrowers.

You have probably heard the statistic that 80 percent of all businesses fail within the first five years. You can see why those business owners pose particular risks for lenders. Conversely, in this era of corporate downsizing and reengineering, small businesses—the strongest sector of the economy at present—are creating most of the new jobs today. Let's see how the industry copes with these special problems.

SELF-EMPLOYED BORROWERS

This is a quote from the underwriting manual of a large lender, "The self-employed borrower represents a high risk in mortgage lending, as their income is directly related to the business. Not only must we determine the actual income received by the borrowers, but the viability of the business to continue to support that income."

Self-employed borrowers are generally defined as those who have 25 percent or more ownership in a business. This definition includes everyone from the one-person law firm to someone who owns 100 percent of a 100-employee machine shop. The first hurdle the self-employed borrower has to face is the longevity of the business. As a general rule, the requirement is that the borrower must have been self-employed and demonstrated profitable operation for at least two years. As a result of widespread downsizing, lenders ought to be better prepared to consider exceptions to this rule, particularly when someone's position was eliminated and he or she was awarded a contract with the former employer to provide same service as an independent contractor.

The underwriter will look at the borrower's 1040s as an indication of income and then look at the financial health of the business to determine its ability to adequately support the borrower.

VARIABLE INCOME

Compared with salaried borrowers, self-employed borrowers, almost by definition have income that varies. People who are paid commissions or bonuses are treated similarly.

First, in any of these scenarios, underwriters will calculate income in several ways and almost surely use the lowest-income answer to determine qualifying ratios. They will use the word *conservative* to justify this, although I think that *accuracy,* a quantitative concept, is more relevant than a qualitative concept like conservative. If you think this isn't fair or reasonable, do not underestimate the fact that this approach dominates underwriting practices for many lenders.

There are good and bad reasons for this. First, no lender wants to fund a loan for someone who had only one good year, because they know that this borrower may be in trouble in years 2, 3, and 4. On the other hand, there is a tendency among underwriters to assume that the worst-income year will repeat itself.

How Lenders Evaluate Variable Income

To lenders, income is either increasing, decreasing, or staying the same. When encountering someone with rising income, the underwriter will throw out the most recent year if it's the best one. Yet when they evaluate the file of a borrower with declining income, the underwriter will count only the most recent year—the worst one. If you detect Murphy's law at work, you're right.

In practice, the underwriter will average the income on the 1040s for the past two years and then compare it with year-to-date (YTD) income in the current year. If the YTD income is the same or higher than the two-year average, the income used for qualifying will be the average calculated. If the YTD income is lower than the two-year average, current income is used. People are generally fairly accurate about their current income and their prospects for the future, yet the underwriting process evaluates history, not the future. You can see why the collision of these opposing forces causes more underwriting battles than any other reason I can think of.

Many self-employed borrowers have successful businesses. If they are incorporated, the corporation pays them a salary that may be somewhat less than their "share" of the income as determined by the percentage of their stock ownership. Of course, a business needs cash in order to grow, and the more successful it is, the greater its cash needs to finance inventory, accounts receivable, manufacturing equipment, and so forth. It is possible that paying the owners a larger salary could have a negative effect on the business's growth. But even when a business clearly has the financial capability to pay more than it does, underwriters often assume that if it could pay more, it would; so they typically don't count corporate earnings that are not actually paid out as income reported on a W-2.

If you need more income to qualify than is shown on your 1040, a more detailed analysis will be required. A competent underwriter will be able to help you. When a business's cash flow is higher than its taxable income, the underwriter can add back to taxable income voluntary payments to a pension plan or retirement program, depreciation, and other noncash charges—although they will have to deduct principal payments on debt.

Bonus Income

When a borrower receives a bonus in addition to salary, the underwriter needs to determine the average amount of the bonus under the presumption that future bonuses will be comparable.

It is also important to determine the current base income. Let's look at the case of Bill Stewart, who has applied for a loan. Here's what the documentation in the loan file shows:

1994 W-2	1995 W-2	1996—five months YTD, per pay stub
$49,400	$51,040	$25,345

Alternative 1 analysis. The underwriter calculates the average income per month from the 1994 and 1995 W-2s (using $49,400 and $51,030), which works out to $4,185 per month. Let's say this isn't enough to qualify for the requested loan. That means Bill needs to "find" more income, so he encourages the underwriter to use 1996 income as well, as follows.

Alternative 2 analysis. Average 1995, 1995, and 1996 YTD income equals $4,337 per month. Let's say that this is closer to the objective, so we want the underwriter to take an even more in-depth look at the borrower's income. Here's what the Verification of Employment form returned by the employer shows:

	1994	1995	1996
Salary	44,000	47,250	20,145 (current annual base is $50,000)
Bonus paid	5,400	3,790	5,200

With this additional detail, we can perform the following calculations.

Alternative 3 analysis. The average bonus is $5,400 plus $3,790 plus $5,200 divided by 36 months, or $400 per month. Adding this to the $50,000 base ($4,166 per month) gives us a final income of $4,566 per month.

You can see that three very rational methods developed three different answers: $4,185, $4,337, and $4,566. The last figure is the most accurate and is 9 percent higher than the initial calculation. This 9 percent is the difference between yes and no to the loan request. *It should be readily apparent that it is imperative to get a loan officer who understands the preceding analysis and who is willing to help you portray your income as accurately as possible.*

Commission Income

Bernard Welch is a commission salesman who works for a company that sells most of its merchandise to stores for the Christmas season. The following income is shown on his W-2s and on his last pay stub:

	1994	1995	1996—9 months YTD
Commissions	58,000	62,000	39,000

Many underwriters would calculate qualifying income as follows: Take the current year's earnings of $39,000, divide it by 9, multiply by 12, and get annualized income of $52,000 per year ($4,333 per month). That is less than either 1994 or 1995, so they would deny the file because of "declining income."

But remember what I said about the Christmas season? Bernard actually earns 40 percent of his income in the last 25 percent of the year (October, November, and December). He is going to earn $65,000 this year, *more* than in 1994 or 1995. Although we are 75 percent through the year, $39,000 is only 60 percent of his annual earnings. Another 40 percent, not 25 percent, is still to come. For this loan to be approved, a month-by-month spreadsheet for each year will demonstrate that income actually grew from year to year. Bernard should also get a letter from his employer, probably from the sales manager, explaining his income.

If bonus or commissions make up more than 25 percent of a borrower's total compensation, he or she will have to bring in two years' 1040s, not just the W-2s. This is to verify that something else isn't going on. In particular, borrowers with commission income are likely to be paying business expenses, such as business entertainment and car expenses, that are not reimbursed by the employer. These expenses are tax deductible if the borrower files a Form 2106, and the underwriter will deduct this amount from the bonus income.

OTHER EXCEPTIONAL QUALIFYING SITUATIONS

Closely held corporations. John Hastings owns one-third of a closely held corporation with two others, and the company has accumulated $150,000 in cash on which taxes have already been paid. The partners kept the money in the company because they didn't want to declare a dividend and wanted to keep open the possibility of using that cash instead of borrowing from a bank. Each of the shareholders considers that he has $50,000 in the "company bank." Problem: Many lenders will not count that money as earned income even though the company could have declared a bonus and paid it out. Furthermore, some lenders will not allow the $50,000 to be withdrawn for a down payment or used toward liquidity requirements. If this applies to you, ask about this special requirement while you are loan shopping so you can find a lender who is flexible in this regard.

S corporations. Many lenders simply do not understand S corporations, companies that have most of the attributes of a partnership but that are legally corporations. The S corp is a creation of the IRS that allows such corporations to be treated as partnerships for tax purposes. Some businesses are, for all intents and purposes, partnerships that are incorporated for some other reason—for example, to protect the stockholders from individual liability. Many underwriters do not know how to evaluate the income of such a shareholder and, in fact, may not count income.

Unlike the K-1 from a partnership, there is no box on an S corporation's K-1 to list the cash actually distributed to an owner. This completely negates the obvious fact that no businessperson would ever elect to have his or her business treated as an S corporation unless the company were able to distribute cash on which the stockholder is paying tax. Here, too, you will have to find a lender who understands your income. Once you are satisfied with the training, experience, and competence of your loan rep in this regard, have the lender review your application and all the tax returns. You want to get what is referred to as *credit approval* up front, *before* spending money on an appraisal.

Limited partnerships. In the early 1980s, an individual could invest in a limited partnership to the tune of, say, $10,000; because of accelerated depreciation or other charges, the company might have a huge tax loss, of which our partner's share was, say, $30,000. If you were in the 50 percent tax bracket, you got a tax refund of $15,000. You got your $10,000 back plus another $5,000, and you still owned your share of the partnership. You can understand why they were so popular with high-income people during the years when the marginal tax rates were higher than they are today. The Tax Reform Act of 1986 changed all that. The IRS no longer allows (most) passive losses to be written off against earned income. That pretty well ended the limited partnership binge, but alarmingly, in 1997, more than 10 years later, most underwriting manuals still have not been updated. As ridiculous as it sounds, underwriters still want to see the K-1s from these mostly inconsequential partnerships to see whether you are a general partner (and thus have some liability for losses) and whether you are making cash contributions to the partnership to cover its losses. If you have a lot of partnerships, this can be very annoying; now that you know about this, the best thing to do is to get the K-1s up front and include them with your application.

If you are a general partner, and the partnership has a loss, the presumption is that someone has to "fund" the loss—and that's you! If the K-1 shows a capital contribution, it will be deducted from your income. Finally, when a partnership sells or liquidates a property or a partner withdraws the CPA will make a noncash adjustment to the partners' capital accounts. That adjustment may look just like capital contribution of cash, so if that applies to you, get your CPA to write a letter explaining it and submit it with your loan application.

Look for more lenders to emulate Citicorp's Citiquik program. If you meet its credit scoring standards and qualify on the basis of income as shown on your 1040, you don't have to show the company tax returns, year-to-date profit and loss statements, or K-1s.

Divorced borrowers. If you are divorced and paying alimony or child support, and you are trying to get a loan, you should be aware of the special rules that apply to you. Fannie Mae and Freddie Mac policies consider court-ordered support payments to be a "recurring bill" just like a car payment. The judicial system thinks it is splitting income between the parties, and the IRS treats such payments as tax deductible to the payer and as taxable income to the payee, but the mortgage industry doesn't look at it that way. It's way out of step. Consequently, unless you have a mammoth income, look for problems. Bill and Susan Taylor have been granted a divorce, with Susan getting the old family home and spousal support of $750 per month. With the divorce behind him, Bill wants to buy a home for himself. Here's their situation:

	Before Divorce (per month)	Alimony (per month)	After Divorce (per month)
Bill's income	$4,000	−750	$3,250
Susan's income	$1,000	+750	$1,750
Total income	$5,000		$5,000

Bill has $3,250 income, and Susan has $1,750. Make sense?

Not! Our industry looks at his income *as if* he still makes $4,000 but went out and bought a new car with a $750 monthly payment. Assuming a $1,000 per month housing payment and an existing $250 car payment, this is how the underwriter will look at it:

Top ratio	1,000/4,000 =		25%
Bottom ratio	Housing	$1,000	
	Alimony	$750	
	Car payment	$250	
	Total	$2,000/$4000 =	50%

How many lenders are going to approve a loan using these figures? Not many, especially if the LTV is more than 80 percent. In contrast, compare this situation with that of Frank Parker, a borrower who makes $3,250, which, you will note, is *exactly* the same as Bill's income after he pays alimony. The underwriter would make these calculations:

Top ratio	$1,000/$3,250 =		31%
Bottom ratio	Housing	$1,000	
	Car payment	$250	
	Total	$1,250/$3,250 =	38%

Frank's application would be approved almost everywhere. We have two borrowers with *identical income,* yet the industry calculates Bill's ratios as 25/50 and denies the loan, while Frank's come out to 31/38 and his loan is approved.

The good news is that while Fannie Mae and Freddie Mac show no inclination of changing their policy, several national portfolio lenders will underwrite to a different standard for their portfolio programs. They will deduct alimony and child support payments from gross income, not treat them as bills. If you are divorced and pay alimony, run your numbers to see what they look like. If you have such a problem, don't bother fighting a losing battle with a rigid, unsympathetic lender. Start out with a mortgage broker. He or she will be able to find a compatible source much faster than you can.

Delegated PMI Underwriting

I've explained how difficult it can be to find just one underwriter to approve your loan. If your loan request is over 80 percent LTV, you have to go through it all again with another underwriter because you must also be underwritten by one of the private mortgage insurance (PMI) companies. Not only does that step add two or three days to the approval process, it introduces another hurdle you must leap over to earn final and complete approval. Therefore, if your loan has an LTV higher than 80 percent, I recommend taking it to a lender who has *delegated underwriting* authority. With such a lender, the PMI company has authorized the lender's underwriters to do PMI underwriting, as well as you have to convince only one person to understand your file.

EZ QUALIFIER AND STATED-INCOME LOANS

If you fall into one of the problem categories I've defined in this chapter, you know that you may have a tough time getting a loan even though know you can afford the house payment. I recommend that you look for an EZ Qualifier–type loan. They come in a number of forms with different names, such as no-doc, EZ Qual, no-income-verification, stated-income loans, and even ones where you do not even have to state your income. Typically, you fill out the application as for any other loan, but the lender does not ask you to *document* the income via 1040s, W-2s, paycheck stubs, or Verification of Employment forms. The lender still calculates ratios, but uses the income stated on the application. For many borrowers with unusual circumstances, these loans provide the only means to buy a house.

Consider the case of Bob Wright, a real estate developer who experienced severe financial difficulties in the early 1990s when the real estate industry went through a crunch. As commercial rents fell and occupancy declined, his company lost money for several years. He was able to pay his bills on time and avoided foreclosure on his buildings by using his savings. When rental rates increased, his company returned to profitability, and he signed up a number of new long-term tenants. With his income prospects looking good, Bob decided to buy a new home. If he were to submit a full-doc application, the underwriter would deny it. Two years of losses have dragged down his average income, so he wouldn't qualify. The solution is to state his current monthly income on his application and submit it under EZ Qual guidelines. The lender doesn't get into all the documentation about the bad times, and Bob's loan will be approved.

Not So Easy

By now, you're no doubt wondering why everyone doesn't avoid all the headaches posed by full-documentation loans and take the easy way out. The reason is that EZ Qual programs have their disadvantages as well.

First, most lenders are not as liberal on loan-to-value ratios for EZ Qual loans as for full-doc programs. Here's a typical LTV matrix comparing the two:

	Full Doc	**EZ Qual**
Purchases and rate/term refinances	95% to $300,000	80% to $300,000
	90% to $400,000	75% to $400,000
	85% to $500,000	70% to $500,000
	80% to $650,000	65% to $650,000
	75% to $1,000,000	N/A
	70% to $1,000,000	N/A
Cash-out refinances	80% to $300,000	70% to $300,000
	75% to $400,000	65% to $400,000
	70% to $500,000	N/A

You can see that the lenders are demonstrating risk aversion here, and I don't blame them; after all, they're parting with a lot of money. If they can't verify income to support the loan, they must rely almost solely on the equity in the home to protect them.

A second disadvantage is the added liquidity requirements. Lenders take more risk with EZ Qual loans, but they may require that you have $10,000 or $20,000 in the bank—enough to weather a few storms. One large lender requires that you have an amount equal to 75 percent of your annual income in the bank.

Others ask that you have six months' worth of housing payments in the bank. Be sure to ask up front; otherwise you may lose precious time, or worse, the home. This is another area where experience and competence are essential and where a mortgage broker can really help you out. Note, in determining liquidity, lenders usually count 100 percent of your cash, 75 percent of the value of stocks and bonds, and 50 percent of the value of IRA or pension plan balances. They don't count all of it because of the tax consequences of such liquidations.

A third disadvantage is that most EZ Qual loans come at some additional cost. In addition to being more restrictive on LTV, most lenders will add to the rate, the points, or both. Often, the charge is reasonable, such as ¼ point to fees—and even that may be eradicated if the LTV is less than 70 percent. Other lenders, however, may add ¾ point to fees or ⅛ percent to the rate. Be sure to ask the right question up front, "What is the extra charge for your EZ Qual programs?," not "What are your rates?," because a lender will not reveal these add-ons unless you ask.

Fourth, many lenders now require EZ Qual borrowers to sign a release form that allows the lender to check with the IRS about the borrower's income. Several large national lenders now require this for all full-doc loans, too, before the loan is funded. The following IRS forms are used: 4506, 95-01, or 88-01. These forms allow the lender to find out from the IRS the income you declared on your last two years' 1040s. If your adjusted gross income for each of those years was $20,000, and you put down on your application that your income was $50,000, expect trouble. You could be accused of loan fraud, a felony punishable by heavy fines and imprisonment. Some borrowers, such as our Bob Wright who experienced tax losses for several years, would be penalized by a lender using this system. As a response to this negative factor, some lenders will not require you to sign one of these forms. They recognize that a laid-off aerospace engineer or someone in real estate may actually make $50,000 in a new or rebuilt career but that he or she might not want to show 1040s for the period of lower income. If this situation applies to you, I recommend that you ask about the use of these forms when you are interviewing lenders.

Today, some lenders will not even ask you to state your income on the application. This is helpful for anyone who has been out of the country and is returning to a business that may not have shown any taxable income for a couple of years.

Finally, the EZ Qual loan area is a very fluid segment of the business right now, and I expect it to become more liberal. As I write this, one lender is doing 95 percent LTV EZ Qual loans for amounts up to $300,000. However, the lender has added one more hurdle—a FICO score higher than 700. Yes, it's restrictive, but not unreasonable, and there are no add-ons to the price.

CONCLUSION

As a borrower with special income circumstances, do not assume that you are necessarily relegated to an EZ Qual. Portfolio lenders, such as an S&L that plans on keeping loans in its portfolio, can be more flexible because they don't have FNMA looking over their shoulders. They can approve a loan that makes sense if they like an applicant's property and other aspects of the transaction. I encourage you to check out such sources.

Some lenders will use a concept called *residual income*. A couple with an income of $2,000 per month has fewer dollars left over after paying taxes and monthly expenses than someone making $10,000 per month. *Residual income* is the amount left after paying taxes and other expenses, so the higher-income family has more dollars every month, or more residual income. It costs only so much to feed and clothe a family, so lenders may be more lenient in qualifying people with larger incomes. If your income is over $75,000 per year, but your ratios are too high and you've been turned down by an A lender, I'd bring up this concept, particularly with a portfolio lender. My experience is that the better lenders are more understanding.

When interest rates go up, qualifying theoretically gets harder because it takes more income to qualify for every dollar of loan. However, other expenses (food, clothing, education) are more or less constant, so as rates go up lenders typically loosen credit standards. I can remember getting lots of 35/45 loans approved when rates were high in the early 1980s.

Finally, sort of as a last resort, choose a B/C lender. B/C lenders love it every time FNMA and FHLMC tighten their standards. Their experience is that FNMA and FHLMC are way too strict anyway, and these lenders are very happy doing "FNMA turndowns. This is the area in the mortgage industry that has experienced the most growth in the last year or so (1996–1997), and I suspect this will continue. You can also expect A lenders to start their own B/C departments. If they can't approve you under an A program, they'll kick your application over to the B/C department and do your loan at a higher rate. *Hint:* If you get such an offer, be careful. Almost all B/C loans have prepayment penalties associated with them, typically 3 percent for three years or 80 percent of six months' interest—about 4 percent. That's a lot! That means you have to pay more, and you have to pay it for a long time! If you have to go this route, ask about paying another 1 point now to buy out of the prepayment period after 1 year. That gives you a year to clean up your problems and refinance into an A loan.

If your income is complicated, my best advice to you is this: Find the most competent, experienced loan officer you can. Be very direct in asking questions about each lender's underwriting procedures and policies. You do not want your loan sent 1,000 miles away for underwriting. Do not underestimate the importance of having your loan handled in a local office where your loan officer and the branch manager can keep tabs on it and, if necessary, come to the rescue.

REFINANCING

KEY POINTS

- Many homeowners do not know the current status of their mortgage. Therefore, they cannot determine when a refinance could benefit them.
- Refinancing just because everyone else is doing it is foolhardy.
- Any refinance plan should be undertaken within the context of a larger financial plan, not just to reduce the monthly payment.
- There are many reasons for refinancing, and each one involves a different strategy

No topic in real estate financing is subject to more misconceptions than refinancing. In brief, refinancing is the right of every borrower. It is your right to terminate the contract by repaying the loan in full when you wish. By contrast, unless you are in default, your lender cannot come to you and say, "You're paying only 7 percent and we can invest the money we lent you at 10 percent now, so we want to terminate the contract and have you pay the money back."

Sadly, the right to refinance is not exercised as intelligently as it could be, because most homeowners do not remember the details of their current loan, and therefore cannot make meaningful comparisons with alternatives. If you are contemplating a refinance, before continuing, put the book down, dig out your loan documents, and make some notes to remind yourself of the details of your current loan.

SHOULD YOU CONSIDER A REFINANCE?

In 1993 and early 1994 there was an avalanche of refinance business because long-term interest rates dropped below 7 percent. Millions of homeowners who had purchased their homes between 1980 and 1992 had 8 to 11 percent mortgages, and they all wanted to trade in for a better rate. But it wasn't falling rates that actually propelled this refinancing binge. That first wave of astute people initiating refinances made the news; that news alerted millions of other, less-tuned-in people, and that was what created the onslaught. My point is that by knowing your loan terms, you will be better prepared to make a decision regardless of what others are doing—or not doing.

Should you consider a refinance? Yes! I want you to throw away everything you ever heard about a mortgage being a loan for life. That concept went out with the era of 1 percent inflation, 3 percent interest rates on savings accounts, and 6 percent mortgages. A loan is a financial instrument not significantly different from stocks and bonds. You wouldn't think of buying stock and holding it for 30 years, would you? Of course not. Even the most static long-term investors reevaluate their holdings on a regular basis. You should look at your mortgage the same way. This is cyclical world, and homeowners can often find an alternative loan to better meet their changing circumstances. People start families, get promotions, become empty nesters, and retire. Obviously, no one type of loan is best in all of these circumstances.

Knowing When to Refinance

Too many people are intimidated by the refinancing process and are thus hesitant to find out how a refinance might benefit them. They think that someone is going to sell them something of no value and they'll end up losing money. They concentrate on the negative, *cost,* rather than on the positive, *savings.* Nationwide, this is a boon to lenders because people's inertia means they keep high-yielding loans in their portfolios. When pressed, however, lenders admit that perhaps as many as 20 percent of borrowers could benefit from a refinance but just don't know it.

It is the "sheep syndrome" that most often motivates people to consider refinancing. Homeowners hear through the grapevine that everyone else on the block is doing it, and they want to jump on the bandwagon. This is the wrong reason to refinance. You should *always* be open to reevaluating your needs, regardless of what others are doing.

Evaluating a refinance is really quite simple—and painless. You can do it yourself or with the help of an expert. The key is this: Add up the costs and add up the benefits. If the benefits exceed the costs, refinance. If the costs outweigh the benefits, do not. The money you spend refinancing should be regarded as an investment. Your return on that investment is the savings on your loan in the form of reduction in interest expense.

Let's view this graphically by looking at Figure 16.1. Say your loan is currently at 9 percent and you find out that rates have fallen to 7 percent. If you maintain your current loan, you'll be on the top line of the graph. If you refinance, you'll be on the bottom line. In this example, you save the difference, 2 percent per year. If it costs a total of 2 percent (for example, $2,000 on a $100,000 loan) to refinance, you'll get your money back in one year, as shown by the crosshatched block on the graph.

Let's try another example. Assume that rates have fallen to only 8 percent, not 7 percent. You can see from Figure 16.2 that it takes twice as long—two years—to recoup your refinancing costs, because you are saving only 1 percent per year. Of course, determining costs and benefits may not be quite that easy, but it is a logical process.

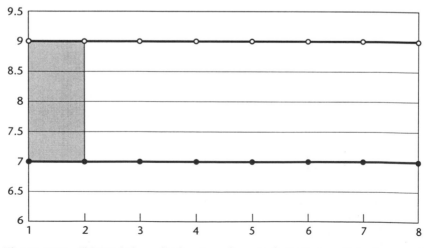

Figure 16.1   Determining whether to refinance from 9 percent to 7 percent.

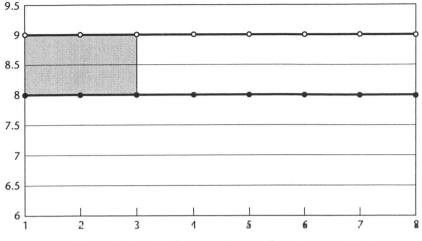

Figure 16.2   Determining whether to refinance from 9 percent to 8 percent.

The Larger the Loan, the Greater the Benefits

Perhaps you've heard it said that it takes at least a 2 percent drop in interest rates before it makes sense to refinance. This is because there are some fixed costs in refinancing your home. With an average-size loan of $60,000 or $70,000, it *does* take a 2 percent drop in rates before a refinance makes sense. But for those with larger loans, it is easier recoup those costs with a much smaller drop in rates. Let me demonstrate.

I'm going to use zero-point loans for this example, and I define a "good deal" as one where you recoup the costs of the refinancing within two years. In the following chart, line 2 (origination costs) shows what might be considered reasonable costs, which I've increased on the larger loans to reflect their slightly higher costs. Line 3 (savings per year necessary) is line 2 divided by 2 because we want to recoup costs in two years.

	Loan 1	Loan 2	Loan 3
Loan balance	$50,000	$250,000	$500,000
Origination costs	$1,500	$2,000	$2,500
Savings per year necessary to recoup costs	$750	$1,000	$1,250
Rate decrease required to create savings	1.5%	0.4%	0.25%

As you can see, it takes a 1.5 percent drop in rates to generate $750 per year in savings. This is what's needed to recoup (in two years) the $1,500 costs of refinancing a $50,000 loan—hence the 2 percent rule. The average loan in this country is $68,000; the average house is worth about $105,000. When you look at it this way, you see why someone with a $50,000 loan is far less likely to refinance; rates have to make a major move before he or she could benefit.

On the other hand, the homeowner with a $500,000 loan can afford to be more opportunistic about his or her loan. In general, borrowers with large loans should almost never pay more in points than they can recoup in two to three years. Because they can benefit significantly from relatively modest shifts in the market, they should have a friend in the mortgage business who can regularly update them on market conditions, just as a stockbroker calls clients about investment opportunities. Needless to say, I am not advocating that such borrowers refinance every time the rates drop ¼ percent, but you can see that it *could* make sense.

When a borrower is buying what is probably his or her last home, particularly if retirement is approaching, it is safe to assume that it is also the borrower's last loan, in which case it makes sense to pay more points and buy down the rate.

REFINANCING EXAMPLES

Example 1: *Refinancing to a Lower Rate*

Julie Harrison bought her home at a time when rates were high. Let's assume that she has a $150,000 loan at a rate of 10 percent. She knows that rates have fallen, so she is considering a refinance to a lower rate.

This is a refinance the sole purpose of which is to lower the rate. With a 10 percent fixed-rate mortgage, it's easy to establish that as a starting point. Julie calls a few lenders and determines that rates are 9 percent for zero points but that she will have to pay the other loan costs. She calculates that she can save $1,500 per year, 1 percent of $150,000. Next, she finds out what the costs are. Let's look at Julie's costs to refinance.

Appraisal	$275
Credit report	$50
Processing and underwriting fees	$500

Title insurance	$450
Settlement or escrow	$450
Flood certification	$15
Tax service	$75
Reconveyance fees	$75
Recording fees	$100
Total	$1,970

Julie's benefits are $1,500 per year and her costs are $1,970. She can now figure out how quickly she can recoup her costs:

$$\frac{\$1,970}{\$1,500} \times 12 = 15.76, \text{ or around 16 months}$$

This is a good investment, so she should do it. Every year thereafter, she saves another $1,500. In my experience, if you can recoup your costs in less than 24 months, you should proceed with the refinance. If, however, this is a long-term situation for Julie, it will probably be advantageous for her to pay some points rather than take the zero-point loan. For a further discussion of this important topic, refer to Chapter 11. In brief, most buy-downs—the trade-off of rate for fees—have a breakeven of between three and four years. If Julie is sure that she will be in the house that long, it will be to her advantage to pay the points. But it is important to do the initial analysis at the zero-point rate. Then calculate the value of additional buy-downs as we did in Chapter 11.

An overlooked but important factor is the *term* of the new loan. If Jane took out her initial 30-year loan seven years ago, she's almost certainly going to be offered another loan amortized over 30 years. That means that between loan 1 and loan 2, a total of 37 years will have elapsed before she owns a home free and clear. When she refinances, I recommend that she increase the payments on her new loan to pay off her home within 30 years of the initial loan. She should also follow this strategy if she buys a new home. People may stay in a home for only seven years, but they should attempt to pay off their most recent home within 30 years of purchasing the first one. If Julie bought her first home at age 30, she should try to pay it off by the time she reaches 60.

To accomplish this, she should figure out the additional payment required to amortize the new loan in 23 years. In this example, the refinance would lower Julie's obligatory payment from $1,316 to $1,207, but would add seven years to the payment period. If she were to keep making a payment of $1,316, she converts the interest rate savings into additional principal reductions, thus reducing the term of the new loan to 21½ years. *This is an excellent move, and I recommend a similar strategy to every borrower.* If Julie's income is such that she would be comfortable making an even larger payment, she should consider shortening the maturity of the loan even further, perhaps to 15 years, which would reduce the rate yet again. Refer to the Chapter 17 for more details.

Example 2: *Short-Term Refinancing*

Edward Martin has a 9 percent loan, which he would like to refinance, but his employer has told him that he might be transferred in a year or two. He wonders whether he can save money in the intervening period. Edward should not consider the same refinance plan as Julie, because he's not going to be there to benefit from long-term rate protection, which is the purpose of a fixed-rate loan. A one-year T-bill ARM makes more sense. These are always available with start rates 2 or 3 percent under current rates. Instead of an 8 percent fixed-rate loan, Edward is offered a 6 percent ARM with no points. The benefit of an ARM is three times greater because Edward can lower the rate for the first year from 9 percent to 6 percent. This 3 percent difference multiplied by $150,000 equals $4,500 savings in the first year, and the costs are the same as Julie's, $1,970. Edward can recoup the costs in only 5.25 months. If it turns out that he is still around in year 2, the rate will go up to index plus margin, say 7.5 percent. That cuts his savings down to $2,250 (9 percent minus 7.5 percent equals 1.5 percent times $150,000) in the second year, but that's okay, because he recovered his costs long ago.

Be warned, however, the lender is subsidizing this loan through the below-market 6 percent teaser rate. Sometimes the lender will want to ensure that you stay around for a while by insisting on a prepayment penalty for the first three years of the loan. A penalty of 2 percent of the balance is $3,000, which would wipe out most of Edward's savings! If you are going use this refinancing strategy, *be sure you check with prospective lenders about prepayment penalties,* and go with a lender that doesn't charge one.

Example 3: *Empty-Nest Refinance*

Morgan and Mary Benson's kids are finally out of college, so they have more disposable income. They wonder if they can own their home free and clear when he retires. A 15-year loan will ensure their objective and is sound financial planning. Also, 15-year loans are cheaper, usually about ½ percent lower than 30-year loans. Even though the monthly payment is greater than for a 30-year loan, the important point is that all the savings are converted into principal reduction. Morgan and Mary could accomplish their objective even more quickly by boosting their monthly payment even higher.

Too many homeowners simply do not comprehend the tremendous savings that accrue to them by shortening the maturity of their loan. In fact, this may be the most overlooked option in the mortgage industry. Why? Well, not surprisingly, once you have established a good payment record, the lender wants you around for a while, paying all that profitable interest. Paying your loan off more quickly is exactly the opposite of what lenders want, so they don't mention this option to their customers. For more information on this important alternative, refer to Chapter 17.

Example 4: *Falling-ARM Refinance*

Nancy Pearson secured an adjustable rate mortgage when she bought her home, but rates have fallen, and she's considering a refinance to protect herself from future interest rate fluctuations. This is an excellent strategy, because every borrower with an ARM should get a fixed-rate loan when rates fall, assuming he or she will be in the home for at least three or four years. Even if Nancy's ARM is at the same rate as a fixed-rate loan, she should do it. She should regard the costs of the refinance as the premium on an insurance policy in the following manner. Let's assume Nancy will be in her home for 10 years; if it costs $2,000 to refinance, her "insurance policy" costs her only $200 per year. Sounds like cheap protection, doesn't it?

Nancy's boldness is an exception. My experience is that people are more resistant to this type of refinance than to any other. As I write this in 1997, millions of homeowners have ARMs tied to one-year T-bills and CDs on which the current rate is in the 8.25 to 8.75 percent range, and COFI ARMs are about 7.5 percent. FNMA 30-year loans are about 7.25 percent and the FIRMs, such as 5/1 loans, are 7 percent and lower. On a $200,000 loan, savings of 1 percent amounts to $2,000 per year! People could switch from an 8.5 percent ARM to a 7.25 percent fixed-rate loan and recoup the costs of refinancing in six months or less. Let me reiterate the first point I made in this chapter: Maintain an ongoing awareness of your loan so that when an opportunity arises, you know it and can take advantage of it.

Example 5: *Neg-Am Refinance*

Jack and Sue Freeman have an 8 percent ARM, but they heard about a loan starting at 3.5 percent and think this loan might be better for them. Jack and Sue need to be careful here. With such low start rates, the lender is almost surely advertising a negative-amortization loan. Some people hear a low start rate and just become mesmerized by it. Yes, their payments can go down dramatically. I've done COFI loans with start rates as low as 2.95 percent, and if you are paying 8 percent, your payment is going to drop substantially. So what's wrong with this?

The start rate applies for only the first three months of the loan, after which the interest rate goes to back up to index plus margin, about 7.4 percent in this case. So the real savings is only .6 percent, not 4.5 percent, and the borrower still has an adjustable rate mortgage. Dropping the rate from 8 percent to 7.4 percent is not enough of a benefit to justify spending a couple of thousand dollars on the refinance. Are the better alternatives? Try this one.

At this same time Jack and Sue were offered this deal on an ARM, conforming 15-year fixed-rate loans were at 7.375 percent with zero points. Why have an adjustable loan at 7.4 percent when you can have a fixed-rate loan for 7.375 percent? If Jack and Sue don't like the higher payment of a 15-year loan, how about a 5/25 loan or a 5/1 FIRM, both of which are fixed for the next five years, also at 7.375 percent with zero points? Either of these alternatives is better than another ARM. As a general rule, if you going to switch ARMs, look at the index plus margin and find out where rates are going. Read Chapter 6 on ARMs for more information.

Example 6: *Cash-Out Refinance*

Ted and Margaret Walton's kids are starting college next year and they need extra cash to pay tuition. Does it make sense to refinance to get the cash? I have to admit that I tapped some of the equity in my home to pay tuition when I had two kids in college at the same time. Certainly, one way to accomplish this is to refinance and take out some cash. In retrospect, however, financing four years of education with a 30-year loan doesn't make sense. A better choice is to get an equity line and, after the kids graduate, make accelerated payments to reduce it to zero as quickly as you can. Refer to Chapter 17 to learn more about equity lines.

Having said that, there is a reasonable exception to what I just said: When you have a nonoptimal loan and are considering refinancing anyway, then it makes sense to refinance and take out the extra cash you need. As of this writing, 30-year fixed-rate loans are about 7.5 percent and the equity lines are from 8.5 percent to 9.5 percent, so for Ted and Margaret, it's cheaper to refinance than to get an equity line.

In general, whenever you refinance and use some of the proceeds to pay for a college education or for something depreciable like a car or a boat, work out an amortization table that will show you how quickly you can get the loan balance back to its prepurchase level.

Example 7: *Expansion or Remodel Refinance*

Brian and Fran Wilson are considering adding a bedroom, expanding the family room, and remodeling their kitchen. Should they finance the work with a home-improvement loan, or should they refinance with a larger loan? Because the improvements to the property are permanent, I think it's perfectly acceptable to finance them with a long-term loan. But Brian and Fran still need to do some rate analysis. If they have a nonoptimal loan that justifies refinancing, it makes sense to go ahead and refinance the whole loan, taking out extra money at the same time. If, however, their existing loan looks good compared with current alternatives, then they should examine their options, because it generally costs at least $2,000 to refinance the primary loan. By comparison, a home-improvement loan may cost only $500, and many equity-line loans are free. If Brian and Fran aren't able to justify the $2,000 plus costs with savings on a new first TD loan, then a refinance just adds $2,000 to the cost of their project and should be rejected.

OTHER REFINANCING INFORMATION

Prepayment penalties were instituted by the industry to ensure yields on loan portfolios for a longer period of time. Although they almost disappeared in the 1980s, you may still run across them, so it's important to be aware of them. They have reappeared in the 1990s for two reasons. First, the volatility of interest rates has caused a higher rate of loan payoffs, upsetting portfolio managers' calculations and reducing profitability. Second, the widespread use of zero-point loans, in which a lender subsidizes the loan, reduces profitability in the first year. Lenders want to avoid these losses, so they have begun reintroducing prepayment penalties.

Even if your note calls for a prepayment penalty, the law in your state may limit its enforceability. For example, the law may give the lender the right to collect a penalty only for the first five years of the loan, after which collection cannot be enforced, in spite of what the loan document says. Again I urge you to read your loan documents. If necessary, check your rights with an attorney. Don't always believe your lender, because the person you talk with may not be well informed.

If your loan has such a penalty, and it is enforceable, there's still a way to avoid paying it. Lenders will frequently give you the option of switching to another type of loan they offer—their motivation being to keep you as a customer. Nine times out of ten, the new loan won't have a prepayment penalty. In addition, they may charge only $250 for the new loan. Ignore the other terms of the new loan, because once you have it, if it's not what you want, you can then refinance into the loan you *do* want—*without* the penalty.

Three-Day Right of Rescission

Refinance transactions of an owner-occupied residence are subject to a RESPA-mandated three-day period during which you have the right to rescind the transaction. The rescission period is designed to protect consumers from hasty decisions made under high-pressure tactics. Say a homeowner pays for something, such as new aluminum siding, by taking out a second mortgage on his or her property. If a problem arises and the homeowner stops payment, his or her home is at risk of foreclosure.

This kind of thing happened often enough that Congress decided to act. In addition to Truth in Lending disclosures, the

Consumer Credit Protection Act of 1968 granted customers a period during which they could reconsider a financial commitment that would put their homes at risk. During this cooling-off period, people can take the forms home to study or to discuss with a lawyer or some other expert for validation. The refinance of the loan on a residence is covered by this law, although refinance of rental property is not.

Here's how the right of rescission works. Let's say you sign loan documents on Thursday. The three-day period starts at midnight that day and the three days are Friday, Saturday, and Monday. (Sundays and holidays don't count; perhaps you can't think about it on those days.) You can cancel the transaction during this period, but if you don't, the loan could fund on Tuesday. If you sign on a Monday, the three-day period runs Tuesday, Wednesday, and Thursday; the lender could theoretically fund the loan on Friday, but we almost never do that because the settlement agent cannot make the payoff to the previous lender until Monday. That means the borrower would have to pay interest on both loans over the weekend, usually over $100 in extra interest payments. So when you refinance, be sure to work with your lender to schedule the funding in the middle of the week, and transfer the money electronically to ensure the previous lender gets the funds quickly.

Interest Payments in a Refinance Settlement

In a refinance, allocation of interest is very confusing to many people. First, mortgage interest is paid *in arrears*. That is, when you make your regular mortgage payment on the first of the month, you are paying the interest that accrued during the prior month, plus a small amount for principal reduction. Let's say that you are settling (closing) on August 10. When you made your payment on August 1, you paid the interest that accrued during July. The lender deserves another 10 days' interest for the time you used its money; therefore you deposit 10 days' interest with the settlement agent or escrow company that is handling the transaction, and they send it to the lender. The new lender is giving you money for the remaining 20 days of the month, so you need to deposit interest for that lender, too.

In this way, you pay one month's interest, and it's split between the lenders: 10 days' worth to your previous lender and

20 days' worth to the new lender. There is some good news, though. You don't have to make a payment on the first of the next month—you've already paid the interest. Your first payment isn't due until the first of the *following* month.

CONCLUSION

I want to close this chapter the same way I started it: by admonishing you to "stay in touch" with your mortgage. Millions of otherwise financially astute homeowners forfeit billions of dollars every year because they don't know the details of their mortgage, don't stay in touch with a mortgage expert, and don't take advantage of money-saving alternatives. Don't be one of those people.

FIFTEEN-YEAR LOANS AND ACCELERATED PAYOFFS

KEY POINTS

- The majority of the public thinks a 30-year loan is the standard loan. This chapter makes a case for the 15-year loan.
- You can save a huge amount on interest if you make higher payments.
- Biweekly payment plans are beneficial for some people, and you don't need to pay someone else to do it for you. It's not complicated; you can handle it yourself.

Compared with other amortization alternatives, the 30-year loan has two features that make it a compelling loan for many people: It has a very low payment, and it is the easiest to qualify for. The payment is low because it is essentially an interest-only loan in the early years; that is, only a very small percentage of the payment is going toward principal reduction. At an interest rate of 10 percent, for example, 95 percent of the payment is going to interest and only 5 percent to principal. Keeping the payment low is important to first-time home buyers who are stretching themselves to buy the largest home they can. Thus, the 30-year is their loan of choice. But for a significant number of other home buyers, qualifying is not a major issue. For many of them, the 30-year loan is not the best choice.

In fact, 99 percent of all lenders offer loans that are fully amortized in 15 years. Let's examine the benefits of those loans. At any given time, perhaps 30 percent of borrowers should have a 15-year loan, yet it enjoys only about a 5 percent share of the market. That other 25 percent is missing an opportunity for significant savings.

A MORTGAGE IS A TOOL

A loan is a tool; it enables you to buy a home when you have accumulated only a small percentage of the purchase price. On the day escrow closes, the mortgage is your friend. Thereafter, you should treat it as your enemy and try to eliminate it as soon as you can. This is accomplished by reducing the principal quickly, which does *not* happen with a 30-year loan.

From the lender's perspective, most of the risk of approving a loan occurs during the first year. If, for one reason or another, borrowers are unable to make their payments, their problems usually become apparent during this time period. After that risky first year, however, lenders have a vested interest in keeping your interest coming in for as long a time as possible. Remember, most loans are sold in the secondary market, so your "lender" is merely the collector of the payments—and is paid handsomely for doing so. The fee is based on the loan amount, and the lender/service is happy if the loan balance stays high. If a lender has a servicing portfolio of $1 billion in January, and if the principal reduction is 5 percent during the year, the portfolio has been reduced to $950 million by December, and the lender's servicing income has declined by 5 percent. Obviously, lenders are not as keen on 15-year loans, which pay off even faster, thus reducing their income still more quickly.

BENEFITS OF A 15-YEAR LOAN

Look at Figure 17.1 to see graphically what happens with different amortization periods. The graph shows the relative distribution of interest and principal on a 30-year loan. Note that more than two-thirds of the payments go to interest—over twice the amount of the initial principal balance.

Now let's look at the same loan on a 15-year amortization schedule. In Figure 17.2, note that the interest paid drops from $215,928 to $93,427 and is *less* than 50 percent of the total payments. Also keep in mind that the interest rate on 15-year loans

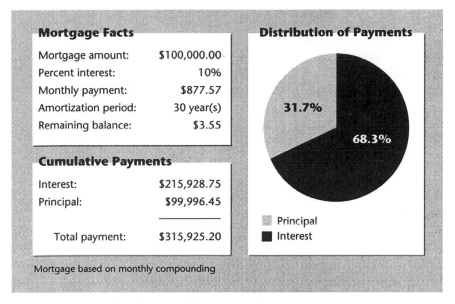

Mortgage Facts	
Mortgage amount:	$100,000.00
Percent interest:	10%
Monthly payment:	$877.57
Amortization period:	30 year(s)
Remaining balance:	$3.55

Cumulative Payments	
Interest:	$215,928.75
Principal:	$99,996.45
	———————
Total payment:	$315,925.20

Mortgage based on monthly compounding

Distribution of Payments

31.7%

68.3%

▨ Principal
■ Interest

Figure 17.1   Distribution of interest and principal on a 30-year loan.

is about ½ percent less than on 30-year loans. If you redo the calculations at 9.5 percent instead of 10 percent, you will find that the total interest paid drops even further, to $87,961—compared with $215,928. Now you can understand why I think 15-year loans are so terrific.

One of the arguments in favor of 30-year loans is that the homeowner can deduct mortgage interest from taxable income, a significant benefit. Criticism of the 15-year loan is the loss of tax deductions after 15 years. That misses the point. Unless the marginal tax rate is 100 percent, when you write a check, it still costs you money, just not as much. If we look at the taxes saved with a 30-year $100,000 mortgage compared with a 15-year loan, the difference over 15 years is only a little over $20,000. Even if you consistently invest the taxes saved (that's a big if), the benefit is only marginally better—not enough to compensate for the fact that after 15 years, the person with the 30-year loan still owes $75,000 on the original $100,000 he or she borrowed. The 30-year borrower paid $37,000 less in the first 15 years, but in the second 15 years, he or she still has to pay another $125,000, while the 15-year borrower pays zero!

It *is* true that if you were to take the money you save as a result of making lower payments on the 30-year loan—about

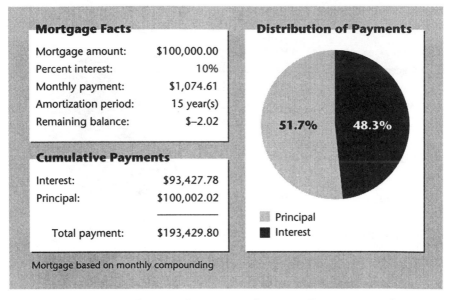

Figure 17.2   Distribution of interest and principal on a 15-year loan.

$200 per month in our example—and invest it, you *could* come out ahead. But that's true only if you can get a return on those funds that's at least as high as the note rate. If you have an investment account that gives you a return of exactly 7.5 percent, those funds will grow and be equal to the remaining loan balance after 15 years. You then could just write a check out of that to pay off your mortgage. But if your average yield is lower than the note rate, you lose. How many people get those kinds of returns? Of course, well-managed mutual funds and high-yield bond funds do this today, but the average consumer doesn't make use of the vehicles that allow him or her to earn that kind of return consistently year after year. And you must make the investments consistently or you lose.

Earning a Return on Investment of 20 Percent

Most arguments against 15-year loans are theoretical and ignore one very practical fact—they are cheaper. Figure 17.3 demonstrates that a 15-year loan is typically priced well below a 30-year loan. For jumbo loans greater than the conforming limit

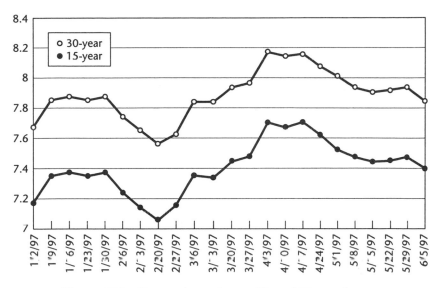

Figure 17.3   Comparing rates on 15- and 30-year loans.

(currently $227,150), the differential is typically even greater. Thus, with a 15-year loan, not only do you benefit from the accelerated payoff, but you save on the interest rate as well.

No doubt some of you are thinking, "His analysis is good *if* I keep the loan until maturity. But I'm going to sell my house in a few years and buy another. Can I still benefit from a 15-year loan?" That's a good question. The trick is knowing how to measure this advantage over a shorter term. Remember that even if there were no difference in rate, whenever you send in extra money on your mortgage payment, you get a return on investment equal to the note rate; that is, if you had an extra $1,000, there would be no difference between making a new investment with a 7 percent return and making a principal reduction on your 7 percent mortgage—except that when you pay down your loan, your yield is locked in, and very few investments offer that kind of guarantee.

My approach to analyzing this situation treats the ¼ to ½ percent lower interest rate as a bonus for being willing to commit to a 15-year loan's higher monthly payment. Then I assign this "bonus interest" as the marginal return on investment of the additional payment. Let me show you what I mean on a $100,000 loan, assuming this time a ⅜ percent difference.

	Rate	Interest	Principal
30-year loan	7.5%	$625	$74.21
15-year loan	7.125%	$593.75	$312.08
Difference	0.375%	31.25	$237.87

Your reward for committing to the $237.87 extra payment is a $31.25 bonus. Divide that $31.25 by $237.75 and you're up 13 percent on top of the 7 percent return you were getting anyway—a total ROI of 20 percent. Obviously, this kind of ROI is tough to beat in any market, but it's especially good today when CDs are yielding only 3 or 4 percent.

Saving versus Investing

Let me get a little philosophical here. When most people talk about *saving* $200 per month, they make it sound as if they were investing that money. The fact is, the majority of people do not *save* these kind of funds; they *spend* the money on something else. *Spending* money is different from *saving* it. Thus, an additional advantage of the 15-year loan is that it encourages discipline, forcing borrowers to build equity in their home.

Financial discipline is in short supply these days. The very fabric of our economy is powered in great part by the engine of consumption. Most peoples' wish lists include items such as a new house, a new car, a new refrigerator, or a new TV, rather than alternatives such as making additional deposits to the 401(k) plan at work, adopting a systematic investment plan, or saving for the kids' college education. In the last 17 years in which I have been a mortgage broker, many clients have told me, "I want the 30-year loan but we intend to make extra principal payments to pay it off faster." But when they come into my office again five years later, perhaps to refinance or to buy a new home, 80 percent of them haven't paid an extra nickel. The truth is, a lot of people simply do not have the self-discipline to make this commitment on their own, or other things pop up every month that take priority over paying something extra on their mortgage. I encourage you to examine your motivation and discipline when making this decision. Your choice will have a long-term financial impact: Own your home free and clear 15 years from now, or still owe 75 percent of what you do today. The 15-year loan is one of the most powerful investment tools available for home-owners.

If you go through this kind of analysis on your loan and it seems as if the 15-year loan is just too much for you, consider a 20-year loan. Most lenders offer 20-year loans at the same price as their 30-year loans, but several national lenders price the 20-year loan about halfway between 30- and 15-year pricing. That should be an incentive for you to shop around. Another alternative is the 10-year fully amortized loan. This is not for everyone, but for someone who is already a few years into a 15-year loan, the pricing is the best in the market, about ¼ percent under jumbo 15-year pricing, making it the lowest fixed-rate loan in the market!

[WARNING] Beware of what I consider the worst alternative, the 40-year loan. True, the payment is lower on a 40-year loan than on a 30-year loan, which might make a difference in qualifying, but on a $100,000 loan, lowering the payment from $665 to $621 is inconsequential compared with not building any equity.

ALTERNATIVE RAPID AMORTIZATION PROGRAMS

For a number of reasons, a 15-year loan is unattainable for some people, especially if they can't qualify for it because the under-writer won't count a portion of a borrower's real income. For people who wish to adopt an accelerated payment schedule any-way, I work out special amortization tables to help them make additional payments that will help meet their objectives.

[TIP] If you are skilled at Excel or Lotus 1-2-3, these tables are included in all computer spreadsheet programs these days, and you can run sample amortization schedules yourself. If you do not have a computer, have a friend run one for you. You can also order a worksheet from me using the form at the end of the book or by going to my Web site at http://www.loan-wolf.com.

Whatever your methodology, I encourage you to be aggres-sive in adopting a savings plan. Foremost among your goals should be making the maximum possible contribution to tax-advantaged retirement programs, such as a 401(k) at your place of employment. After that is taken care of, adopt a rapid amorti-zation schedule for your loan.

Biweekly Payment Plans

There are 26 biweekly periods in a year, and if someone were to make one-half of his or her mortgage payment every two weeks, it would amount to the equivalent of 13 monthly payments, thus amortizing the loan more quickly. The problem is that most lenders and loan servicers do not have a mechanism for collecting payments on a biweekly basis. They are set up to accept 12 monthly payments per year and perhaps an occasional extra payment. They do not have processing methods to accommodate 26 payments per year (nor do they want them).

Some entrepreneur figured out that it is possible to accommodate borrower and lender by establishing a special escrow account to accept the 26 payments from the borrower and then, once a month, disburse loan payments to the lender, including the extra amount. Using this method will pay off a 30-year loan in about 23 years—a definite benefit. What's the catch? Well, there are two. Most, if not all, services require that the payment be deducted every other Friday from your bank account. This is fine for many people, but for those who like to make payments when it is convenient for them, this feature is problematic. The other, and more significant, catch is that this process is expensive. Most services charge a setup fee of $400 or $500 and then tack on an annual processing fee. I do not question that providing this service should come at a price, but I think that borrowers can do this themselves at little or no cost. Let me show you how.

Remember that making a biweekly payment means there are 13 biweekly periods in a year. If you make 26 half payments, it's the same as making 13 payments. There are three ways to accomplish this:

1. Make a thirteenth payment once a year, either in December or at some other time.

2. Spread out the thirteenth payment by adding 8.33 percent to every payment.

3. If you get paid every two weeks, set up a savings or money market account and transfer one-half of your payment into it every two weeks; then make the payments to the lender as appropriate. (Be sure to maintain whatever minimum balance is required to earn interest on the balance in the account.)

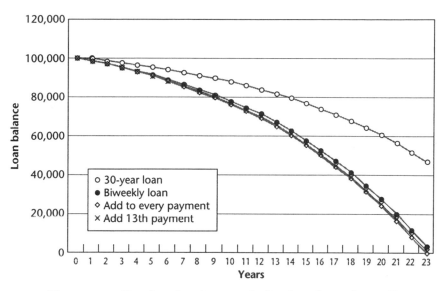

Figure 17.4   Results of various methods of accelerated payoff.

Look at Figure 17.4, which shows the principal reduction for each method just described compared with a biweekly payment. You can see that each of these methods produces an almost identical result, and mine won't cost you anything.

SUMMARY

Accelerated payment plans that pay off loans quickly are a highly underrated savings and investment plan for many people. If the additional payment is not a financial strain, you should consider a 15-year loan when you purchase a home. Those whose loans are above-market rate and who are attracted by the merits of my arguments should consider a refinance, because the interest rate differential—an extra ½ percent—will provide more incentive to help finance the cost of the transaction. For others whose with loans that are at or below the current market rate, adopting an accelerated plan of any type will yield significant long-term benefits.

EQUITY LINES, SECONDS, AND REVERSE MORTGAGES

KEY POINTS

- Although at one time not very respectable, second trust deeds and equity lines offer some consumers unique opportunities to meet their financial needs.
- Reverse mortgages offer older homeowners the opportunity to convert equity in a home to a more comfortable lifestyle.

Once upon a time, not so long ago, in a galaxy not very far away, there was a world inhabited by needy borrowers and shady lenders. This was the world of second trust deeds, where desperate borrowers, driven by unusual circumstances, sought lenders who were eager to profit from others' misfortune. In the penultimate reaches of this world, if you missed a payment, someone in a long, black coat with an unusual first name would come calling on you. The human condition being what it is, I'd suspect that loan-sharking is still around, but most people do not think of that when they hear some television infomercial promising to solve their financial woes. "Lost your job?" they ask, "We don't care. Overwhelmed by bills? We don't care. Come to XYZ Funding! Money in as little as 48 hours upon verification of equity." When you hear that, you know that the land of 15 percent 10-point loans is not in another galaxy, it's only a phone call away.

Those are the lenders that we in the industry call "hard moneylenders." The difference between them and the lenders I represent is simple: The lenders I deal with go to extraordinary lengths to assure themselves that borrowers can and will make the payments on their loans. Hard moneylenders transfer that responsibility to borrowers. If they don't make the payments, the lenders will take away their homes.

Recently, however, the *second trust deed* has earned a new a sense of legitimacy within the safe haven of the commercial banks. It is interesting and informative to explore this world because second trust deed lending is now a legitimate business for both borrower and lender. Seconds get their name from the fact that they are recorded by your county clerk as a lien against your property in a *second* position, after your normal mortgage, which is in *first* position. If you already had a first and a second, the next loan would be a *third.*

THE ADVENT OF EQUITY-LINE LOANS

An equity line is really just a specialized form of second, one where the balance can go up and down. They became popular after the passage of legislation that affected the deductibility of interest. Previously, the interest you paid on all types of loans was deductible on Schedule A of your tax return, which reduced the cost of borrowing. When, in 1989, Congress started to phase out deductibility of interest on all personal loans *other than* real estate loans secured by your principal residence and a second home, it meant you couldn't deduct interest on car loans, boat loans, college loans, credit card debt, and so forth.

This change in the tax laws posed a threat to business as usual at the bank. Not being able to deduct interest paid on such loans meant effective interest costs were raised by 30 or 40 percent. In a business where even a small rise in the cost of borrowing chokes off purchasing of certain items, the banking industry immediately saw the threat to their business and responded by offering *equity-line loans.* These loans may be used for any purpose and are secured by the equity in your home—*which makes the interest tax deductible.* Securing such loans is relatively easy. You are approved for an amount consistent with your income and the equity in your home. Let's say that your home is worth $100,000 and the current balance of your first trust deed loan is $50,000. Using a yardstick of 80 percent LTV, the equity in your home represents another $30,000 in borrowing power ($100,000 × 80 percent = $80,000 − $50,000 = $30,000). And you don't have to take all that money at once. Usually, the bank gives you a checkbook, and whenever you want money, you just write a check. You pay back the loan monthly, usually making interest-only payments for the first 10 years, and then making higher payments that will amortize the loan, if you are still in the house.

Benefits of Equity-Line Loans

With your equity line in place, you can go down to your automobile dealer, buy a car, and instead of going out and shopping for a loan, simply write a check for it. Unlike the car loan, the interest on your equity-line loan is deductible on Schedule A of your 1040. You can understand why people like them. The banks like them, too. First, it replaces many car loans and other unsecured personal lines of credit, so the risk factor is lower. Unlike a car loan, where someone can drive the bank's collateral to Mexico, the house doesn't move. The banks discovered that the payment record improved, too, because people were pledging the equity in their homes as collateral. As a result, equity-line loans have become very popular with both borrowers and lenders. Recent statistics show that more than 25 percent of homes have equity lines on them.

Features and Uses of Equity Lines

In addition to tax deductibility, another advantage of the equity line is that you can repay the loan, then take it out again for another purpose later, pay that back, and so forth. With a normal second TD, you just get it and pay it back. The uses for equity lines are limited only by your imagination, although here are some of the most common:

- To purchase a car, boat, or recreational vehicle
- To finance a college education or other educational expenses
- To finance home improvements
- As a debt consolidation loan to pay off credit card debt or other unsecured debts
- To pay taxes for self-employed people whose cash flow is uneven

- As regular monthly income for people who get huge bonuses once a year and pay off the equity line with the bonus

These are all constructive uses of equity-line loans. But people *can* be carried away with them and forget that they must be paid back. If you secure an equity line, be sure to work out a repayment plan before you write the check. You do not want to finance groceries for 30 years. As a rule of thumb, schedule the repayment period to be at least as equitable as the rate of physical depreciation of your purchase. For example, if you use your equity line to buy a car, repay it in three or four years so that the balance is zero when you want to buy your next car.

If you are using an equity line as a debt consolidation loan, add up what you would have been paying on your old loans and pay at least that same amount so you'll amortize the debt over just a few years. (Note, this is *not* the obligatory minimum payment! Your purpose is to *pay off the debt,* not just lower the payment!)

$\boxed{\textit{WARNING}}$ Equity-line loans are recommended only for those people who have the discipline to repay them. Too often, the equity-line checkbook gives people the feeling that the money is free! If you are not a well-disciplined person, walk the other way.

Pricing

The major banks have become competitive on equity-line loans. The pricing can be extraordinarily complex. In brief, here are the details:

- Pricing is usually tied to the prime rate. For larger loans, those over $75,000, it can be at the prime rate, which is 8.5 percent as I write this, or perhaps .25 percent over prime. That's very attractive. For smaller loans of $25,000 or so, pricing might be prime plus 1 percent or prime plus 2 percent. It may also be tied to the six-month CD rate plus 3 or 4 percent, putting the actual rate in the 9 percent range today.
- Recently, many lenders have been offering 90, 100, and even 125 percent LTV loans. I recently received a fax from a lender offering 135 percent LTV loans. Once LTV goes

over 80 percent, however, the rate usually goes up to 12 percent or even higher. (*Note:* interest on the loan balance that exceeds the value of your home is *not* deductible.)

- For the first period, frequently called the *draw period* (perhaps 10 years), your monthly repayment is either interest only or a flat percentage rate of the outstanding loan amount (for example, 1 percent of the balance). If you owe $17,000, you pay $170 per month.

- After the draw period, the loan goes into a mandatory repayment period during which it is fully amortized, typically over the next 20 years.

- The up-front costs are lower than on a typical first TD mortgage loan.

- The interest is almost always variable.

- An annual fee may be charged whether the account is used or not.

- There are lenders that offer free equity-line loans to the most creditworthy borrowers. When I say free, I mean *free:* no appraisal cost, no title insurance, no escrow, no funding fee, nothing. Lenders will pay brokers $400 to originate such loans for them. If you add $400 to the other costs, you can assume that the bank is paying about $1,000 to get that loan on the books. So you know that the bank is planning to make much more than $1,000 over the life of the loan.

- Lenders other than the big banks have also gotten into the equity-line business. Usually, the loans they offer are like other loans where you pay for the appraisal and other costs. They might require only a "drive-by" appraisal, a cheaper report that does not require a physical inspection of the property, and the title policy may be only a $100 "special" instead of a full policy.

Unlike the highly competitive market for A loans, the features and pricing of equity lines are highly variable between lenders, so you will have to make a bunch of phone calls. Start out by talking with friends and neighbors; narrow it down quickly to companies that are offering the kind of loan you want. Check with the big national lenders, the local commercial banks, and your credit union, if you are a member of one.

TRADITIONAL SECOND TRUST DEEDS

You already know that an equity line is really just a specialized form of second TD, one where the balance can go up and down. The traditional second is not like that. You borrow $15,000 at 10 percent and pay it back over, say, five years at $318.17 per month. These loans are still alive and well and available in many places. A common one is the home improvement loan. Seconds make up a respectable segment of the business these days, to some degree because so many borrowers refinanced at 6.5 or 7 percent in 1993 or 1994. When they want to add a swimming pool, they aren't going to refinance their primary loan because that would increase that lovely 6.5 percent loan to 8 percent. A better method is to finance it with a second TD loan. The same thing goes for almost any other home improvement.

Seconds are amortized over a shorter period of time than normal first TD mortgages, usually 5, 7, 10, or 15 years. Typically, they have fixed interest rates, commonly above 10 percent, and the interest rates do not vary on a daily basis as do the rates on first TD loans. You may get a choice—for example, 10 percent and 2 points, 10.5 percent and 1 point, or 11 percent and no points. You will also be expected to pay the up-front costs, although they will be less than on a first TD.

Certain home improvement loans have another desirable feature: The lender will calculate the loan on the basis that you've already made the improvement. Let's say that you have a $100,000 home but owe $80,000 on your first TD. You are already at 80 percent LTV, so many lenders aren't going to be eager to lend you more money. But you want to add a bedroom and expand the family room at a cost $12,000. The lender doesn't want to be at 92 percent LTV as would a "normal" lender, so the appraiser goes out and looks at the property and your plans. The appraiser says, "If the improvement were made, it would make the home worth $110,000. The bank then might be willing to lend you $8,000, or maybe even the entire $12,000, depending on their policy. If you want to do something like this, check with your contractor, because many of them have arrangements with banks to "finance" their jobs at reasonable rates.

Another good feature of the home improvement loan is that the lender will be looking over the contractor's shoulder, making sure the construction is being done right and that suppliers and subcontractors are being paid on time.

To decide which is best for you, an equity line or a fixed-rate second, gather the numbers and plow through them to determine *total loan costs* over the period of time it will take to get the money, use it, and pay it back. Obviously, the shorter the period, the better a no-cost equity line will look, but the risk is that the interest rate may rise.

NINETY PERCENT EQUITY LINES AND SECONDS

Perhaps elated by rising property values and an improving economy, lenders have begun to offer 90 percent equity lines. For some purposes, such as landscaping a new home, even paying interest of 10 or 11 percent may be very cheap money compared with the alternative—putting it on your credit card. That tax-deductible 10 percent is a bargain compared to your credit card's non-tax-deductible 18 percent. For other purposes, be cautious. All the preceding warnings apply even more, because the equity cushion left to protect you is less.

NO-EQUITY LOANS

Last year, for reasons that are unclear to me, lenders started offering 100 percent LTV seconds and even *125 percent* LTV seconds. After those loans fund, *you have no equity left,* hence the name. That means if you have a $90,000 mortgage and your home is worth $100,000, the lender will offer you an additional $35,000, for a total debt of $125,000. We'll see how that shakes out. One of the most insidious by-products of no-equity loans is that the homeowner is shut out from being able to refinance the underlying primary loan. Lenders who are doing these loans are convinced that they are following prudent underwriting practices by approving these loans. They are using tight standards and doing them for only A-paper borrowers. As one underwriter said, "We aren't lending money to people who aren't paying their bills. We think they'll pay us, too." Perhaps they are right.

Having said that, *Loan Origination News,* an industry publication, recently reported that 125 percent LTV loans are the hottest new products today. I think they are hot because lenders are making obscene profits on them, making the cost of borrowing to consumers very high. Those lenders target people with substantial credit card debt, and their sales pitch of lowering the interest cost from 18 percent to 12 percent can sound attractive. However, the first year's cost may be over 20 percent, and interest on any loan amount over 100 percent LTV is probably not tax deductible. I hope that you have taken to heart all my advice about doing business with reputable people. If you really need such a loan, I would not respond to a telephone solicitation; hang up and find a reputable lender in your own hometown instead.

Title 1 Loans

A special case of these no-equity loans is the Title 1 loan, named after the HUD law that enabled it. The limit is low, between $15,000 and $20,000 at this time, and the money must be spent to improve your property. For certain very specific purposes, this may be the perfect loan. On the good side, lenders don't ask a lot of questions. You don't even have to tell them what the loan is for other than to improve your home. On the bad side, even though it is possible to get rates in the 10 percent range, on typical loans the rate is more likely to be 13 percent, and most lenders charge 5 to 10 points. That's pretty expensive money and, in my view, makes it a loan of last resort.

TAX RESTRICTIONS

Congress realized that as soon as the tax benefits of borrowing were phased out, homeowners would start getting equity lines to pay off their car loans. And so they did. When Congress floated the idea of limiting or eliminating the deductibility of interest on second homes, I funded some loans for clients who used the proceeds to pay off the mortgages on their second homes. Finally, Congress did limit the deductibility of interest. To the best of my understanding, this is what you can and cannot do, but check with your CPA, attorney, or other tax adviser for advice on the current law before you take action.

- When you first purchase your home, you establish acquisition indebtedness. To that number you may add the cost of any permanent improvement to the property (for example, adding a new bedroom).

- The limit is determined by adding another $100,000. You may not deduct interest on any loan amounts greater than the limit. If you have enough equity, however, you can still get an equity line larger than that because the bank won't care about your tax issues; you just won't be able to deduct interest on an amount over the limit.

- Finally, there is also a limit on total indebtedness of $1,000,000.

Let us work through an example:

Home cost	$100,000
Original loan	$80,000
Improvements	$35,000
$100,000 cushion	$100,000
Total limit	$215,000

With the average home in America worth about $105,000, most people are not going to be affected by the rules. Again, if you think you are, or might be, affected by these rules, consult your adviser.

THE REVERSE MORTGAGE

The reverse mortgage is a special type of loan that has piqued the public interest in the last few years. A reverse mortgage is a way for a senior citizen who is "house rich" and "cash poor" to convert the equity in his or her home into a monthly income. This is a very realistic and practical alternative to selling the house, converting the equity into income-producing investments, and living in a rented property for the rest of his or her life.

FHA had the first program on the market, followed by FNMA's program; because there is such keen interest, no doubt there will be others. Having said that, at least one major private firm that offered these loans has announced that this division is for sale, indicating its performance was less than stellar. Let's look at a few common features of the programs.

- Borrowers must be 62 or older.
- The property must be owned free and clear, although existing indebtedness can be paid with the funding of the reverse mortgage.
- The property must be a single-family detached home, an approved condominium project, or a planned unit development.

Working in Reverse

When the reverse mortgage is in place, the terms provide that the owners will receive a certain monthly income, very much like an annuity. They will continue to receive payments as long as one of them continues to live in the property, and a surviving spouse or other co-owner may continue to receive benefits even though the total amount paid out exceeds the value of the house. To that extent, reverse mortgages are a wonderful tool for some people. Note, too, that qualifying, as for a normal loan, is irrelevant because you don't have to figure out whether the borrowers can make payments—the lender is making payments to the owners, not the other way around. This type of mortgage carries with it many of the features of an insurance policy. As in all insurance, if you do the insurance underwriting properly and get a big enough pool of participants, everything works out just fine. That's one reason why the current major participants (FHA and FNMA) are huge institutions that can afford such risks.

On the negative side, reverse mortgages are very expensive to institute. Costs of 5 and 6 points are not uncommon. In addition, the purveyors of these loans are, in some cases, people who either don't know what they are doing or are incompetent. As with the 125 percent LTV loans, firms advocating reverse mortgages seem to be making extraordinary profits, paid for by people who can ill afford to be doing so. If you think that a reverse mortgage may be the solution for you, review it within the boundaries of a comprehensive financial plan developed with the help of a professional in the field, preferably an attorney or a financial planner with whom you have already had successful dealings.

CONCLUSION

Equity lines are an important part of today's mortgage market. Because of the tax deductibility of interest on such loans, and because of their low acquisition costs, homeowners should evaluate them as potential solutions for many of their financial problems.

Traditional second trust deeds also fill an important niche in the world of lending. The field is wide open, and as time progresses, more and more legitimate lenders will enter this segment of the business. Although the loans are typically much smaller than regular first TD loans, shop carefully. On a percentage basis, the costs can be high. Although $1,000 in fees doesn't seem too high on a $200,000 loan, that same amount is 5 *percent* on a $20,000 second. On top of, say, a 10 percent interest rate, that means you'd be paying 15 percent the first year. Is it worth it? Perhaps, but you need to run the numbers carefully.

Reverse mortgages are a gift from heaven for elderly homeowners who are struggling to make ends meet in a postretirement world. As with many exotic financial products with limited distribution, this is not as competitive a field as the rest of the lending business, so I would be especially careful. Deal with only the most reputable people whose credentials you have thoroughly checked out.

As a consumer, during the coming years you will be bombarded by mailers and other solicitations urging you to get one of these loans. As good as they sound, remember that they all come at a cost, sometimes a high cost. The higher the pressure to select one, the more cautious you should be.

NO-COST AND ZERO-POINT LOANS

Salesmanship is the art getting someone to suspend his normal sense of caution and disbelief long enough for you to get into his wallet.

—ANONYMOUS

KEY POINT

- There is no such thing as a free lunch. Zero-point and no-cost loans come at a price, no matter what they promise.

The California Department of Real Estate made the following announcement when it forbade mortgage brokers from advertising zero-cost loans to the public: "Advertising claims . . . of 'no cost' or 'no fee' loans are patently misleading and are in violation of Business and Professional Code Section 10235." That public-service announcement was released to put an end to shady promotions that have proliferated in recent years. Slick telemarketing reps would phone homeowners with a script like this: "If I could show you how you could lower your mortgage payments by $200 per month, and if I could do it for free, would you be interested?"

We have discussed at length how the marketing departments at the large lenders try to manipulate borrowers and get them to believe something that isn't what it appears to be. The no-cost loan is the epitome of the huckster's art, the ultimate misdirection, and it is responsible for borrowers paying tens of millions of dollars in extra interest. Usually, these loans are a terrible deal for consumers, but when people hear the word "free," they are interested. If it sounds too good to be true, it *isn't* true. No-cost loans are particularly insidious because they pander to the consumer's natural desire to save money. Getting a loan isn't cheap by any standard, so this sales pitch can sound like a miracle to the unsuspecting homeowner.

As you know by now, I'm against people wasting money on points or anything else. You should pay points *only* when it is to your advantage to do so. I've arranged lots of zero-point loans, but only when they were warranted because of the customer's needs. As a general rule, if you are going to be in a property for more than three years, it makes sense to pay points. By refusing to pay a dollar in points now, you are giving up three dollars in future benefits—a poor bargain. Of course, those who are trying to convince you that it's a good deal always talk about *now,* not the future. Let's analyze in detail a typical situation in which perhaps a million borrowers found themselves.

BORROWER BEWARE!

Let's assume that you have a $200,000 loan at 9.5 percent and the payment is $1,700 per month. The loan rep who called you said that he or she could lower the payment to $1,500, thus fulfilling the promise made in the pitch: to save you $200 per month. When you do the math, it means the rep has to lower the rate from 9.5 percent to 8.25 percent. That sounds good to you, so you proceed to fill out the application.

The loan is processed and approved, you sign the docs, the loan funds, and everybody's happy, right? So why is this a bad deal? The reason is simple. You, the borrower, focused on the word *free,* and you never stopped to evaluate whether it was the *best* deal for you. Had caution reared its head, you might have mused to yourself, *If someone I never heard of can do that for me, I wonder what else is available.* Let me illustrate a better approach.

Originating loans is my business. I provide advice and counsel to people and arrange financing for them. I do it well by providing value for them, and I get paid for doing that. But I am their *agent,* and they are allowed to know how much money I make on their transaction. If they want, they can negotiate my fee. Typically, I earn from 1 to 1½ points on my deals, depending on loan size and the complexity of the transaction. My customers and I think this is fair.

By comparison, lenders use zero-cost loans to disguise the fact that they make *huge commissions.* All of the costs are buried, including the commission. If you ever ask a question about compensation, you're likely to get this response: "Look, this isn't costing you anything. It isn't relevant what I make on the transaction." Most people do not know how to respond to this kind of statement so they let it go. They shouldn't. To see how this whole process works, let's go through a transaction in more detail.

Let's say a borrower comes to me and asks me to do the following loan, and we agree that 1 point is reasonable compensation on the deal. He'll pay all the other fees, say another $2,000. If the market allows lenders to market a zero-cost loan at 8.25 percent, it will also allow me to secure a 7 percent loan at 1 point, as I agreed to do with my client. This would lower his payment, not just $200, but a whopping $371 per month. Let's compare the two loans using as our benchmark the total amount of interest paid over the first five years and the loan balance at the end of five years. Here's how it breaks down:

Rate	Points	Costs	Payment	5 years' interest	Loan balance at end of 5 years
8.25	0	0	$1,502	$80,720	$190,568
7	$2,000	$2,000	$1,331	$68,099	$188,263
Difference	$2,000	$2,000	$171	$12,620	$2,305

Clearly, the borrower saves a lot more with a loan I arrange. He pays $4,000 ($2,000 in points and $2,000 in costs), but he pays $12,620 less interest, a net saving of $8,620. In addition, he owes $2,305 less on the loan the loan I arrange. Bottom line, I save my client $10,924 compared with the zero-cost lender. That's almost $3 in savings for every $1 up front, and that's just in the first five years.

It's not that zero-cost transactions are inherently bad, but when they are advertised, the inducement of no initial cost is almost invariably a smokescreen that enables the lender to make more profit than on normal transactions. The broker in this example received a gross commission of 3 points for delivering an 8.25 percent loan in a 7 percent market, a total of $6,000. Out of that, the lender pays the $2,000 costs and keeps $4,000 as a net commission, twice as much as I make. What does the customer get in return? Simple: a more expensive loan, one that costs almost $11,000 more over the first five years.

Let me state this another way. If the telemarketer were completely truthful, he would have said:

> *We offer a loan where you pay nothing—no points and no costs. By saying it's free, we try to induce you into making an application with us. We like it because we make $4,000 on it.*
>
> *Or you could agree to pay points and costs and get a much lower rate. We would only make $2,000 on this loan, and over the next five years, this alternative will save you more than $11,000 over the zero-cost loan I first offered you.*
>
> *Which do you prefer?*

No one ever says this, but that's exactly what's going on. There are a number of journalists and other writers who still write that homeowners should get zero-point loans because they are risk-free. As we have seen, such reasoning is faulty and mortgage people don't agree with the journalists.

One reason behind the proliferation of these loans is that some wholesale lenders pander to mortgage brokers who market these loans by offering a fee structure that encourages these deals. I frequently see flyers offering rebates of 3 and 4 points. Those rebates aren't being offered for the benefit of the end client, the borrower. They are being offered to induce brokers to do zero-cost loans. In spite of the Department of Real Estate's warning, this sales gimmick is still being pitched on a regular basis. I saw an infomercial on TV last week, and during the half-hour show, I'll bet they said, "At XYZ Mortgage, you never pay any fees," a dozen times. Only once did they mention that the rate would be "slightly higher." In my mind, 8.25 percent is significantly more than "slightly higher" than 7 percent. It's misleading.

FLIPPING AND PREPAYMENT PENALTIES

Ironically, this practice can bite the lenders back. In the example, the lender who funded this loan made an investment of $206,000; he funded a $200,000 loan and paid $6,000 to the broker in the form of the 3-point rebate. Because the interest rate was higher—8.25 percent, well above the market rate of 7 percent—the payment was $171 higher, too. After three years, the lender received 36 payments, each $171 higher, so they lender recouped the extra $6,000 it paid the broker. If the loan stays on the books for longer than 36 months, the lender finally comes out ahead. But the lender is in trouble if the borrower comes in after six months and says, "You know, rates have fallen even further and I'm going to refinance again. Here's the $200,000 I borrowed from you." The lender squirms because it recouped only about $1,000 in extra payments in those six months, and it has to take a loss of $5,000. There's no way to recoup that money, as every loan transaction stands on its own.

Some brokers even made a practice of going back to the same borrower six months later and "flipping" the borrower themselves, offering the same deal I would have done for them in the first place—7 percent at 1 point. Remember that deal *still* offers $11,000 in savings over five years. This broker makes $2,000 on the second deal in addition to the $4,000 it netted on the first transaction—a total of $6,000 in six months on a $200,000 loan.

How do a lenders protect themselves against being bitten? In the form of prepayment penalties, of course. When lenders offer you a zero-point deal, they are giving you something of value for no immediate income for themselves. They have to make a profit somewhere along the line, and if it's not now, it's got to be later. A prepayment penalty is their way of ensuring that you stick around. Prepayment penalties are not discussed by loan reps because they are a negative factor, and salespeople don't like to talk about negatives. But many large lenders are requiring penalty clauses on all loans for which they have to pay a rebate of more than ½ point. If you are contemplating a zero-point or zero-cost loan, even with a lender who is treating you fairly, don't get caught. Ask if there is a penalty; if there is, inquire about comparable pricing without the penalty. You'll probably like the alternative better.

SHOULD YOU EVER CONSIDER A ZERO-POINT LOAN?

There are times when a zero-point loan does make sense. As we learned in examining rate-versus-fee alternatives, it takes three or four years to recoup the cost of points paid to secure a lower interest rate. If you are going to have the loan for only one or two years, then you shouldn't pay points. Let me share a few situations in which I can make a case for zero-point loans:

- Frank and Mindy Hughes purchased a new home in February, but it took the builder six months to finish the home. When they entered into the agreement to purchase the home, rates on a 30-year fixed-rate loan were 7 percent, and they were elated. But during the next five months, rates rose to 8.5 percent. They still want the home, but they're concerned about the higher payment. Unless there are some pretty dark economic storm clouds on the horizon, I would recommend they consider a zero-point 3/1 FIRM. Such a loan is likely to be about 7.25 or 7.5 percent. Their payment isn't much higher than they anticipated, and because they didn't pay points, they won't mind refinancing next year when rates fall (I call this a "disposable" loan). Yes, there is some risk that rates won't come down far enough to allow them to refinance in three years, and it turns into an ARM in year 4, but the ARM rate is likely to be only 8.5 percent, which is what they were going to pay anyway. They saved a total of 3 percent, so they have a cushion built up.

- John and Martha Garcia have a 9.5 percent loan but think that they may sell their home in a year or two. They should consider one of the zero-point one-year T-bill ARMs that are widely available at start rates under 7 percent. They'll save 2.5 percent the first year, enough to recoup their costs, and probably less the next year. But by then they're out of the house and into the next one. As we discussed, beware of prepayment penalties on loans like this.

- James and Nancy Jordan have purchased a $700,000 home, putting $200,000 down and securing a $500,000 loan. You will remember from our earlier discussion about refinances that people with such large loans can benefit from a refinance in the event of even minor changes in interest rates. If James and Nancy can secure a zero-point loan at 8 percent, they can benefit from a refinance even if rates slide to 7.5 percent. I'd do it myself and hope that rates would fall. However, if rates get to historic lows—for example, 7 percent represents the lowest rate over the last 25 years—then James and Nancy should consider paying points and buying down the rate even further, because that rates will move even lower. The lower the rate, the less likely it will be.

- Henry and Marie Tucker are first-time home buyers. They have managed to save 5 percent for a down payment and have enough cash left over to meet the lender's and PMI company's reserve requirements, but they are really short on closing costs. This is going to be a long-term acquisition for them so they'd like to pay points, but they just don't have the money. There is a solution, however, and it involves getting the seller, whether it's builder of a new home or the owner of a resale, to pay nonrecurring closing costs. Let's say the home is worth $100,000. The seller isn't likely to agree to a $100,000 sale price and then pay $2,000 in costs, which is tantamount to selling the home for $98,000. So your initial offer might be something like this: "Price to be $98,000 and seller to pay $3,000 of buyer's nonrecurring closing costs." Say Henry and Marie finally settle on the following: "Price to be $103,000 and seller to pay $3,000 of buyer's nonrecurring closing costs." It is almost impossible for appraisers to tell the difference between a $100,000 and a $103,000 home anyway, and, frankly, other buyers are getting these concessions, too, so it's okay from the market standpoint. Lenders have very specific policies about how much they will allow, typically 3 percent of the purchase price in 95 percent LTV transactions and higher amounts as the down payment increases. When they complete the transaction, Henry and Marie can use the $3,000 to pay points to buy down the rate and, in effect, finance the points with the higher sales price. You can see that knowing exactly what you can and can't do with your lender is another advantage of getting prequalified before house-hunting.

CONCLUSION

If someone calls you and offers a zero-point or zero-cost deal, or if you see an ad for one, be very wary. Most of them are what I call "sucker loans." The deal may look good to you because "free" offers are tempting. Refinancing makes sense for many people, as we discussed in Chapter 16. If a zero-cost refinance looks attractive, you should investigate further, but you should use a reputable, trustworthy lender and rely on the principles and procedures you have learned throughout this book.

TECHNOLOGY:
THE INTERNET AND
SOFTWARE

KEY POINTS

- The Internet is the key to access an enormous amount of valuable mortgage information that can dramatically improve your chances of getting the right loan and saving money.
- Through the Internet, you can seek loans from companies across the country, some of which may be more efficient and offer lower pricing than your local lenders.
- Commercially available software can help you analyze your situation and make better decisions.

From my point of view, the definition of an efficient market is one in which both buyer and seller have the same information, or at least access to the same information. In the stock market, certain investors may be smarter than others, but all of them have access to an enormous amount of information about public companies. This is also true in the real estate market. Both buyer and seller have access to the same information about recent sales of comparable homes. On the other hand, this is *not* true of the mortgage market. Lenders have far more information about rates and programs than do home buyers, who are interested in this information only once every 5 or 10 years. Even the rate surveys regularly published in newspapers on Saturday mornings are advertisements paid for by lenders; they are made to look like independent surveys. As I have admonished repeatedly, your goal as a home buyer and borrower is to find someone who will share this information with you and educate you about loans and the process of getting one so that you can you make informed decisions about what is best for you and your family. Today, technology, in particular the Internet, has made equal access to this information possible.

THE MORTGAGE INDUSTRY ON-LINE

The Internet has the capability to expand your knowledge and speed up the learning process. It levels the playing field, empowering borrowers by giving them easy access to information that traditionally has not been available to them. Although there is no accurate way to determine this, I would hazard a guess that there are over 10,000 sites purporting to offer information about mortgages. Needless to say, some of these are terrific and some are not. As with all sources of information, it is still the responsibility of the individual to verify facts and check out authenticity of the sources. In any case, there is substantially more information than you can find in your local newspaper or even in some of the finance-oriented national magazines, and most of it is accurate, timely, and reliable.

The big lenders are very visible on the Web. They have the resources to display fancy sites costing $100,000 or more to develop. Keep in mind that a beautiful Web site is no guarantee of a customer-friendly operation. Behind a pretty face may lurk a huge bureaucracy that is just as indifferent to customers as its counterpart in your city. It is important to know how to analyze the information you find on the Internet, and this book will help.

To get you started, I'm going to recommend some Web sites to check out and then show you how to use the information you find. Although there is a lot of hype about Internet connectivity and millions of people have Internet access, many millions more do not. For those who don't have such access but who are intrigued enough to have read this far, let me suggest that you get a friend to help. Almost everyone I know who is on the Web is delighted to introduce the "unconnected" to its possibilities. Failing that, many libraries and community colleges offer computers with Internet access, along with people to assist you. I would guess that in the future, community services will offer education programs for home buyers that will include Internet access.

To understand the organization of the material that follows, you need to understand that an Internet Web site has an address, just as you do, but a Web address is known as a Uniform Resource Locator (URL) and looks something like this (my company's site): http://www.loan-wolf.com. If you tell your computer's Internet browser to Open Location and then type in my URL, it will find and display my home page. Let's look at some useful sites.

Government Sites

> **http://www.hud.gov**   This is the URL of the Department of Housing and Urban Development under which the Federal Housing Administration governs loans and lenders. The FHA library offers publications on line, such as the Guide to Closing Costs at http://www.hud.gov/fha/sfh/sfhrestc.html. This is the booklet that lenders must give you when you apply for a loan, but you should read it sooner than that.
>
> **http://www.va.gov**   This is the URL of the Department of Veterans Affairs, which administers VA loan programs.
>
> **http://www.ftc.gov**   This is the Federal Trade Commission (FTC) site, which contains a terrific reference library of guides to loans, credit repair, and other items of interest to homeowners.

LEARNING ABOUT RATES ON-LINE

When shopping for a loan, the big question everyone wants answered is, "What are your rates?" The Internet is a good place to find the answer to that question, but first I want to explain what you will find so you can better integrate the information into your decision-making process.

As I've stated repeatedly, the conventional 30-year fixed-rate loan that will be sold to Fannie Mae or Freddie Mac is a commodity. Every lender who sells loans to FNMA or FHLMC will get the same price, meaning the cost of acquiring money is substantially the same for all of them. There are minor exceptions to this statement, but they usually are not apparent in the retail market or in the prices you see. Ultimately, to you, the difference between one lender's price and another's is determined by the markup they apply to their cost of funds.

Rate Markup

Typical retail businesses buy merchandise for $5 and sell it for $10, what is referred to as a 50 percent markup. At the end of the season, those retailers have a 25 percent off sale and sell their products for $7.50. Much of the public thinks that the mortgage business is conducted the same way, that if one lender is at 9 percent, another will have a sale rate of only 6 or 7 percent. Wrong! The total markup on loans is only about 3 percent, not 50 percent, and there are a lot of costs that need to be covered by that 3 percent.

The markup for mortgage money twofold. One portion pays for servicing the loan—that is, collecting the payments and remitting them to the owner of the mortgage. That portion is about 1.5 percent and originates in the secondary market. To consumers, it is neither visible nor negotiable.

The other 1.5 percent is the markup to the retail customer. That 1.5 percent has to pay the salaries of the loan rep, the processors, the underwriters, the document staff, the people who fund the loans, and certain overhead expenses such as rent and management. Industry trade groups gather data from lenders, and these data show that the loan origination function actually loses money. The reason lenders can stay in business is that they sell the servicing rights on some of their loans—remember, it's worth about 1.5 percent—to other companies; the profit from such sales covers their losses. In short, the loan origination business is one with very slim margins, and there is not much room for discounting—meaning that the pricing differences among lenders on the standard FNMA/FHLMC-type loans is going to be very small.

Enter the Internet

Some types of loans, especially the easier ones (to borrowers with clean credit and W-2 income), can be originated on the Internet at a lower cost than they could be funded by a fully staffed local lender with higher overhead. Remember that lenders are looking for borrowers who are easy to deal with, those who will have a higher approval rating and will cost less to handle. They think they can find these borrowers on the Internet. If their costs are less, lenders can lower pricing and still make money. As a well-qualified smart shopper, your goal is to use the on-line information to find one of these lenders and secure a loan at a better price than less-informed consumers are getting at the same time.

Although you can use one of the many Internet search engines such as AltaVista or Infoseek or directory services such as Yahoo!, using standard keyword searches of words like *mortgage* or *real estate loan* will yield literally hundreds of thousands of responses, which is practically useless because no one can deal with information on that scale. To give you a head start, I'll list several sources that I know to be valuable in one or more areas. As you become more familiar with the way the information is organized, you can go off on your own search missions.

Quasi-governmental Sources

http://www.freddiemac.com The Federal Home Loan Mortgage Corporation (Freddie Mac). At this site, go to the News page, and follow the route to the PMMS, the Primary Mortgage Market Survey. (*Primary* refers to the market between borrowers and lenders, as opposed to *secondary,* the market between lenders.) This is one of the most valuable sites on the Internet for mortgage shoppers. A sample of its survey is shown in Figure 20.1. From this information, you can compare what you are being offered with the rates posted by more than 100 major lenders across the country. If you are just starting your search, you immediately know what rates most people are getting. If you are an above-average borrower, you should get an above-average deal, and from the Internet, you'll know what "average" is. If you are well along in the process and are getting ready to lock, use the information to keep your lender honest.

http://www.fanniemae.com The Federal National Mortgage Association (FNMA). This site offers a great deal of information about FNMA's programs, especially new ones that may be of interest to you. Be sure to spend some time here.

Other Nonbiased Sources

http://www.hsh.com HSH Associates has a wealth of information gathered weekly from 2,500 to 3,000 lenders. In

PRIMARY MORTGAGE MARKET SURVEY RESULTS

30-YEAR FIXED-RATE MORTGAGE

	US	NE	SE	NC	SW	W
Average	7.74	7.68	7.75	7.82	7.74	7.74
Fees and points	1.7	2.0	1.6	1.4	1.7	1.8

15-YEAR FIXED-RATE MORTGAGE

	US	NE	SE	NC	SW	W
Average	7.25	7.16	7.25	7.375	7.24	7.26
Fees and points	1.7	1.9	1.6	1.3	1.7	1.8

ADJUSTABLE RATE MORTGAGE (ARM)

	US	NE	SE	NC	SW	W
Average	5.53	5.30	5.63	5.69	5.47	5.56
Fees and points	1.3	1.7	1.2	1.0	1.4	1.2
Margin	2.78	2.80	2.80	2.8	2.77	2.74

Figure 20.1   Freddie Mac's Primary Mortgage Market Survey.

addition, you'll find comprehensive historical data on the performance of each index used by purveyors of ARMs. HSH also has a low-cost service for finding rate data in your area.

http://www.briefing.com   This is Charter Media's site. For a modest charge of $6.95 per month, you can tap into the latest news on the stock and bond market. You'll also find financial charts and a valuable mortgage commentary. You really should access this source. I'd recommend charting the yield on the 30-year bond *every day* while you are shopping, right up until you lock in your rate. In Chapter 10, we learned how much money you can save by locking in at the right time, and this will help you determine that time.

http://www.dbc.com   The Data Broadcasting Corporation site has current data on Treasury securities with all maturities. You can also use this site and briefing.com to update the prices of stocks in your portfolio.

Other Sources of Real Estate Information

http://www.ired.com The Internet Real Estate Directory, known among insiders simply as *ired,* is the top site for real estate information. You'll find a directory of links to over 10,000 real estate–oriented sites, including links to a huge number of lenders. This is a very valuable service because sites are rated, so you needed waste time chasing after losers. Do not miss this one.

http://www.fair.com The Homebuyer's Fair is one of the very first real estate–oriented sites on the Net, and it's still one of the best. In addition to information, the Webmaster offers commentary, evaluating the information. There are also a number of tools you will find nowhere else—a "don't miss" site.

Directories of Lenders

The organizations listed in the previous section are independent sources, not paid or supported financially (or only minimally so) by lenders. A number of other sites are registries of lenders, similar to the Yellow Pages. Some will list anyone who asks to be included; others will include only those firms that have paid for the privilege. Here are a few good ones:

http://www.LoanPage.com LoanPage, in addition to a comprehensive list of lenders, has two types of on-line applications and a printable loan application that is virtually a duplicate of the standard FNMA Form 1003. You can print it out yourself and use it to fill out your application; it precludes having to talk with a lender just to get the form. (You will have to configure your printer to print the form on legal-size paper. Merely setting your printer control from Letter to Legal may not work. In Windows go into Control Panel/Printers or in Win 95, Start/Settings/Printers. Right-click on Properties, select Paper, switch to legal-size paper, and click on **OK.** In other systems, refer to your computer's manual.)

http://www.nfsn.com The National Financial Services Network provides mortgage loan data as well as information on many other kinds of consumer loans, insurance, and other financial services.

http://www.mortgagemart.com   Mortgage Mart is a similar service. Although it is affiliated with a lender, it has a lot of valuable information.

http://www.microsurt.com   Microsurf has over 5,000 pages of data and a directory of lenders. It is more rate-driven than most, which can give you a good idea about current rates offered in your area.

http://www.mortgage-net.com   AAA National Mortgage Directory has a large number of lenders on its list.

http://www.interest.com   Mortgage Market Information Service is another very comprehensive source of information.

ACTUALLY FUNDING A LOAN FROM AN INTERNET LENDER

Remember when Automatic Teller Machines were first installed? Many people were reluctant to use them; they preferred to continue going inside the bank to cash their checks or make deposits. The issue was one of trust. People were loathe to trust a machine to handle their hard-earned money. Of course, in the past 10-plus years, most of us cannot imagine what we did without them. I think mortgage lending on the Internet will have to go through the same process before its use becomes widespread. My experience in cyberlending is less than one year, but I have originated over $4 million in loans in that short start-up period. I have spent a great deal of time with my clients, trying to understand their motivation and concerns about the Internet, and my conclusions are based upon the feedback I received from them.

- Most people start out with the goal of saving money, but they really want interaction with a knowledgeable person to guide them through the loan process.
- The public is justifiably concerned about security issues on the Internet, particularly transactions involving money and transfer of sensitive, personal financial information. The development of secure servers will deal with this issue, and, frankly, traditional systems have to take over at some point in the process. No matter how an application is filled out, the borrower eventually has to sign it and

mail or ship it with all the supporting documentation to the lender to get the ball rolling.

- It's difficult to determine whom to trust when you meet people in person. It is even more difficult when a lender is a thousand miles away.

The question is, are the advantages of doing business on the Internet worth the risk? The answer is yes for some people and no for others.

In general, the demographics of those who are on-line indicate that many of them will feel comfortable using the Internet for such transactions. Here's why:

- They have more education.
- They have above-average incomes.
- They have fewer problems with qualifying and credit.
- They have greater familiarity with real estate, home buying, and technology.

If this profile describes you, consider the Internet as a source for a mortgage. Otherwise, you might be more comfortable dealing with a lender who can hold your hand; the education process is more easily accomplished across the table in the traditional method.

THE FUTURE OF THE MORTGAGE INDUSTRY ON-LINE

As with all new technologies, the on-line world of cyberspace is both full of potential and fraught with growing pains. No doubt the public is excited about the so-called information superhighway. Its application to the mortgage business is still groping because there is a difference between disseminating information and conducting commerce. The former task is vastly easier than the latter. The information about real estate and mortgages is enormously useful to consumers, and I encourage anyone who takes steps to use it, but I also recommend that you proceed with caution. There will be those who benefit greatly from the Web, but there will be victims as well. If you take the time to approach the Web with caution, you can benefit. The following are among the many advantages I see:

- If you live in an area that is not well served by lenders, the Internet can be a godsend. On-line lenders offer programs and pricing not available from local contacts. I secured a loan on a home in Alaska at a lower cost than offered by companies with local offices.

- From a lender's viewpoint, there is a limit to the area any firm or office can serve. For example, I work in Orange County, and of the 2,000 or so loans I have funded in my career, I'd estimate that 98 percent of my clients either lived here, were moving here, or lived here and were moving elsewhere. But on the Internet, I can help clients anywhere, and so can many other bright, honest lenders who are successful in their own hometowns.

- A typical mortgage company pays its loan reps between one-third and two-thirds of the commission generated by a loan transaction. If a company funds a $100,000 loan and the gross commission is 1.5 points, or $1,500, the loan rep (salesperson) is going to get from $500 to $1,000 and, in terms of value added, may be worth every penny. In contrast, if you structure a mortgage operation to respond to Internet inquiries, you probably don't need to pay someone $500 or $1,000 to handle the transaction.

The savings for the customer who goes on-line are going to come, I believe, from organizations that don't try to handle every need on the Internet. They can reduce staff costs by choosing not to handle all kinds of loans for all kinds of borrowers. That's what I have done at my Web site. Because of the greater difficulty in distance communication, I have chosen to do low-cost loans for creditworthy people with easy-to-document income. My costs for doing that kind of loan are lower, and I am happy to pass those savings on to customers. Several other lenders are applying exactly the same criteria to specially priced programs available only on the Web. I think we will see much more of that in the future.

As to disadvantages, I see the following:

- There are companies that offer loans in every state. To do that, you need to have a huge organization that operates in a bureaucratic manner. That's okay for getting a credit card but the feedback I get is that these lenders are not customer-friendly.

- Some lenders promise all things to all people. I saw one that promised 60,000 programs. That sounds like hype to me, and I'd be concerned about follow-up.

- Several of my clients have asked for references, which I gladly provided; they called back a few days later and we did business. I recommend that strategy to everyone because it is harder to assess character and trustworthiness on the Web than in your hometown.

- I have said a number of times that ideas are more important than quotes. Because of the ability to display so many rates, there are some borrowers who will look at nothing else, to their peril. This is probably even more dangerous on the Web in your own hometown. If you find the right lender, the rates will work themselves out.

COMPUTER PROGRAMS AND THE MORTGAGE BUSINESS

Both FNMA and FHLMC have introduced computerized loan approval programs. FNMA has various products under the MORE-NETPlus program, including Desktop Originator and Desktop Underwriter. FHLMC's program is called Loan Prospector. Both organizations use what is called *artificial intelligence* to evaluate data. Lenders can take the relevant information from an application and transmit it to the agency, where it is combined with credit and appraisal data; the approval or denial is issued within an hour. Pretty slick. As with any program, computerized or not, there are some glitches that need to be worked out, but I am sure that Fannie Mae and Freddie Mac as well as some jumbo lenders are committed to the success of these programs. They will continue to invest whatever it takes to make these systems cost-effective and consumer-friendly.

The following is an example of my own experience with computerized loan approval programs. I had been discussing a refinance with an out-of-state borrower, but our conversations had been intermittent because rates were a little high for his refinance to make sense. One day the rates dropped significantly. I called him and he said, "Let's do it." Importantly, approving his loan was not initially dependent on having an appraisal or title report or escrow instructions. All I needed to do was to fax his loan application and credit report to the lender that afternoon.

The lender submitted the material to Freddie Mac using Loan Prospector, and I received the approval by quitting time. They next morning I talked with my client and we selected the rate that made the most sense. I locked it in, we ordered the loan documents, they were shipped to him that afternoon, his title company received them the next morning, and he went in and signed. It took another week to get the appraisal, title report, and escrow instructions—total elapsed time to funding, 10 days. Compare that with the normal 45-day process, during which time you call your lender weekly to ask, "Have you heard anything yet?"

I also use FNMA's Desktop Originator and have found it to be equally expeditious. The strength of these systems is that the decision can be rendered up front, with the assumption that the follow-up documentation will prove true, as it does most of the time anyway. That is more user-friendly than the normal loan process, which says, in effect, I can't make a decision on your loan until I have *all* the information. These computerized programs will make it possible to move well-qualified borrowers through the system more quickly and at lower cost, and will enable greater resources to be applied to the marginal or problematic borrowers.

I have used computer spreadsheets ever since I started in the business in 1980. I started using Visicalc on a Franklin Ace 1000 computer, then Lotus 1-2-3 on an IBM PC, and now I use Excel on a computer with a Pentium processor that is 200 times faster than my original computer. I still use these programs many times each day, and you have seen a number of the worksheets in this book. If you are reading this chapter, you are probably computer literate and could benefit from such worksheets. If you just want to do some of the easier calculations and don't want to invest money (that is, if you aren't yet serious about buying a home and are just trying to learn about the financial part of it), a complete array of calculators has been developed by Hugh Chou. You can find them at http://www.ibc.wustl.edu/~hugh.

In addition, a number of stand-alone programs have been created that can also be very useful. QUALIFYR is a very useful program, as is PMI OUT, how to get your lender to relieve you from making private mortgage insurance premium payments. The other is RE-FI, which will help you evaluate whether you should refinance your mortgage.

MORTGAGE WIZARD is a slick program that I use all the time. In addition to doing the normal payment calculations, you can view interest-versus-principal breakdowns graphically, run a complete amortization table showing accumulated interest for any chosen period, or analyze the benefits of making increased payments. Figures 17.1 and 17.2 are from Mortgage Wizard. PC-LOAN is a useful program that allows you to compare two loan programs side by side.

Finally, one of the most interesting developments is the Smartloan. In addition to a number of Wizards, you can complete an application using the most user-friendly interface I have yet encountered. When you're finished, you can e-mail it to a lender through the program's sponsor, FormNet, Inc.

As a service to my readers who want to use their computers to crunch data, I have assembled many of these programs on a CD-ROM and on diskettes. You can purchase these directly from me by using the order form in the back of the book or at my Web site, http://www.loan-wolf.com.

PUTTING IT INTO PRACTICE

For the most part, as an Internet borrower, you are going to be looking at Web sites of companies you have never heard of, which means you must be just as cautious as you would when dealing with a lender in your hometown. Implement the suggestions I gave earlier in the book about choosing the right loan. And spend some time surfing relevant Web sites to become familiar with what's out there in cyberspace. Believe me, it won't take long before you're able to separate the cyberwheat from the cyberchaff, to develop your own criteria about which sites are valuable.

Take a look at my Web site at http://www.loan-wolf.com. Although it may lack some of the bells and whistles of the sites of the national lenders with big budgets and a full-time Webmaster, you will find good, honest information that will point you in the right direction. In general, concentrate on Web sites that provide information in a way that is appealing and understandable. We all learn in different ways, so shop the Internet as I recommend you shop hometown lenders. You'll soon develop a feel for it and will find a lender that speaks to you; then you can buy with confidence.

Reread Chapter 10, "Shopping for a Loan and Negotiating with a Lender." The rules are no different, except that on-line you are not going to be able to meet face-to-face with your lender. Ask for references. Specifically, ask for the names, phone numbers, and date of funding of the last three borrowers for whom the lender funded loans. (This prevents the lender from picking and choosing.) When you call the references, confirm the dates and ask them how well they were treated and how the interchange of information was handled. Assuming you receive positive responses, call your lender and interview him or her according to the outline in Chapter 10.

At the same time, collect information from www.freddiemac .com and www.hsh.com. Then you will be prepared to compare current rates offered by your lender with the data you have assembled.

Next, ask your lender to confirm by fax or e-mail the pricing and other fees you will be charged. This may be a little controversial, but you must protect yourself. If you are within 30 days of closing, give very serious consideration to locking in the rate and points to remove the opportunity for the lender to make changes. Knowing when to lock in is a tough call, and your decision must be based on your feelings about your relationship with your lender. If you trust the lender, you can afford to be more opportunistic.

Finally, if your on-line experience was successful, broadcast it. Write or e-mail the lender with your impressions. You can see what some of my clients have said on the testimonial page at my Web site. This will help other borrowers who come along to benefit from your experience and to proceed with less trepidation. Similarly, don't be shy about broadcasting negative interaction. This can protect fellow borrowers and potentially motivate a less-than-professional lender to seek another method of generating business.

EPILOGUE:
ON THE NEED FOR REFORM
AND OTHER THOUGHTS

I want to close by reiterating the point I made at the beginning. Indeed, it is the point that compelled me to write this book in the first place: Three out of every four homeowners either get the wrong loan or pay too much for it. By now, I hope you feel confident about your ability to be the one in four who gets a terrific deal on the right loan.

FORMS, MORE FORMS, AND REFORMS

Most people are in a heightened emotional state when they are buying a home. That is totally understandable; it goes with the territory. First-time home buyers often become overwrought at the enormity of the decisions they face. Home ownership is a very important component of our national wealth and economy. To most Americans, owning their own home is a lifelong goal. Indeed, this achievement is one of the major components of the American dream. That's why, over the years, the federal and state governments, and the mortgage industry itself, has sought ways to expand home ownership, beginning with giving people the information they need to help make this all-important decision.

    The objective of giving borrowers the disclosures mandated under the Truth in Lending Act, the Real Estate Settlement Procedures Act (RESPA), and other various state regulations is that they be given accurate facts about loan performance and costs so they can apply for a loan that best suits their needs. Further, they must be given accurate disclosures of costs at the time of application and again when the loan funds. To that end, borrowers are given the following documents:

The HUD booklet *Buying Your Home*

The Good Faith Estimate of Closing Costs

Itemization of Amount Financed

Notice to Customer required by Federal Law and Federal Reserve Regulation Z

Transfer of Servicing Disclosure

The problems with the disclosure process are as follows:

1. Some lenders view the forms and the process as an inconvenience (after all, they prompt the borrower to ask questions), and they simply neglect to give borrowers the disclosure forms within three days of application.
2. The forms intimidate many home buyers, and thus they do not give them more than cursory examination. Those who do try to understand the forms are confused by industry terminology or bewildered by the mathematics.
3. More alarming, many of the frontline people in the industry do not themselves understand the forms and so are incapable of answering borrowers' questions.
4. The primary means of determining whether one loan is better than another (that is, APR, which is mandated by the law) is fundamentally flawed.
5. The method mandated for disclosing performance of adjustable rate mortgages (ARMs) is also flawed because it does not give consumers the information they need to make an intelligent decision.
6. Unscrupulous lenders may lie about rates and costs to induce customers to apply with them; they then take advantage of the customers by changing the terms of the loan, charging more and delaying final disclosure until the borrower has no other choice.
7. The three-day Right of Rescission is a major inconvenience to many people. For the full refinance of the pri-

mary loan on a residence, borrowers are involved in the process for 30 to 60 days. Of course, they should be offered the opportunity to wait three more days if they want to, but they should also have the right to easily waive this option.

RECOMMENDATIONS

Currently, a mortgage industry task force is working with HUD to improve the disclosure process. The following are my recommendations and suggestions to improve the mortgage lending and the process of transferring information:

- Make the disclosures easier for the average homeowner to read and understand. Follow the example of the Securities and Exchange Commission (SEC), which overhauled the manner in which public companies report to their stockholders. Disclosures *can* be written to be understandable by customers, not just to ensure legal compliance.
- Conclude that APR is not a meaningful way to differentiate mortgages. Develop a new method that focuses on amortizing points and other fixed costs over the borrower's likely period of ownership, *not* over the term of the loan.
- Require that ARM disclosures include a graphical representation of the performance of the chosen index plus its margin compared with other common loan indexes plus their common margin.
- For transactions involving mortgage brokers, offer a form wherein the borrower and the broker define the nature of their relationship—fiduciary or otherwise—and agree on the broker's compensation, not just on the rate and fees of the loan. Change the HUD-1 to better reveal the broker's compensation in the transaction.
- For every loan, lenders have a number of rate-versus-fee options to which the lenders and the market are indifferent (that is, they are neutral). Require that lenders present to borrowers all rate-versus-fee options they offer.

- Develop a replacement policy for the current mandatory three-day Right of Rescission. Perhaps it should apply to equity-line loans or cash-out refinance transactions, but exempt any refinance of the primary loan where the loan amount is greater than, say, $100,000.

- Implement more stringent enforcement to reduce the ability of unscrupulous lenders to take advantage of the unwary public.

WHAT IS REALLY IMPORTANT?

I'll reiterate that many people, particularly first-time home buyers, are emotionally distraught when buying a home. Some even come to believe that their lives will be meaningless unless they can buy the home immediately. This is simply not the case. Let me share *my* priority list for your consideration:

- Developing a sense of spiritual well-being
- Maintaining good health
- Cultivating strong, healthy relationships with your family and friends
- Providing for a comfortable retirement
- Building a rewarding and fulfilling career

You can do *all* of these without ever owning a home. If you find out that you can't buy the particular home you want, remember that there are many, many other homes out there. If you can't quite qualify for the loan you want, settle for a smaller loan or a smaller home. Or do additional planning, save more money, clean up your credit—whatever it takes to meet your goals *next* year. The mortgage industry may have faults, but it is pretty rational most of the time. Denial of an unwise loan may actually be a blessing at that moment in time.

HISTORICAL INTEREST RATES

We've all seen newspaper headlines such as "Fed Increases Interest Rates" or "Mortgage Rates Rise." To anyone in the market for a new home, this news is read with a sense of foreboding.

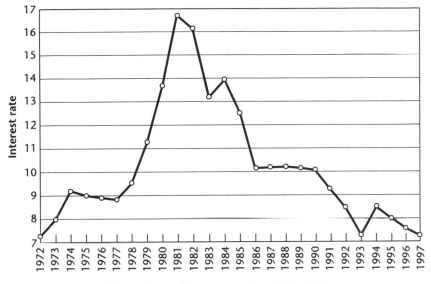

Figure 21.1   Mortgage rates, 1972–1997.

I have seen people get practically apoplectic over a ⅛ percent rise in rates. Certainly, interest rates do have an effect on the affordability of housing to marginal home buyers, but those of you who feel particularly sensitive to interest rates should look at Figure 21.1, which shows the rates on 30-year fixed-rate mortgages for the last 25 years.

This graphic illustration should make you feel better. I do not know what interest rates are or have done between 1997 and whenever you are reading this, but during this period, the housing market had some tough years. The thrift industry has had an even tougher time of it, but most of the homeowners survived. We will have more tough times, and everyone will survive those, too. When you hear that rates are going up, don't be discouraged, because it isn't the end of the earth. Take a deep breath, and keep right on going.

Finally, over the years, I have collected some little aphorisms that have resulted from my reflections on the human experience. Many of these have come from the interactions with my clients as they have coped with the problems of buying their homes. To some extent, these are answers to the questions that life poses to all of us sooner or later, and I'd like to share them with you here. I hope you enjoy them and take them to heart:

1. People will do what *they* need to do, and you gotta let 'em do it.

2. Your worth as a human being is measured not by what you accumulate or what you achieve, but by what you give away.

3. When people meet someone who knows someone they know, they often say, "Isn't it a small world?" No it isn't—it's a very *big* world, 24,000 miles around with 6 billion people on it. However, it is a *connected* world.

4. Success in life comes from finding something you can do well and that makes you happy—then doing it to the very best of your ability.

5. The task you are most reluctant to tackle is almost certainly the one you most need to do.

6. We all have similar experiences in life. The important thing is to pay attention. Each event should be a learning experience, and if you do it right, you will only experience the negative ones once.

7. You are measured not by what you believe in but by what you *do!*

8. By the time people become mature, they have a well-developed set of beliefs that define how they think the world works. However firmly we hold onto our beliefs, we should have the openness to examine them from time to time and the courage to say, "I was wrong."

9. Life is not a training exercise—it is the real thing. You only get to do it once and you have to get it right the first time.

10. Deal with what is on your plate now, not what might be there tomorrow.

11. Be happy with what you have, where you are, now.

12. Don't quit.

CONCLUSION

Buying a home is a marvelously satisfying experience. I still remember the joy of my first night in my first home, so one of the pleasures of my job is helping people realize *their* dreams. Home ownership is better and cheaper when you make the right decisions along the way. I hope this book has been both enjoyable and meaningful and will help you make better decisions in buying and financing your home. Above all, I hope it encourages you to make a financial plan, to treat your mortgage as part of that plan, and to remember to reexamine your mortgage on a regular basis, so you can make wise choices when opportunity calls. Good luck!

APPENDIX

MONTHLY PAYMENT TABLES

If you don't have a computer or a fancy calculator, use the following tables to determine what your approximate monthly payment would be at the various interest rates for 15- and 30-year loans.

15-YEAR LOANS

Loan Amount	Monthly Payment at Various Interest Rates					
	5%	6%	7%	8%	9%	10%
50,000	395	422	449	478	507	537
60,000	474	506	539	573	609	645
70,000	554	591	629	669	710	752
80,000	633	675	719	765	811	860
90,000	712	759	809	860	913	967
100,000	791	844	899	956	1,014	1,075
110,000	870	928	989	1,051	1,116	1,182
120,000	949	1,013	1,079	1,147	1,217	1,290
130,000	1,028	1,097	1,168	1,242	1,319	1,397
140,000	1,107	1,181	1,258	1,338	1,420	1,504
150,000	1,186	1,266	1,348	1,433	1,521	1,612
160,000	1,265	1,350	1,438	1,529	1,623	1,719
170,000	1,344	1,435	1,528	1,625	1,724	1,827
180,000	1,423	1,519	1,618	1,720	1,826	1,934
190,000	1,503	1,603	1,708	1,816	1,927	2,042
200,000	1,582	1,688	1,798	1,911	2,029	2,149
210,000	1,661	1,772	1,888	2,007	2,130	2,257
220,000	1,740	1,856	1,977	2,102	2,231	2,364
230,000	1,819	1,941	2,067	2,198	2,333	2,472
240,000	1,898	2,025	2,157	2,294	2,434	2,579
250,000	1,977	2,110	2,247	2,389	2,536	2,687
260,000	2,056	2,194	2,337	2,485	2,637	2,794
270,000	2,135	2,278	2,427	2,580	2,739	2,901
280,000	2,214	2,363	2,517	2,676	2,840	3,009
290,000	2,293	2,447	2,607	2,771	2,941	3,116
300,000	2,372	2,532	2,696	2,867	3,043	3,224
310,000	2,451	2,616	2,786	2,963	3,144	3,331
320,000	2,531	2,700	2,876	3,058	3,246	3,439
330,000	2,610	2,785	2,966	3,154	3,347	3,546
340,000	2,689	2,869	3,056	3,249	3,449	3,654
350,000	2,768	2,953	3,146	3,345	3,550	3,761
360,000	2,847	3,038	3,236	3,440	3,651	3,869
370,000	2,926	3,122	3,326	3,536	3,753	3,976
380,000	3,005	3,207	3,416	3,631	3,854	4,083
390,000	3,084	3,291	3,505	3,727	3,956	4,191
400,000	3,163	3,375	3,595	3,823	4,057	4,298

30-YEAR LOANS

Loan Amount	Monthly Payment at Various Interest Rates					
	5%	6%	7%	8%	9%	10%
50,000	268	300	333	367	402	439
60,000	322	360	399	440	483	527
70,000	376	420	466	514	563	614
80,000	429	480	532	587	644	702
90,000	483	540	599	660	724	790
100,000	537	600	665	734	805	878
110,000	591	660	732	807	885	965
120,000	644	719	798	881	966	1,053
130,000	698	779	865	954	1,046	1,141
140,000	752	839	931	1,027	1,126	1,229
150,000	805	899	998	1,101	1,207	1,316
160,000	859	959	1,064	1,174	1,287	1,404
170,000	913	1,019	1,131	1,247	1,368	1,492
180,000	966	1,079	1,198	1,321	1,448	1,580
190,000	1,020	1,139	1,264	1,394	1,529	1,667
200,000	1,074	1,199	1,331	1,468	1,609	1,755
210,000	1,127	1,259	1,397	1,541	1,690	1,843
220,000	1,181	1,319	1,464	1,614	1,770	1,931
230,000	1,235	1,379	1,530	1,688	1,851	2,018
240,000	1,288	1,439	1,597	1,761	1,931	2,106
250,000	1,342	1,499	1,663	1,834	2,012	2,194
260,000	1,396	1,559	1,730	1,908	2,092	2,282
270,000	1,449	1,619	1,796	1,981	2,172	2,369
280,000	1,503	1,679	1,863	2,055	2,253	2,457
290,000	1,557	1,739	1,929	2,128	2,333	2,545
300,000	1,610	1,799	1,996	2,201	2,414	2,633
310,000	1,664	1,859	2,062	2,275	2,494	2,720
320,000	1,718	1,919	2,129	2,348	2,575	2,808
330,000	1,772	1,979	2,195	2,421	2,655	2,896
340,000	1,825	2,038	2,262	2,495	2,736	2,984
350,000	1,879	2,098	2,329	2,568	2,816	3,072
360,000	1,933	2,158	2,395	2,642	2,897	3,159
370,000	1,986	2,218	2,462	2,715	2,977	3,247
380,000	2,040	2,278	2,528	2,788	3,058	3,335
390,000	2,094	2,338	2,595	2,862	3,138	3,423
400,000	2,147	2,398	2,661	2,935	3,218	3,510

LENDERS' WHOLESALE RATE SHEETS

The idea of these rate sheets is to show readers that the mortgage business is more complex than they might have thought. One look at these charts and the question, "What are your rates?" seems pretty silly.

A LENDER'S WHOLESALE RATE SHEET
FIXED-RATE LOANS

15-Year Fixed Conforming (up to $227,150)				15-Year Fixed Jumbo (up to $650,000)			
Rate	*15-day**	*30-day*	*45-day*	*60-day*	*Rate*	*15-day**	*30-day*	*45-day*	*60-day*
6.125%	2.000	2.125	2.250	2.375	6.250%	2.750	2.875	3.000	3.125
6.250%	1.500	1.625	1.750	1.875	6.375%	2.250	2.375	2.500	2.625
6.375%	1.000	1.125	1.250	1.375	6.500%	1.750	1.875	2.000	2.125
6.500%	0.625	0.750	0.875	1.000	6.625%	1.375	1.500	1.625	1.750
6.625%	0.250	0.375	0.500	0.625	6.750%	1.000	1.125	1.250	1.375
6.750%	−0.125	0.000	0.125	0.250	6.875%	0.625	0.750	0.875	1.000
6.875%	−0.500	−0.375	−0.250	−0.125	7.000%	0.250	0.875	0.500	0.625
7.000%	−0.875	−0.750	−0.625	−0.500	7.125%	−0.125	0.000	0.125	0.250
7.125%	−1.250	−1.125	−1.000	−0.875	7.250%	−0.500	−0.375	−0.250	−0.125
7.250%	−1.500	−1.375	−1.250	−1.125	7.375%	−0.875	−0.750	−0.625	−0.500
7.375%	−1.750	−1.625	−1.500	−1.375	7.500%	−1.125	−1.000	−0.875	−0.750
7.500%	−2.000	−1.875	−1.750	−1.625	7.625%	−1.375	−1.250	−1.125	−1.000
7.625%	−2.250	−2.125	−2.000	−1.875	7.750%	−1.625	−1.500	−1.375	−1.250
7.750%	−2.500	−2.375	−2.250	−2.125	7.875%	−1.875	−1.750	−1.625	−1.500

30-Year Fixed Conforming (up to $227,150)				30-Year Fixed Jumbo (up to $650,000)			
Rate	*15-day**	*30-day*	*45-day*	*60-day*	*Rate*	*15-day**	*30-day*	*45-day*	*60-day*
6.125%	4.000	4.125	4.250	4.375	6.500%	4.000	4.125	4.250	4.375
6.250%	3.375	3.500	3.625	3.750	6.625%	3.375	3.500	3.625	3.750
6.375%	2.750	2.875	3.000	3.125	6.750%	2.750	2.875	3.000	3.125
6.500%	2.125	2.250	2.375	2.500	6.875%	2.125	2.250	2.375	2.500
6.625%	1.500	1.625	1.750	1.875	7.000%	1.500	1.625	1.750	1.875
6.750%	0.875	1.000	1.125	1.250	7.125%	1.000	1.125	1.250	1.375
6.875%	0.375	0.500	0.625	0.750	7.250%	0.500	0.625	0.750	0.875
7.000%	-0.125	0.000	0.125	0.250	7.375%	0.000	0.125	0.250	0.375
7.125%	-0.625	-0.500	-0.375	-0.250	7.500%	-0.375	-0.250	-0.125	0.000
7.250%	-1.125	-1.000	-0.875	-0.750	7.625%	-0.750	-0.625	-0.500	-0.375
7.375%	-1.625	-1.500	-1.375	-1.250	7.750%	-1.125	-1.000	-0.875	-0.750
7.500%	-2.000	-1.875	-1.750	-1.625	7.875%	-1.500	-1.375	-1.250	-1.125
7.625%	-2.375	-2.250	-2.125	-2.000	8.000%	-1.750	-1.625	-1.500	-1.375
7.750%	-2.750	-2.625	-2.500	-2.375	8.125%	-2.000	-1.875	-1.750	-1.625

Premiums

Fixed jumbo $650,000—$1mm maximum:
+0.250% to rate
Assumable (exclude CA, CT, FL, ID, MA, MT, ND, NH, NJ, NY, RI):
• 15-yr fixed only +0.500% to rate
Second home conf fixed note rate add-ons:
• Purchase 80.01–90% LTV +0.125%
• Rate/term refi 75.01–80% LTV +0.125%
• Cash out refi up to 65% LTV +0.125%
Investor (fixed only): +0.500% rate, +0.500% fees
Convertibility: +0.500% fees, +0.125% margin

• High-rise condos (nonconf fixed): +.500% to fees
• High-rise condos (all ARM products): +.125% to rate

* 15-day lock option not available until further notice.

Long-term Locks—Add to 60-day Price

	Fees due at lock
90-day purchase	+0.500 pts
120-day new const. only	+1.000
180-day new const. only (fixed)	+0.750, +.250 to rate
180-day new const. only (ARM)	+1.500

A LENDER'S WHOLESALE RATE SHEET
CONFORMING ARM LOANS

1-year Treasury ARM (up to $227,150)
Nonconvertible
See Premiums Section for Convertibility
Option

CAPS: 2.000 / 0.000 / 0.000
MARGIN: 2.750   **INDEX:** 5.220

Rate	15-day*	30-day	45-day	60-day
5.000%	0.625	0.750	0.875	1.000
5.125%	0.375	0.500	0.625	0.750
5.250%	0.125	0.250	0.375	0.500
5.375%	-0.125	0.000	0.125	0.250
5.500%	-0.375	-0.250	-0.125	0.000
5.625%	-0.500	-0.375	-0.250	-0.125
5.750%	-0.625	-0.500	-0.375	-0.250
5.875%	-0.750	-0.625	-0.500	-0.375
6.000%	-0.875	-0.750	-0.625	-0.500
6.125%	-1.000	-0.875	-0.750	-0.625
6.250%	-1.125	-1.000	-0.875	-0.750
6.375%	-1.250	-1.125	-1.000	-0.875
6.500%	-1.375	-1.250	-1.125	-1.000

3/3 Treasury ARM (up to $227,150)
Nonconvertible, Convertibility Not
Available

CAPS: 2.000 / 0.000 / 0.000
MARGIN: 3.000   **INDEX:** 5.360

Rate	15-day*	30-day	45-day	60-day
5.500%	1.875	2.000	2.125	2.250
5.625%	1.500	1.625	1.750	1.875
5.750%	1.125	1.250	1.375	1.500
5.875%	0.750	0.875	1.000	1.125
6.000%	0.375	0.500	0.625	0.750
6.125%	0.000	0.125	0.250	0.375
6.250%	-0.250	-0.125	0.000	0.125
6.375%	-0.500	-0.375	-0.250	-0.125
6.500%	-0.750	-0.625	-0.500	-0.375
6.625%	-1.000	-0.875	-0.750	-0.625
6.750%	-1.000	-1.000	-1.000	-0.875
6.875%	-1.000	-1.000	-1.000	-1.000
7.000%	-1.000	-1.000	-1.000	-1.000

3/1 Treasury ARM (up to $227,150)
Nonconvertible
See Premiums Section for Convertibility
Option

CAPS: 2.000 / 0.000 / 0.000
MARGIN: 2.750   **INDEX:** 5.220

Rate	15-day*	30-day	45-day	60-day
5.500%	2.000	2.125	2.250	2.375
5.625%	1.625	1.750	1.875	2.000
5.750%	1.250	1.375	1.500	1.625
5.875%	0.875	1.000	1.125	1.250
6.000%	0.500	0.625	0.750	0.875
6.125%	0.125	0.250	0.375	0.500
6.250%	-0.250	-0.125	0.000	0.125
6.375%	-0.500	-0.375	-0.250	-0.125
6.500%	-0.750	-0.625	-0.500	-0.375
6.625%	-1.000	-0.875	-0.750	-0.625
6.750%	-1.250	-1.125	-1.000	-0.875
6.875%	-1.500	-1.375	-1.250	-1.125
7.000%	-1.500	-1.500	-1.375	-1.250
7.125%	-1.500	-1.500	-1.500	-1.375

5/1 Treasury ARM (up to $227,150)
Nonconvertible
See Premiums Section for Convertibility
Option

CAPS: 2.000 / 0.000 / 0.000
MARGIN: 2.750   **INDEX:** 5.220

Rate	15-day*	30-day	45-day	60-day
5.875%	1.750	1.875	2.000	2.125
6.000%	1.375	1.500	1.625	1.750
6.125%	1.000	1.125	1.250	1.375
6.250%	0.625	0.750	0.875	1.000
6.375%	0.250	0.375	0.500	0.625
6.500%	-0.125	0.000	0.125	0.250
6.625%	-0.500	-0.375	-0.250	-0.125
6.750%	-0.750	-0.625	-0.500	-0.375
6.875%	-1.000	-0.875	-0.750	-0.625
7.000%	-1.250	-1.125	-1.000	-0.875
7.125%	-1.375	-1.250	-1.125	-1.000
7.250%	-1.500	-1.375	-1.250	-1.125
7.375%	-1.500	-1.500	-1.375	-1.250
7.500%	-1.500	-1.500	-1.500	-1.375

(Continued)

A LENDER'S WHOLESALE RATE SHEET
CONFORMING ARM LOANS *(CONTINUED)*

7/1 Treasury ARM (up to $227,150) Nonconvertible See Premiums Section for Convertibility Option					10/1 Treasury ARM (up to $227,150) Nonconvertible See Premiums Section for Convertibility Option				
CAPS: 5.000 / 0.000 / 0.000 **MARGIN:** 2.750 **INDEX:** 5.220					**CAPS:** 5.000 / 0.000 / 0.000 **MARGIN:** 2.750 **INDEX:** 5.220				
Rate	*15-day**	*30-day*	*45-day*	*60-day*	*Rate*	*15-day**	*30-day*	*45-day*	*60-day*
6.125%	2.375	2.500	2.625	2.750	6.125%	3.375	3.500	3.625	3.750
6.250%	1.875	2.000	2.125	2.250	6.250%	2.750	2.875	3.000	3.125
6.375%	1.500	1.625	1.750	1.875	6.375%	2.250	2.375	2.500	2.625
6.500%	1.125	1.250	1.375	1.500	6.500%	1.750	1.875	2.000	2.125
6.625%	0.750	0.875	1.000	1.125	6.625%	1.250	1.375	1.500	1.625
6.750%	0.375	0.500	0.625	0.750	6.750%	0.750	0.875	1.000	1.125
6.875%	0.000	0.125	0.250	0.375	6.875%	0.250	0.375	0.500	0.625
7.000%	-0.250	-0.125	0.000	0.125	7.000%	-0.250	-0.125	0.000	0.125
7.125%	-0.500	-0.375	-0.250	-0.125	7.125%	-0.625	-0.500	-0.375	-0.250
7.250%	-0.750	-0.625	-0.500	-0.375	7.250%	-0.875	-0.750	-0.625	-0.500
7.375%	-1.000	-0.875	-0.750	-0.625	7.375%	-1.125	-1.000	-0.875	-0.750
7.500%	-1.250	-1.125	-1.000	-0.875	7.500%	-1.375	-1.250	-1.125	-1.000
7.625%	-1.500	-1.375	-1.250	-1.125	7.625%	-1.500	-1.500	-1.375	-1.250
7.750%	-1.500	-1.500	-1.500	-1.375	7.750%	-1.500	-1.500	-1.500	-1.500

Notes

* 15-day lock option not available until further notice.
1-yr ARM prepayment penalty: improve fees by 1.0 point.
Note: 1-yr ARM premiums in excess of the following available only in
conjunction with the prepayment penalty option:
  • Purchase: −1.000
  • Refinance: −0.500
Lower note rates now available on fixed-to-adjustable-rate products.
Call for pricing.

GLOSSARY

3/1, 5/1, 7/1, and 10/1 ARMs Also called *fixed interim-rate mortgages* (FIRMs), these are 30-year loans that are fixed for an initial period (the first digit) and then typically become generic ARMs tied to 1-year T-bills for the remainder of the 30 years.

5/25 and 7/23 mortgages These are 30-year amortized loans that are fixed for the first five or seven years. They typically have a "conditional right to refinance" for another 25 or 27 years. The right to refinance is contingent upon the property still being the primary residence, the payment record being good, and other factors, but it is intended to be almost automatic for most borrowers.

acceleration clause Condition in a mortgage that may require the balance of the loan to become due immediately if regular mortgage payments are not made or for breach of other conditions of the mortgage.

adjustable rate mortgage (ARM) A mortgage whose rate changes according to a formula specified in the loan document. (See Chapter 6.)

adjustment interval In an ARM, the time interval between adjustments, typically six months or annually.

agreement of sale Also know as the *purchase agreement, sales agreement, deposit receipt, offer to purchase,* or *contract of purchase,* according to local custom. When executed by both parties, it is the contract that defines selling price, specific terms, and conditions under which the seller agrees to sell and a buyer agrees to buy a property.

amortization A mortgage payment plan whereby a portion of each payment is applied to the interest, and the balance is applied to reducing the principal to ensure that the loan is fully repaid within the specified term.

annual percentage rate (APR)   An inept attempt by Congress to give consumers the ability to differentiate between loan programs by requiring lenders to disclose the "true" cost of borrowing. It is a flawed solution to the problem. (See Chapter 11.)

application fee   Some lenders charge an up-front application fee to cover some of the costs of processing the loan application. Most lenders collect only enough to cover the out-of-pocket cost of an appraisal and credit report.

appraisal   An opinion of value of a property as of a given date, prepared by an expert who is usually licensed by the state in which he or she resides. For residential loans, the report is invariably prepared on a FNMA or FHLMC form. (*Note:* Realtors frequently provide homeowners who are potential clients with an estimate of value or a market analysis showing recent comparable sales and other market data. The conclusion they reach may be very accurate or not, depending on the ability of the Realtor. Such a report is not an appraisal, and some states preclude using the word *appraisal* to describe it.)

assessed value   The value of a property for tax purposes according to the tax assessor of the jurisdiction in which the property is located. This number bears very little relation to the current market value of the property.

assumption   The process whereby a purchaser of a property is substituted for the original borrower upon approval of the lender. The original mortgagor is to be released from further liability in the assumption.

Assumption should not be confused with purchasing a property "subject to" the current mortgage, where the new buyer makes the payments but the original mortgagor remains personally liable if the purchaser fails to make the monthly payments. The Garn–St. Germain bill in the mid-1980s generally gave lenders the right to require payoff of the loan upon sale of the property. In my view, it is a dangerous practice to purchase a property and not telling the lender, hoping that they will not notice. This deprives them of their rights to demand payment of the loan. See **due-on-sale clause.**

Older FHA and VA loans are virtually the only fixed-rate loans that are assumable. ARMs, on the other hand, are always presumed to be "at market rate" and are almost universally assumable at the discretion of the lender.

Although it sounds as if assuming a loan will save you money, usually that is not the case. The only loans that are widely assumable are ARMs. If you assume an ARM, it may cost you 1 point to assume the loan, and you miss the benefit of a teaser rate.

balloon payment loan   A loan for a fixed period of time, such as five years, at which point in time the borrower must repay the entire loan amount in a lump sum plus accrued interest.

basis point   One basis point equals ¹⁄₁₀₀ of 1 percent, or .01 percent. This term is used mostly by bond people, who are involved in the mortgage business because so many loans are securitized. If you look in your paper and see that the yield on the 30-year bond fell from 7.87 percent to 7.82 percent, you would say that it fell 5 basis points. A ¼ percent drop would be equal to 25 basis points.

buy-down   The process by which a borrower pays more in up-front discount points to get a lower loan rate (see **discount points**). This can also refer to a buy-down in which the lender or homebuilder subsidizes the first few years of the loan by giving the borrower a lower interest rate, frequently at a higher cost later.

COFI   The Cost-of-Funds Index, the average cost of savings deposits in the 11th District of the Federal Home Loan Bank Board, a common index used by savings banks, particularly those in California.

caps   On an ARM, there may caps or limits on how much the interest rate or payment rate may vary. With no-neg ARMs, there is usually a cap of 1 percent every six months, or 2 percent per year. With a neg-am ARM, there is usually a 7.5 percent limit on the payment. (See Chapter 6.)

cash-out refinance   A refinance transaction in which the new loan balance is higher than the old loan balance plus closing costs. The opposite is a *no-cash-out refinance,* which presumes that there is less likelihood of fraud because there has been no instantaneous tangible economic gain to the borrower.

closing costs   The expenses in addition to down payment that buyer normally incurs in the settlement process. The agreement of sale negotiated previously between the buyer and the seller may state in writing who will pay each of the costs:

Lender's fees

Loan origination fee

Discount points

Processing, underwriting, and document fees (garbage fees)

Tax service

Flood certification

Wire transfer fee

Fees to others

Recording deed and mortgage

Escrow or settlement fees

Attorney's fee

Lender's title insurance premium

Deposits and expenses which are not related to the loan

Property taxes

Homeowner's insurance premium

Condominium association transfer fee and dues

Mortgage insurance premium

condominium   A type of planned unit development in which the buyer purchases individual ownership of a dwelling unit and a share of the common areas and facilities that serve the project. For example, you may own unit 14 and a one-sixtieth interest in the pool and clubhouse facilities of your project.

It is very important to know that lenders frequently have a number of restrictions in lending to owners of condominiums. As a basis for this, it is helpful to understand that as the owner of a condominium unit, the value of your unit as collateral for the loan is not its full sales price. The other part is your share of the value of the association's owned assets (pool, clubhouse, common area, and so forth). The value of these assets is beyond your individual control. Their ongoing value is a function of the willingness of all your fellow owners to continue to pay dues to the association so it can maintain values of commonly owned property.

construction-defect lawsuit   In many areas, condominium associations have sued the builder or developer of the project, alleging various defects in material or workmanship in construction of the units. You should know that many lenders will not lend on a unit in a project in which a suit is pending. Still others will not lend in such a project even after successful litigation until all the defects have been corrected, perhaps several years.

contract of purchase   See **agreement of sale**

conventional mortgage   A mortgage loan not insured by HUD or guaranteed by the Veterans Administration.

cooperative housing   Also known as a *co-op* and *stock co-op*. This is a form of ownership, frequently of an apartment building, in which the property is owned by a corporation, the stockholders being the residents of the dwellings. In a cooperative, the corporation owns title to the real estate. The resident purchases stock in the corporation that entitles him or her to occupy a unit in the building. The resident does not own the unit, but has the right to occupy it. Except in New York City, where they are common, financing co-ops is far more difficult than financing condominiums.

credit report   A report by a credit-reporting agency that reveals the borrower's history and current status of obligations.

debt-to-income ratio   Also known as the *qualifying ratio,* this is the ratio of housing expense to income.

deed of trust   In many states, the word *mortgage* is used, but the security instrument whereby the property is used as security for the loan is actually a deed of trust. There are three parties to the instrument: the borrower, who is called the *trustor;* the *trustee;* and the lender, known as the *beneficiary.* The borrower transfers the legal title for the property to the trustee, who holds the property in trust as security for payment of the debt to the lender, or beneficiary.

default   Each note will contain provisions outlining the conditions under which the loan is in default, at which time the lender has the right to start foreclosure. The most common reason for this, of course, is the failure to make payments on time. Generally, if payment is not received 30 days after the due date, the mortgage is in default.

　　Other events causing default are failure to pay property taxes, failure to keep adequate insurance in force, and failure to maintain in an acceptable condition (for example, knocking the house down).

deferred interest   In the case of neg-am ARM, when the obligatory minimum payment rate is insufficient to pay the interest that is accruing, the unpaid interest is added to the principal amount of the loan. Also known as *negative amortization.*

delinquency   The failure to make mortgage payments on time.

demand   The document issued by a lender showing the current mortgage balance and interest due. Upon payment of those sums, the lien is reconveyed.

discount points   Money paid to a lender at closing to obtain a lower interest rate. Lenders offer a number of options. (See Chapter 11.)

down payment   The cash portion of the purchase price—that is, the difference between the sales price and the initial mortgage amount.

due-on-sale clause   The clause in a mortgage that allows the lender to demand payment in full when the property is sold. So-called assumable loans still have a due-on-sale clause, but they also give a prospective new owner the right to assume the loan upon application and payment of a fee.

earnest money   The deposit money given by the buyer to the agent or settlement agent upon the signing of the offer to purchase, actually called the *deposit receipt* in some places. This shows that the buyer is serious about purchasing the house. If the sale goes through, the earnest money is applied against the down payment. If the sale is not consummated, the earnest money is either forfeited or returned to the buyer, depending on the terms of the purchase agreement.

encumbrance   A legal right or interest in land that affects a good or clear title. Usually, the agreement of sale will provide that the seller deliver a preliminary title policy or the results of a title search within 10 or 15 days. The purpose of the title search is to reveal the existence of such encumbrances and to give the buyer the opportunity to determine whether he or she wants to purchase the property with the encumbrance or how it can be removed.

Some encumbrances, such as easement rights, special assessments, or restrictive covenants conditions, covenants, and restrictions (CC&Rs) of community associations, "run with the land" and may not be negative. Others, such as mortgages, judgment liens, pending legal action, or unpaid taxes, are invariably extinguished through settlement process.

equity The value of an owner's interest in his or her property. Equity is the difference between the property's fair market value the total of the unpaid mortgage balance and any outstanding liens or other debts against the property.

escrow In California and some other states, the settlement agent who handles the closing of a purchase transaction is an escrow company. In other states, escrow accounts, also known as *impound accounts* in some areas, are lender-established accounts into which the borrower makes regular payments and from which the lender periodically pays some or all of the following on behalf of the borrower: mortgage insurance premiums, property tax payments, and/or casualty insurance premiums.

These are usually required by mortgage insurance companies where the LTV of the original loan was greater than 80 percent. The reason for this is that on such loans, the borrower's equity in the property is not high, and if the lender were to have to foreclose, it does not want to have to pay back taxes.

flood insurance In a federally related transaction (99.9 percent of all loans), a lender will require that the borrower purchase flood insurance if the property is located in a designated flood zone as determined by government maps. The flood certification costs about $20 and is paid to a company that checks the location of the property relative to flood boundaries. Flood certification is required even if you live on top of a mountain.

FHLMC An acronym for the Federal Home Loan Mortgage Corporation, or Freddie Mac. Similar to FNMA, Freddie Mac is also a purchaser or loans. Loans that conform to FNMA/FHLMC standards are referred to as *conforming loans.*

FHA See **HUD.**

FNMA Acronym for the Federal National Mortgage Association, or Fannie Mae. A quasi-governmental organization that purchases mortgage loans from banks, S&Ls, and mortgage bankers, groups them in pools, and sells security interest in the pools to institutional investors. Such sales make up a portion of the secondary market.

foreclosure After an event of default, the legal process whereby a lender enforces payment of debt secured by a mortgage or deed of trust by taking and selling the mortgaged property. The beneficiary notifies the trustee of the default, whereupon the trustee proceeds to sell the property at a public sale. Normal foreclosure is nonjudicial foreclosure, where the proceeds of the sale apply against the loan. If the proceeds from the sale are not sufficient to pay off the loan, the lender may not pursue other legal action to collect the deficiency. Lenders' rights vary from state to state.

fully indexed rate   The rate calculated by taking the index value and adding the margin to it. For example, a lender might offer an introductory rate of 6 percent, but if the index value is 5.75 percent and the margin is 2.75 percent, the fully indexed rate would be 8.5 percent. Every analysis of an ARM should include this calculation.

hazard insurance   Also called *homeowner's insurance, fire insurance,* or *casualty insurance,* these policies protect the homeowner against damages to the property caused by fire and other common hazards. It is invariably a requirement of the lender that you provide for insurance coverage and that the lender be named as an additional insured party so that its interests are also protected.

HUD   U.S. Department of Housing and Urban Development. The Federal Housing Administration (FHA) within HUD insures home mortgage loans made by lenders and sets minimum standards for such homes. HUD is also charged with enforcing RESPA and other housing-related laws.

impound   See **escrow.**

index   A number used by a lender to calculate the new interest rate at a change date. Used on all ARMs and on 5/25 and 7/23 loans.

interest   The price paid for borrowing money.

interest rate cap   The maximum interest rate that can be charged on an ARM, also called the *ceiling rate.* This is frequently 6 percent over the initial interest rate. The cap can also be an interim cap, which limits the amount by which the interest rate can be increased within a specified time interval, frequently 2 percent per year.

jumbo loans   Loans larger than the current conforming limit established by FNMA and FHLMC, currently $227,150.

lien   A claim by one person or entity on the property of another. Commonly, this is security for money owed, such as is created when you buy a property. Such claims may also include obligations not met or satisfied, judgments, and unpaid taxes, materials, or labor.

loan-to-value (LTV)   The ratio of loan amount to the value of the property.

lock-in   A lender's commitment or guarantee that it will fund the mortgage at the rate and points agreed upon if the loan funds within the lock-in period, typically 15 or 30 days.

mortgage   A lien or claim against real property given by the buyer to the lender as security for money borrowed.

mortgage commitment   A written notice from the a lender saying it will fund the mortgage loan to enable a buyer to purchase a house.

mortgage insurance premium (MIP)   The payment made by a borrower for a policy that protects the lender in the event of default. In the case of conventional mortgages, premiums are paid to the private mortgage insurance (PMI) carrier that insured the loan. In the case of government loans, the premiums are paid to HUD (in the case of FHA loans) or to the Veterans Administration (in the case of VA loans).

mortgage note   A written agreement to repay a loan. The agreement is secured by a mortgage, serves as proof of an indebtedness, and states the manner in which it shall be paid. The note states the actual amount of the debt that the mortgage secures and renders the mortgagor personally responsible for repayment. Used interchangeably with *deed of trust*, although there's a slight difference in meaning.

mortgagee   The lender in a mortgage agreement.

mortgagor   The borrower in a mortgage agreement.

open-end mortgage   A mortgage with a provision that permits borrowing additional money in the future on the same note. In the case of case of conventional loans, these are now quite uncommon. The exception is the equity-line loan, which is an open-end loan.

origination fee   The fee for processing, underwriting, and funding your loan, usually about 1 or 1½ points.

owner's title policy   The policy of title insurance given to the buyer and typically paid for by the seller assuring that the title to the property is free of defects at the date the property is transferred.

PITI   Acronym for principal, interest, taxes, and insurance, which together make up the borrower's housing expense when making the calculation for qualifying.

PMI   Acronym for private mortgage insurance, as applicable to conventional mortgages over 80 percent LTV.

POC   Acronym for paid outside of closing, which is the terminology used to describe funds associated with a loan transaction that do not actually pass through the settlement agent's (escrow) accounts. This would include, for example, funds paid directly to the lender for the appraisal and credit report. It also includes any other funds, such as rebates, paid to a broker in addition to the loan origination fee. Sometimes such rebates are okay, meaning that the borrower and broker agreed to them. *Important warning:* Sometimes the POC fees are rebates paid by the lender to the broker for getting the borrower to pay an above-market rate.

points   A point is equal to 1 percent of the amount of the loan. On a $50,000, 1 point is $500. On a $200,000 loan, 1 point is $2,000. When a borrower pays points, this first includes the loan origination fee. Additional points are called *discount points* and are an offset against interest rate. Lenders will, these days, almost always offer a number of rate-versus-fee combinations, allowing the borrower to choose one that is most suitable to his or her circumstances.

prepayment   Payment of the whole or part of principal amount of a mortgage loan before the due date. Mortgage agreements can restrict the borrowers right of prepayment by either limiting the amount that can be prepaid in any one year or charging a prepayment penalty.

principal   The balance of the loan outstanding. Initially, the full amount of the loan. This is the amount on which the interest payment is computed.

purchase agreement   See **agreement of sale.**

qualifying   The process whereby the lender assesses the borrower's ability to repay the loan.

RESPA   Acronym for the Real Estate Settlement Procedures Act, which governs disclosures to consumers applying for a loan.

rescission   Under RESPA's Right of Rescission, when a residence is refinanced, the borrowers are allowed three days after signing the loan documents to cancel the contract.

refinancing   The process in which a borrower pays off one loan with the proceeds from a new loan. When the new loan is just enough to pay off the old loan (and perhaps some of the closing costs), it is referred to as a *rate-and-term refinance* or a *no-cash-out refinance.* When the new loan is sufficiently large so that the borrower ends up with some cash after closing, it is known as a *cash-out refinance.*

reverse mortgages   Also known as *reverse-annuity mortgages.* (See Chapter 17.)

sales agreement   See **agreement of sale.**

securitization   The process whereby loans are pooled for sale in the secondary market.

servicing   The collection of monthly payments on a loan and administration of escrow accounts.

special assessments   A special tax imposed on a property, and usually all other property in the immediate area, for school or road construction, sewers, streetlights, underground utilities underground, and so forth.

taxes   As applied to real estate, these are property taxes paid to the government, usually the county or state, to support education, police and fire protection, and so forth.

tax service   A contract paid for by the borrower whereby a company checks every tax due date to confirm that the owner has paid property taxes. If taxes are overdue, the service company notifies the lender.

title insurance   First, an *owner's* title insurance policy protects homeowners against loss of their interest in property due to legal defects in title. This is typically paid for by the seller to verify marketable title to the property. Second, and different, lenders require that the borrower purchase a *mortgagee's title policy* to protect the *lender's* interest, ensuring, for example, that the lender is in first-lien position.

trustee   As it applies to real estate, the party or entity given the right to hold property for another. In a trust-deed state, the trustee has the "right of sale" of the property when notified by the *beneficiary* (the lender) that the *trustor* (the borrower) is in default on the note secured by the deed of trust.

Truth in Lending   A law requiring that borrowers be advised of the APR shortly after application.

underwriting   The process in which a lender determines whether a borrower is qualified (using income, credit, employment, and other factors) for the loan for which he or she has applied.

VA   Now known as the Department of Veterans Affairs, the VA administers the loan program that guarantees loans to qualified persons who are or were in the military service.

wraparound mortgage   Also known as the *all-inclusive trust deed* (AITD), this is a type of financing generally provided only by sellers. An AITD combines an existing assumable loan with additional indebtedness into one new loan. The borrower makes a payment on the larger loan, and that party then makes the obligatory payment to the underlying lender, keeping the difference as interest on the additional loan it provided.

INDEX